BANKABLE BUSINESS PLANS

Edward G. Rogoff

Foreword
By
Jeff Bezos
Founder and CEO
Amazon.com

THOMSON
™
TEXERE

Australia · Canada · Mexico · Singapore · Spain · United Kingdom · United States

Bankable Business Plans
Edward G. Rogoff

Published in 2003 by TEXERE, part of the Thomson Corporation. TEXERE, Thomson, and Thomson logo are trademarks used herein under license.

Printed in the United States of America
1 2 3 4 5 6 7 08 09 07 06 05 04 03

For more information, contact Texere, 300 Park Avenue South, New York, NY 10010 or find us on the Web at www.etexere.com.

For permission to use material from this text, contact us by
Tel (800) 730-2214
Fax (800) 730-2215
www.thomsonrights.com

Brief excerpts, as submitted from *The Risk Management Association Book* by The Risk Managment Association © 2002 by The Risk Management Association. Reprinted with permission of The Risk Management Association.

This publication is designed to provide accurate and authoritative information in regard to the subject matter covered. It is sold with the understanding that the publisher is not engaged in rendering legal, accounting, or other professional services. If legal advice or other expert assistance is required, the services of a competent professional person should be sought.

Composed by Cape Cod Compositors, Inc.

Library of Congress Cataloging in Publication Data
Rogoff, Edward G., 1951–
    Bankable business plans / by Edward G. Rogoff.
    p. cm.
    Includes bibliographical references and index.
    ISBN 1-58799-163-2 (alk. paper)
    1. Business planning. 2. New business enterprises—Finance. 3. Business enterprises—Finance. I. Title.

HD30 .28 .R65   2003
658.4'012--dc21   2002042982

In Memory of
My Father
. . . . who made the best plans

Contents

CHAPTER 14
Demonstrate That You Can Manage Conflicting Goals   133

CHAPTER 15
Present Yourself in the Best Light   139

CHAPTER 16
Make a Great In-Person Presentation   147

PART III   BUSINESS PLAN OUTLINES AND SAMPLE PLANS

Acknowledgments

This book has gained immeasurably from the wonderful colleagues with whom I am fortunate to work. Throughout the process, from conceptualization to completion, Mike Shatzkin, my friend and agent, has been essential. Mike possesses one of the most active and creative minds I have ever encountered; you would not be holding this book without his unflagging support and enthusiasm.

At Baruch College's Zicklin School of Business, I work with an extraordinary group of scholars, including Professors Myung-Soo Lee, Barry Rosen, Marilyn Neimark, Robert Foskey, and Carl Ullman, who shared their extensive knowledge about entrepreneurship and contributed their patient and constructive readings of earlier drafts.

Professor Ramona K. Z. Heck at Baruch College has been a pioneer of thought and research in the realm of family business, which permeates virtually every aspect of entrepreneurship and business creation. I have greatly benefited from her work, from being her colleague, and, most of all, from being her friend. Chapter 8, which deals with potential sources of funding, has been greatly improved by her suggestions.

Professor George Haynes of Montana State University, a leading expert on small-business finance, generously provided guidance on identifying the most common sources of financing for small and startup businesses.

Dr. Pat Imbimbo, the Director of the Baruch Career Development Center imparted her expertise about presenting one's qualifications, and Frank Guarino, a business counselor at the Field Center for

Entrepreneurship, contributed his knowledge of SBA loans, a subject in which he is an unrivaled expert. Yael and Avi Levi, graduate students with significant business experience, masterfully helped shape the financial presentations. Another wonderful graduate student, Enoch Anand, provided great help with time lines. Carla Hojaiban, a former graduate student of mine, was an especially insightful reader of previous drafts. There was no more knowledgeable reader of earlier drafts than Milt Kamen, a successful entrepreneur and man of great wisdom. He made significant contributions to the concepts and specifics of this book.

My friend and colleague, Professor Alvin N. Puryear, deserves special mention. Not only did he provide indispensable comments on various drafts, but he has also been the guiding force in establishing the teaching of entrepreneurship as a vital course of study at Baruch. As the founding and current director of the Field Center for Entrepreneurship, Professor Puryear has provided fundamental insights as to how entrepreneurship should be taught, and how a public college can encourage aspiring entrepreneurs. His commitment to these goals has created a superior educational program for Baruch students and faculty, as well as Field Center clients. The opportunity to work with Professor Puryear, Baruch students, and Field Center clients has been crucial to my writing this book.

I also want to thank Dr. Gary Cadenhead, Director of the University of Texas MOOT CORP Competition and Ms. Ann Whitt, the Coordinator of the MOOT CORP Competition, for their help in obtaining permission to use the Zif Medical Devices plan, which was a former winner of this prestigious competition. Professor Arnold Cooper of Indiana University, who was the faculty advisor to the team of David Bean and Joseph Schroeder, authors of the Zif Medical Devices plan, provided help above and beyond what I could reasonably expect, in making additional arrangements for use of this exemplary plan.

As you can tell from reading *Bankable Business Plans*, I believe that libraries are indispensable in completing the research to support a strong plan. I greatly benefited from the expertise of Baruch College librarian Rita Ormsby, who helped identify the superb resources listed throughout this book.

An extraordinary attorney and wonderful friend, Richard Rosenstein, provided expert guidance on legal issues and embodies the quality of lawyer that successful entrepreneurs need.

I have greatly benefited from being married to a wonderful writer and editor, Perry-Lynn Moffitt, who is now, unexpectedly, an expert on writing business plans. Her thoughtful, patient, and cheerful multiple readings of this book have increased its clarity and eloquence many fold.

The team at TEXERE, led by Myles Thompson and Victoria Larson, is to be credited with seeing the need for *Bankable Business Plans*, helping define its focus, and being the source of numerous improvements. Victoria combines creativity, literacy, business knowledge, and an unfailing gift of organization.

Foreword

Jeff Bezos, Founder and
CEO, Amazon.com

The wake-up call for Amazon.com came in 1994 when I read that World Wide Web usage was growing at an astonishing 2,300% a year. The Web was a small place then, but something growing that fast can be invisible today and everywhere tomorrow.

I chose books as the first-best product to sell online. At any given time, there are millions of books active and in print around the world. The largest physical superstores can carry only about 100,000 different titles and mall bookstores typically less than 30,000. Amazon.com would be able to offer the complete selection—millions of books—not just what would fit on the physical shelves. That basic idea—complete selection—was the primary way that Amazon.com was going to add genuine, important value for customers in its early days.

A little after that wake-up call, my wife and I left New York City and headed to Seattle. In the car, I wrote the first draft of what would become the Amazon.com business plan. I continued to work on it for weeks after we arrived in Seattle—ultimately locking myself in a research cubicle at a local library with peanut butter sandwiches for days on end so that I wouldn't be distracted. The more I worked on it, the better the plan became.

The process of writing down my thoughts improved my thinking, and helped me practice mentally and visualize what we were going to do. To be sure, my primary motivation for writing the business plan was to help communicate the idea of Amazon.com to prospective investors, but, in hindsight, an incredibly important benefit that came from writing the plan was crisper, more innovative, more customer-focused thinking.

After months of effort and presenting the Amazon.com business plan to some 60 different prospective investors, I was lucky enough to find about 20 "angel" investors who put in approximately $50,000 each. Raising $1 million dollars is supposed to be hard, and it was. I doubt it would have been possible at all without an organized business plan.

In July, 1995, we opened for business with an office and a 400-square-foot warehouse in the "Color-Tile" building in an industrial area south of downtown Seattle. Our expectations for early sales were modest, and the business plan called for a long start-up period where customers would slowly learn about and adopt this new way of shopping. But we were surprised immediately. To everyone's astonishment, in the first 30 days, with no advertising, we took orders from customers in all 50 states and 45 countries.

At this point, our growth was so much stronger than expected, that most of the details in the business plan were no longer valid. It's probably the rare business plan that survives the first day of the business being open. Nevertheless, the process of writing the plan forces you to think through many different cases. As a result, when something changes, you're better prepared for it.

So while the business plan had called for us to be small, we quickly scaled up as customers around the world discovered Amazon.com and kept coming back. After nine months, we relocated to a 12,000 square foot fulfillment center, and seven months later we occupied a 45,000 square foot facility.

Building on the initial business plan, Amazon.com was able to raise $8 million in venture capital by 1996 and the following year, we went public. Customers kept asking us to sell additional categories of products (they still do this). So we introduced music CDs, DVDs, and videos in 1998. That same year we opened amazon.co.uk and amazon.de in Europe. The following year we added electronics, tools, toys, and software, and we began allowing other people to sell their merchandise at Amazon.com. In 2000, Amazon.com had more than 3 million square feet of fulfillment center space in the United States. And we had also opened sites for France and Japan.

As we gained experience, our business continued to be built on offering customers selection and convenience. In July of 2001, we added a third pillar to our business plan: low prices. We would be the kind of retailer that works relentlessly to lower prices for customers. With growing volume and increasing operational efficiencies, we've been able to share the savings with customers in the form of lower prices—and we're going to keep doing that.

Even though all the details have changed over the years, many of the original concepts outlined in the first business plan remain central to our business. In addition, even though you can't plan on it, we've also been lucky. We're especially grateful to our customers, and if you bought this book (or anything else) from Amazon.com, thank you.

I knew Ed before I started Amazon.com, and I believe his experiences with his own successful ventures and as a professor of entrepreneurship make him an excellent person to guide you from initial idea through the creation of an effective plan that will serve the needs of your customers and investors.

A strong business plan will not only help you locate the early funds you need, but will also clarify your thinking and serve as a starting blueprint for future growth in what is always a changing world.

All the best, and good luck serving customers!

Jeff Bezos

Seattle, Washington
October 2002

Preface

This book is written with one central purpose: to guide you through the process of creating a bankable business plan, so you can obtain the resources you need to start, build, or buy a business.

A *bankable business plan* is one that attracts the approval and financing for your venture by addressing the needs of bankers and other investors while still accomplishing your own goals.

My extensive experience in writing my own successful business plans, helping other entrepreneurs create effective plans, and advising funding sources on how to evaluate submitted plans, has taught me that a strong plan is built on a single basic element: It must meet the needs of financial supporters, whether they be bankers, investors, family members, or partners.

I have personally raised more than $100 million from angels, banks, and venture capitalists to finance my own enterprises by writing bankable business plans that demonstrated how my ventures met the needs of my funding sources. And, with this book, you can greatly increase your chances for success.

In these pages, I will also impart my expertise as a business academician. Since 1992, I have been a professor at Baruch College of The City University of New York, the largest, most diverse business school in the United States, where I created and continue to teach both graduate and undergraduate courses on entrepreneurship and business plan development. As a founding Faculty Coordinator and Mentor—as well as a former Director—of the Lawrence N. Field Center for Entrepreneurship and Small Business at Baruch College, I have advised hundreds of individuals as they established their ventures.

All of my students and clients have learned to build their business plans on this single basic element of meeting their funders' needs. Now, you can learn how to follow this same route to creating a successful, effective, and *bankable* business plan.

In reading this book, you will soon realize that:

$ **Bankable business plans focus on financial issues.** Most other books and programs simply ignore the fact that you're writing a document about an enterprise which, like all businesses, exists to make money. Since the people reading your plan will decide to invest in or lend money to your venture based largely on this document, your plan must address *their* issues. *Bankable Business Plans* not only takes you through the steps of producing quality financial projections, but tells you how to identify and satisfy specific concerns that matter to potential lenders and investors. Moreover, it is the only book that shows you how to make use of the Risk Management Association (RMA) data to establish your plan as credible. Since most bankers and many investors will compare your projections to the RMA data, knowing how to obtain and use these numbers is like being given the answer key to a test ahead of time.

$ **Bankable business plans don't follow formulas.** Most books and software packages about creating business plans urge the reader to follow a template or copy an existing plan without first doing the conceptual work. This method produces a plan that sounds canned, generic, and lifeless, especially to someone who analyzes hundreds of proposals every month. It takes an experienced investor or lender about two seconds to spot a formula plan. Your business concept, and the work you accomplish to bring it to life, will make your plan compelling, and motivate others to support your efforts. *Bankable Business Plans* will show you how to create a unique, exciting, convincing, and thorough description of your proposed venture.

$ **Bankable business plans *do* follow good business thinking.** Creating a business is a process that moves from conceptualization to implementation, and creating a business plan should follow the same sequence. Some books insist that the best way to begin a plan is to answer dozens of highly specific questions, which doesn't work if you haven't done the conceptual work first. Answering a question such as, "What is your profit goal for years one through five?" when you start to work on your plan, is rather like being asked to write a shopping list before you've decided what to cook. *Bankable Business Plans* takes you through the entire process from thinking of your initial idea, to testing it against basic criteria, to researching the market and the competition, to developing strategies, and, finally, to creating a plan for implementation. Since your resulting business plan will be based on the steps *you* took to create *your* business in *your* mind, it will be different from any other business plan—and it will be *yours* alone.

$ **Bankable business plans can be created regardless of your skills.** Many books and software packages assume that their readers are highly computer literate, with extensive knowledge of Windows, word processing, and spreadsheet programs. These are excellent skills to have and can save you tremendous amounts of time, but *Bankable Business Plans* is written for people at all skill levels. Although this book does not pretend to be an accounting text book, it will explain exactly what you need to learn and where you'll find the information to complete your financials. Reading this book is about creating a unique, effective business plan based on your enthusiasm for your venture and your willingness to learn about your industry. The only real skills you need to create a bankable business plan are your passion and your perseverance in learning how to do it effectively.

$ **Bankable business plans serve a specific purpose.** Business plans are documents created with a particular objective, which is usually to obtain financing, test an idea's feasibility, or recruit partners and suppliers. Most books and programs about creating business plans skip this step of defining the plan's purpose, which results in plans that don't address the specific concerns of the potential lender, investor, or partner. *Bankable Business Plans* will enable you to define and accomplish that purpose, including how to:

• Develop convincing financial projections by employing the RMA database.

- Choose which purposes of the plan are crucial to the success of your business.
- Demonstrate that you can manage potentially conflicting goals.
- Identify the basic elements and information that a strong business plan must contain.
- Construct a business plan that expresses your own confidence in your concept.
- Create a business plan that convinces others to believe in your concept.
- Focus on the business issues that are important to the people whose support and involvement you need.
- Make an effective in-person presentation of your plan at a business meeting.

Since my clients have an extremely broad range of business ideas—from New York City pedicabs to a web portal for Africans living away from their home countries—it's important for me to make the language I use to discuss the creation of a business plan as uniform as possible. No matter how you envision your eventual enterprise—as a store, an online service or a firm that reaches your customers by mail order—I refer to the entity you're creating as your *company.* When you start a business of any sort, you're establishing a means of delivering your product or service to a wider group of people. Even if you're setting yourself up as a sole practitioner, it's helpful to think of the way you organize your concept as a type of company with you at the helm making decisions and setting a course.

With my knowledge of what makes a successful business plan—from both the entrepreneur's and the funder's point of view—I can pass all the lessons I have learned along to you, the reader of *Bankable Business Plans.* By following the process in this book, and adhering to the RMA data, you will guarantee that your individual business plan will be as *bankable* as possible.

Edward G. Rogoff

New York City
August 2002

INTRODUCTION

What a Business Plan Is and How It Can Help You Start a Successful Enterprise

When individuals come into the Field Center for Entrepreneurship at Baruch College and sit down in my office, they usually open the conversation with one simple sentence: "I want to start my own business."

The next statement almost invariably includes one of the following four predicaments: "I have a specific idea for a business, but I don't know what to do next," or, "I know what I want to do and how I want to do it, but when I went to the bank for a loan, they said I had to show them something in writing before they would even talk to me," or, "I want to buy a business that I think I can make more successful, but I don't know how to start," or, "I'm an inventor and I've come up with a fabulous new product, but I don't have a clue how to get it manufactured—or sold."

The answer to all of these appeals for advice, whether the individual is opening a restaurant, taking over a competitor's ocarina manufacturing plant (an ocarina is a small, simple wind instrument), building a better mousetrap, selling a new kind of soap, or offering expert financial services to Wall Street investors is: "You need a business plan." Every one of these entrepreneurs is focused on a single goal: to build a successful enterprise that delivers profits and satisfaction to each owner. And no matter what that potential business is, there is one basic tool to employ in achieving that goal: a clear and compelling business plan.

Since I'm always interested in the types of businesses my clients want to develop into profitable and satisfying ventures, I ask them to tell me about their aspirations for the product or service they hope to provide. As they talk, I can sense their excitement and enthusiasm, even if they're uncertain about the next step. My job in this book is to channel your similar passions into that next step: writing a strong business plan.

Bankable Business Plans Are for Starting, Growing, or Buying a Business

Whether you're starting a new business, growing an established business, or buying an existing business, you need to create a strong and bankable business plan. Even though the circumstances may vary and certain strategies and funding sources may be more effective than others, your basic business plan will still follow the same primary principles outlined in this book.

The Power of a Bankable Business Plan

A good business plan is simply a document with a purpose—the power to accomplish a number of goals:

$ **Test the feasibility** of your business idea.

$ **Find the right financial resources** to start your business through investors or partners.

$ **Secure enough debt** by establishing loans, lines of credit, or payment terms.

$ **Identify the key people** to work with you as managers, employees, partners, or consultants.

$ **Establish business relationships** with your customers, suppliers, or distributors.

$ **Create an operational template** for the successful management of your business.

Starting a business and creating an effective business plan both require a great deal of thought before you set pen to paper or fingers to the computer keyboard. To guide you through this process, I have identified ten essential action steps to take. I'll show you how each step will help you create a persuasive plan for your company that follows a streamlined, logical path from the most general principles to the most specific. Before I detail these ten action steps, let's look briefly at some of the essential characteristics of entrepreneurship.

Entrepreneurship Is a Team Sport

The definition of *entrepreneurs* that I like most is, "Entrepreneurs are business people who undertake ventures without regard to the resources under their direct control." Let's face it, limiting yourself to a venture you could do solely with your own resources—both human and financial—would probably result in a pretty small business. Your human resources would be confined to your own muscle and brain power during waking hours only, and your financial resources would be limited to your investments, retirement accounts, house, credit cards, cash in the bank, and those few treasured items, such as the original set of Batman comics that your uncle gave you when you were a kid.

Even if you are enormously wealthy, you probably wouldn't want to risk it all—especially the Batman comics—on your business idea. Assets of around $1 million are not likely to be enough to buy or start the business of your dreams. Most brand-name fast-food franchises sell for more than that. Moreover, you need to be realistic and recognize the possibility that your business could fail and take all your assets with it.

Let's start with the assumption that, on the financial side, you are probably going to need help, either through loans from a family member, a friend, a bank, or a credit card company, or through investments from friends, family, business partners, or an investment group. Lenders let you borrow their money for a set period of time, and are paid interest along with receiving their loan amount, called *principal*, back in full. Investors buy equity or ownership shares in your business, and receive a share of the profits from operations or an eventual sale of the company.

As for the human resource side, do you really think you can operate your business completely alone? Very few businesses work that way. Consultants, freelancers, and individual investors may qualify as true one-man bands but, even for them, success (and sometimes failure) may spoil their solitude and require them to bring in employees or partners. And don't forget suppliers. The most solo operation still requires basic office supplies, such as paper and pencils. And absolutely no business operates without those important people, clients and customers.

No doubt about it, business is a team sport, requiring the contribution of others with different backgrounds, skills, and needs in order for you to build a successful venture, which brings me back to the definition I like and the reality that entrepreneurs must recruit and manage many resources—both human and financial—to create and grow a successful venture. This reality must be built into your business plan right from the beginning, which is why I believe that when you follow the process outlined in this book, you will create the most bankable business plan possible.

PART I

The Ten Essential Action Steps

CHAPTER 1: ACTION STEP ONE

Define Your Company:
What will you accomplish for others and yourself?

CHAPTER 2: ACTION STEP TWO

Identify Your Company's Initial Needs:
What will you require to get started?

CHAPTER 3: ACTION STEP THREE

Choose a Winning Strategy:
How will you distinguish your product or service from others?

CHAPTER 4: ACTION STEP FOUR

Analyze Your Market:
Who will want your product or service?

CHAPTER 5: ACTION STEP FIVE

Develop a Strong Marketing Campaign:
How will you reach your customers and what will you say to them?

CHAPTER 6: Action Step Six
Build a Dynamic Sales Effort:
How will you attract customers?

CHAPTER 7: Action Step Seven
Design Your Company:
How will you hire and organize your work force?

CHAPTER 8: Action Step Eight
Target Your Funding Sources:
Where will you find your financing?

CHAPTER 9: Action Step Nine
Explain Your Financial Data:
How will you convince others to invest in your endeavor?

CHAPTER 10: Action Step Ten
Use the RMA Database:
Check your answers against the answer key.

CHAPTER 1

Action Step One

Define Your Company:
What will you accomplish for others and yourself?

Right from the start, you need to define your business in terms of what it will accomplish for others, including your customers, investors, lenders, suppliers, employees, and, of course, you. If you ask yourself about meeting the needs of each financial and human resource required to start and grow your venture, you will be well on your way to creating a bankable business plan.

Write down all the specific needs your company will satisfy. In the privacy of my office, you can tell me about the personal reasons you have for starting a business: escaping an overbearing boss, not being able to get along with colleagues you didn't hire yourself, or proving to your skeptical father-in-law that you can be a success. Then, set these incentives aside. They may inspire you, but they will have no place in your final business plan. Your personal reasons for starting your business are not of particular interest to the potential investors or funders, who will be reading and analyzing the effectiveness of your concept.

Even if you're eager to start a company that can find a cure for the rare disease that made the feathers on your beloved parakeet fall out, your personal motivation will be of little or no significance to the funding sources or other people whose support you need. Potential investors need to know that your business will be meaningful and marketable to people who can use your product or service. Your deep-seated desire to find a cure, so that your parakeet can grow new feathers, may galvanize you to become a tireless crusader but, unless there is a commercial application for the product you hope to develop, your emotional commitment won't mean much to investors. In fact, they may worry about your continued commitment to the cause, if a cure isn't found in time to work wonders on your ailing pet.

So, concentrate on the external needs your company will meet. What will your product or service enable people to do better, more cheaply, more safely, or more efficiently? Will your restaurant make people's palates delirious with new taste sensations? Will your new mousetrap help people capture mice without feeling sick to their stomachs? Will your new bubblegum scented bubblebath revolutionize the way children agree to take nightly baths?

Think of all the positive benefits your company will provide. Write them down. Admire them. Absorb them into your consciousness. Believe in them. These are the primary motivators that readers of your business plan will respect and value.

What Will Your Business Accomplish for Your Customers?

Let's start with your source of revenue—your customers. Why will they spend their money on your product or service, and why will they return to spend money again? Unless there are strong answers to these questions, your business plan will not make it to first base.

Suppose you're planning to open a pet-supply store in your town. People with pets are obviously buying the food, supplies, treats, and other items at some store in the community, so, why will they want to shop at your place? Will your service be better? Your location more convenient? Your prices lower? Your selection greater? Your hours of operation longer? Your delivery faster and cheaper? Will your store be more fun, a pleasanter place to shop? Unless some of the answers to these and other questions are *yes*, then you won't be accomplishing enough for your customers to build the large and loyal group of shoppers you'll need to operate a successful pet store.

Sometimes, a business is successful simply because demand is greater than the supply. I had a client at the Field Center who wanted to open a day-care center for preschoolers. Her analysis was quite simple: She knew a dozen families that were having trouble finding day-care facilities for their children in their neighborhood. She figured that the demand was there and was woefully underserved. She didn't have to be better or cheaper than her competition. She just had to be in business. She was right, and opened a day-care center that was successful from its first day of operation.

What Will Your Business Accomplish for Your Investors?

Investors are the people or firms that buy stock in your company. Owning stock entitles them to a share of the profits either from general operations or from the sale of your business. Keep in mind that investors have many options. They can buy very secure government bonds, or publicly traded stocks; they can purchase real estate, or invest in any number of large or small businesses other than your own.

Entrepreneurs have an uphill struggle to attract investors, because these other options offer attractive returns and, probably, less risk. Investing in smaller businesses is chancier than buying stocks in large, publicly traded, well-established, and well-financed companies with a long history of profitability. In addition, those companies' stocks are defined as being *highly liquid*, meaning they can be sold at virtually any point very quickly to raise cash or to change investments. Most investments in startups or smaller entrepreneurial ventures are highly illiquid, meaning the investors' money is locked into the company's operating expenses until the business raises additional financing, becomes profitable enough to buy them out, or is sold.

To attract investors in the face of this risk and lack of liquidity, entrepreneurs must offer the potential of very high returns. How high? Well, it's not unusual for investors to expect credible and reasonable projections in the range of 20 percent to 30 percent annual returns before they will buy stock in your company. At this early stage in planning your business, you don't have the detailed financial projections that you will eventually need to show investors, but you can produce some back-of-the-envelope calculations to assure yourself that this rate of return is possible.

Suppose you're thinking of raising money to invest in real estate. It's not unusual for a bank to lend 80 percent or more of the purchase price. If the property you're considering makes a profit of $100,000 per year and you expect to pay ten times that profit, or $1 million to purchase the property, you will need $800,000 from a bank and the remaining $200,000 from investors. If you expect to increase profits to $150,000 per year within three years by raising rents when old leases come up for renewal, then your building will be worth $1.5 million, and the investors' $200,000 will be worth $700,000. That is more than a 50 percent annual return, and should be enough to make any investor happy.

Of course, there are additional considerations I haven't mentioned yet, such as transaction charges, lawyer's fees, your share of the profits for finding and managing the deal, and the need to spend money repairing the building you want to buy. But, for this stage, you have at least shown that high, attractive returns are possible and you should continue to work out the details.

Many entrepreneurs think they can attract investment for reasons other than financial returns. Your family and friends may simply want to help you start or build your business because they like you and believe in your talent. It is also possible that your business may serve a societal good, such as supporting medical research or helping endangered wildlife. I know this kind of investing does take place. I've actually seen it happen a few times, but my advice to clients is *don't count on it*. Most investors interested in such causes still want to see high projected returns, too. If your plan can't produce significant returns for investors, then perhaps you should change from starting a business to establishing a charity or foundation. A not-for-profit organization may be a more accurate description of what you're trying to accomplish, and there is certainly nothing wrong with that!

What Will Your Business Accomplish for Your Lenders?

Lenders, such as banks, provide your company with debt financing through loans in exchange for which they are paid interest. Because interest rates are generally far lower than the returns expected by most investors who buy stock in your company, lenders require much greater certainty that their principal will be returned and their interest paid. For this reason, lenders are always repaid completely before investors can receive a single penny. Business loans currently have interest rates in the 8 to 13 percent range, depending on the borrower's record, and the amount being borrowed.

To increase the likelihood that lenders will not lose their principal, they usually ask for *security*, which is a claim on an asset they can seize and sell in the event of a payment default. We are all familiar with the concept of a bank foreclosing on a house if the homeowner falls behind on mortgage payments. The same concept applies to business loans, only the security may be tied to an actual business asset such as inventory, receivables, equipment, buildings, or land.

The federal government provides guarantees to small business loans made by banks through the Small Business Administration (SBA). The purpose of this program is to encourage banks to make loans to small and new businesses, because small businesses create most new jobs and generate a large share of overall economic growth. SBA guarantees cover between 50 percent and 85 percent of the total business loan, depending on the loan amount and the program type.

Most banks and other lenders require that business owners also provide a personal guarantee for the repayment of a loan. This means that, in the case of default, the bank can claim these personally owned assets, such as a house, as repayment of the loan. Offering a personal guarantee is a very serious step for an entrepreneur, because lenders will do whatever they have to do to be repaid. I have seen sad cases of people, some of them very wealthy, who lost a large share of their personal assets to banks after signing personal guarantees on a business venture before thinking through the consequences.

Remember: Lenders always want multiple assurances that they will be paid their interest and principal. First, they will look to the profits of your business for repayment, then to the business's assets, and, finally, to you personally. If your business plan can demonstrate that all these sources of repayment are likely, you have a good chance of garnering support from lenders.

What Will Your Business Accomplish for Your Suppliers?

Most businesses rely on purchasing goods to resell or to use in manufacturing other products. The companies that sell these inputs to your business are your suppliers, and they are essential. If you want to open a tea shop, you had best check to make sure that the supply of distinctive teas you'll need is actually available at a price that you can afford. If you're planning to open an architectural design firm, you probably need specialized computer and software systems to lease or purchase.

Suppliers, of course, view you and your fledgling business as a new customer. And every business loves new customers. Right? Well, maybe. Before a computer company installs a very expensive system in your office, they are going to want some of the same assurances a bank requires before making a loan, namely that they will be paid in full or get their computers back. Before a supplier delivers thousands of dollars worth of tea for your shop, she will certainly want to be paid up front, since most consumable goods are not returnable. Over time, as you prove your creditworthiness with your suppliers, they will likely extend you credit, just as you may eventually offer credit to your faithful customers.

This is an issue worth exploring right at the beginning of designing your business. I have seen a private medical office stymied by its failure to obtain essential testing equipment because the supplier didn't want to aggravate its larger client, a nearby hospital. I saw a high-tech manufacturing business fail over some crucial raw materials that simply couldn't be bought, because they were going to the supplier's larger, more established customers.

What Will Your Business Accomplish for Your Employees?

If your venture requires employees—and almost all do—your business plan needs to demonstrate that you have the means to attract and keep people who have the right qualifications and abilities. If you feel certain that you will always be able to hire good employees at the right price in sufficient numbers, think again.

I witnessed a business close down that provided telephone customer support to software companies because they were located in a city without an adequate supply of well-educated, computer-literate people to hire. I have seen restaurants built, but never open, in communities where the owners simply could not recruit a full-fledged staff of cooks, busboys, and waitstaff.

Then, there were the companies with large enough pools of qualified employees, who couldn't afford to match the excellent salaries and benefits offered by their competitors, so they were forced to close down. I have seen several businesses with such poor management reputations that they could only hire people who couldn't get jobs elsewhere. Needless to say, these businesses always underperformed their competition, until they failed or were sold to owners who hired entirely new management teams.

Your bankable business plan must define the types of employees you need and demonstrate that you will be able to hire and retain them. Employees want fair pay, a good place to work, and opportunities for the future. If your budget calls for salaries at market rates or better and you can show what similar businesses are paying for similarly qualified employees, then you have established your ability to hire a good staff. Creating a good place to work depends on you and your management team. Have you managed a staff successfully before? Were your workers satisfied, as evidenced by low turnover rates? Do some of your previous employees want to come work for you again? Positive answers to these questions will indicate that you can provide an attractive work environment.

Opportunities for employees in entrepreneurial ventures arise from two sources: growth and strong management. If your company is growing, there will be opportunities for promoting employees into positions with more clout and pay. Strong management feels secure enough to give its employees the chance to learn different tasks and build new skills. Discussing these issues in your business plan and demonstrating a record that you understand both sources of opportunities for employees, indicates that your company will work as much for its employees as its employees will work for you.

Last, and Perhaps Least, What Will Your Business Accomplish for You?

If you have demonstrated that you can meet the needs of the key groups you must recruit to build a successful business, then you will learn what the business is capable of accomplishing for you. For most aspiring business owners, prime goals include being their own bosses, working at what they enjoy doing, gaining a sense of accomplishment by building a business, and creating the opportunity to make money.

You may be wondering why I didn't mention money first. The answer is that virtually every study of business owners shows that making money, while an important ambition, is rarely the most compelling goal of an entrepreneur. For example, people in family-owned businesses frequently list spending time with their relatives and employing family members as their most important goals.

Of course, your goals are unique to you. However, to establish them in your own mind, you need to do three things:

• **First, state your goals.** They may be some of the ambitions listed here, or they may be issues such as having the opportunity to travel, work with children, or get away from the incompetent bosses you've worked for in the past. Make these personal goals into a list.

• **Second, ask yourself whether your business will accomplish those goals.** Aspiring business owners who ask themselves this question honestly, often realize that their business idea will not produce the fast path to the riches they envisioned. Or that their dream of doing creative work most of the day dissolves as the reality of running a business—selling to clients, keeping the books, or training a new assistant—comes into play. If the way you have defined your business does, in fact, accomplish your goals, then you can move on to the third step.

• **Third, tear the list up!** From here on your task is to convince others that your business will meet *their* needs and that they should contribute their time, money, or expertise to become your investors, lenders, customers, suppliers, or employees.

If you have been able to define your company in terms of what it will do for others, then you have also defined a worthy and potentially successful business concept. But, beware. As we work through the process of creating a bankable business plan, you may find truth to the expression, "The devil's in the details." Issues and problems may arise that cause you to return to this step of defining a new concept, and force you to start over again.

CHAPTER 2

Action Step Two

Identify Your Company's Initial Needs:
What will you require to get started?

Whether you want to buy an existing company with 300 employees, or can start your business by only adding an extra phone line to your home-office desk, you need to make a list of the materials you'll need. Some may be tangible, such as five-hundred file folders and a large cabinet in which to store them all. Other requirements may be intangible, such as time to create a product design or to do market research. You may need to hire an assistant to develop a retrievable filing system for the five hundred folders, or hire a consultant to set up a computer system that's beyond your technical skills.

If you're going to build a better mousetrap, you may have constructed a prototype out of used toothpaste tubes and bent paper-clips at home, but you'll need a sturdier, more attractive model to show potential investors. What exactly will your mousetrap look like? What materials will you need? Do you require money for research and development to improve on your original toothpaste tube and paper-clip construction? Do you need to hire an engineer to draw up accurate manufacturing designs? Should you patent your invention? Will you need to investigate federal safety standards for mousetraps? Should you allow time to test the materials for durability before you start manufacturing thousands of mousetraps? How many mousetraps do you plan to make at first? Should you find out if extensive advertising in the *Wall Street Journal* will be crucial to starting your firm? The answers to these questions will become the budget line items in your list of startup costs for your business.

And, if you're the client who wants to open a restaurant, you'll have to figure out how much money you'll need to cover your rent, equipment, and renovations before you start turning a profit. If you're the bubblebath manufacturer, you may need to purchase specialized software to stamp bar codes on every bottle. If you're the financial-services company entrepreneur, you need a financial model of the business to show potential investors.

Next, do your homework. Call a real-estate broker and look at actual retail spaces in the neighborhood in which you'd like to open your restaurant. Make a chart of the most expensive and least expensive sites by location and square footage. Then, estimate how much space you require and how much money you'll need to allow for rent.

In the mousetrap scenario, you should contact an engineer who can help you create design specifications. Be sure to ask about her fee structure. Will she charge by the job or by the hour? Will you own the designs or will she? And, if you're the client who wants to make bath time fun, check to see if bubblegum fragrance for your kiddie bubble-bath soap is readily available or has to be manufactured from scratch. How much fragrance will you have to buy to make your soap smell yummy? And, if you're the entrepreneur who wants to open a financial services firm, find out what a half-page ad in the *Wall Street Journal* costs. (Hint: It's mind boggling!)

Make a list of all the tangible and intangible resources you need to get your business going. The total estimated price of all of these items will become your startup cost whether you're buying more toothpaste tubes, an ocarina factory, or simply installing a new telephone line on your desk. If there's any item in your estimates that seems unreasonably high (the *Wall Street Journal* ad is a likely culprit), research alternatives. Keep in mind that it's better to include every element you truly need along with a reasonable estimate of the cost of each item, so you don't run out of money or default on your loans. Be honest and conservative in your estimates, but be optimistic, too.

Whether you are starting a business completely from scratch or buying an existing business with hundreds of employees and millions of dollars in revenue, completing this step carefully and diligently is important, because it starts the process of quantifying what you will need. You can think of this step as the first cut at researching and enumerating the resources your business will require. When you have completed the entire process, which is still a few steps away, you will have produced detailed, credible, and compelling financial projections.

You have already defined your business in terms of what it will accomplish for your major groups of resource providers. Now, it is time to make this resource list more specific and begin your research into each item. If you are planning to purchase an existing, operating business, you will probably have an easier time with this analysis of your initial needs. Existing businesses have actual numbers for costs, so research is considerably easier.

However, even for existing businesses it is valuable to review all categories of expenses in detail to determine where you might be able to reduce costs. For example, if you are purchasing a restaurant, you might be able to improve on the prices or terms by changing suppliers. You may also devise a more effective way to advertise and promote the restaurant. While you do have real numbers to work from when you buy an existing business, you still must research the financial figures thoroughly.

For startup businesses, few operational parameters are established, so the number of options to consider may be very large. For example, suppose a group of accountants wants to start a new firm. They probably have a geographic area in mind, based on whom their initial clients are likely to be. Even so, there might be multiple towns or counties to check for possible office space. They need to research the tax laws in each town or county (not a difficult task for accountants!) because these could make a significant difference in their costs. They should talk to businesspeople in the area to find out which locations are regarded as high status and which as low status.

Some new businesses can locate almost anywhere on earth. If you're starting a clothing factory, you might want to consider as many countries as possible to uncover the best shipping rates, labor costs, and tax breaks. You might want to engage a location consultant for guidance, in which case you should explore various options and costs for these services.

By now, you're probably realizing that you will be spending less time with your feet up on your desk thinking conceptually and making grand plans, and more time slogging through the details of your options. At least I warned you.

The Major Expenses

There is no better way to develop expense estimates than to actually go shopping, so, if you like to shop, you'll enjoy this step. In many industries there is often a big gap between asking price and final price, so shopping may reveal realistic prices. For other types of expenses, such as raw materials, data, or skilled workers, obtaining realistic cost estimates can be a challenge.

Your major expenses will consist of:

$ **Real estate**

$ **Employment market**

$ **Employee benefits**

$ **Startup and capital costs**

$ **Advertising and promotion**

Let's look at each of these expenses in detail.

Real estate.   One industry that often has a large gap between bid and asking price is real estate. If you're examining real estate costs, start with newspaper ads, but don't stop there. Call agents and go see available spaces. Discuss what a final price is likely to be. In real estate, as in many other industries, you can never know what price someone will actually accept until you put a firm offer on the table, so ask about other locations and recent deals. This is a time-consuming and sometimes tedious process, but it will pay dividends in a better final deal. After you have seen a number of properties and talked with several agents, you will understand pricing and the tradeoffs on location and amenities.

Employment market.   For most businesses, salary and benefit costs are a major expense. Your ability to find and retain quality employees can be one of the major determinants of your ability to deliver a quality product or service to your customers. This is another estimate you cannot trust to winging it. To obtain accurate salary estimates, you need to talk with employment agencies, employees who do similar jobs at other companies, and managers of companies who handle hiring. You can also try some simulated hiring. By this, I mean you could actually advertise positions for a company that expects to open soon and have people apply for the jobs. From the response you receive, the quality of the people who apply, and the conversations you have with the applicants, you will be able to develop real, bankable knowledge of likely employment costs and availability.

Employee benefits. Employee benefits include government programs such as Social Security, Worker's Compensation, private health insurance, pension plans, stock-option plans, life insurance, and perhaps other types of benefits. This is a very technical, complex, and highly regulated area, which may make it difficult for you to estimate these costs. The alternative is to ask a benefits consultant, a financial planner, or an accountant to give you some guidance. You need to decide what benefits you'll offer and how the costs will be divided between the company and the employees. If you're hiring people who view their jobs as temporary before they move on to better positions, like fast-food employees, then it's best to provide minimal benefits and make their current pay as high as possible. If you're hiring people who see their jobs as long-term career moves, then you should offer long-term benefits, such as pension plans and stock options. Analyzing this expense will enable you to compile a description of the benefits you expect to offer and a cost per employee expressed as a percentage of each salary, a fixed amount per employee, or a combination of the two.

Startup and capital costs. Startup and capital costs for items such as restaurant equipment, filing cabinets, or raw materials for manufacturing, are very dependent on the exact nature of your business. Establishing a metal fabricating company is going to have very different startup and capital requirements from creating a home-based computer consulting business. But, whatever the precise list of startup costs, get bids and speak with as many potential sources as possible.

Advertising and promotion. For many new and established retail businesses, advertising is an important part of the initial plan to attract new or additional customers. I describe a detailed marketing plan in Chapter 5 and give an outline for one in Part III but, in order to establish what you need in an initial burst of advertising, you must consider two issues. First, where will you find your customers? Do they read particular magazines or newspapers, or listen to certain radio stations? Can you purchase a list of likely customers? The answers to these questions will help you create a basic budget for reaching your market. The second issue to consider is that repetition is the essence of advertising. You will need to purchase multiple ads, send multiple mailings, and make multiple sales calls before your message is heard by a large share of your target audience. Be certain to budget enough funds to achieve this critically important repetition.

Once you've identified your company's initial requirements, you will have a much clearer concept of what you'll need to buy, invest, or borrow in order to start your business. This information will become the basis for the credible financial analysis that will be an essential component of your bankable business plan.

CHAPTER 3

Action Step Three

Choose a
Winning Strategy:
How will you distinguish your
product or service from others?

Now it is time to select an effective business strategy for your enterprise, based on your specific business goals. Before you can decide on a winning strategy, however, you have to know what you want to achieve with your concept, such as positive cash flow, personal wealth, profitability, improved market share, or an advantageous sale of an existing business. Strategy is *how* you will accomplish those goals through actions such as advertising and cost control, as well as product characteristics and quality.

This chapter takes you through the process of creating a winning strategy for your business by helping you to understand your industry, define your competitive advantage, and analyze your company's strengths and weaknesses. You will learn that vague strategies, such as "I will have the best product available," are not nearly as powerful, convincing, or successful as specific strategies.

There are two fundamental categories of business strategies: low cost leadership and differentiation. Choosing the best strategies from within these two categories is the first step in developing a strong competitive advantage for your business. Once you understand these two basic categories, you can adapt the best strategies to your business according to the type of industry you have chosen, whether it is in an industry that is emerging, maturing, or declining.

Low-Cost Leadership

Everyone likes to pay the lowest possible price for any product or service, so companies that can offer customers the lowest prices have a strong competitive advantage. Masters of low-cost strategies include WalMart, which uses its enormous buying power to negotiate lower prices from its suppliers, then manages store operations so efficiently, that it can price below its competitors and still make a profit. Dell Computer, regarded as the most efficient manufacturer of personal computers, employs a strategy that allows the company to increase market share by lowering prices, while still remaining profitable and forcing its competitors to lose money if they try to match Dell's prices. Toyota has accomplished the same low-cost leadership in the auto industry.

Many entrepreneurs starting new businesses think they will be able to execute a low cost strategy, but most find out otherwise. It is difficult for a new business to operate more efficiently than existing businesses that are already known to their market, are profitable, and have experienced and knowledgeable management and staff. Existing businesses usually have access to more financing than startups, giving them a big advantage if a price war breaks out.

Differentiation

Designing your product or service precisely to match the preferences of your customers makes your business attractive, and sets it apart from your competitors. Think about the choices you have when you decide to book a hotel room. Hotel companies differentiate themselves with such qualities as room size, location, luxurious appointments, reputation, sports facilities, image, price, and level of service.

Motel 6, for example, is geared to the bargain traveler who isn't interested in amenities, but the company is successful because they've designed their product to appeal to a sizable, yet very specific, group of customers. Your business plan needs to define your target market and state how you will differentiate your product or service to appeal to your potential customers.

Create a Powerful Competitive Advantage

To be successful, every business must have some competitive advantage over its competition. Competition is the enemy of profits: It's great for customers, but bad for business. Competitive advantage is the barrier that keeps competition at bay. The stronger your competitive advantage, the more profitable and less affected by competition your business is likely to be.

The first step in selecting strategies from one of the two basic categories—either low-cost leadership or differentiation—is to identify a competitive advantage for your product or service. How will you establish that your product or service is better, cheaper, more delicious, and/or more convenient? How can you make your company more noticeable than your competitors? What restraints in your business or industry might determine which strategy you choose?

Your competitive advantage may include designing special features not found in rival products. It may entail superior service characteristics such as speedier delivery, a lower price, or more attentive salespeople. Perhaps you're establishing an image or brand of exceptional quality or reputation. Does your product or service bestow a certain status on its users? Does it create more profits or other benefits for your customers' own endeavors?

Suppose you want to open a restaurant that serves squid-flavored pancakes. What will your competitive advantage be? Do you know that the people in the neighborhood devour other squid-based dishes and can't seem to get their fill? Have all the other pancake restaurants in the community failed to include squid-flavored items on their menus? Is squid much cheaper to acquire than other more traditional pancake ingredients, such as bananas? Will that enable you to charge much less for all the items on your menu, including banana pancakes? Will the decor of your restaurant be so enticing to squid lovers that they'll come in to look around and then discover how delicious your squid pancakes can be?

Perhaps you want to position your mousetrap for a primarily upscale market because the best design requires titanium, and manufacturing costs will be so expensive only rich people will be able to afford your product. Maybe the mousetrap is so fantastically effective that wealthy people will want hundreds of them around their vast country estates and polo-pony barns.

Examples of strong competitive advantages include:

$ **A patent**, which prevents anyone else from using your product without your permission. Pharmaceuticals are protected by patents for significant periods of time, making them both high priced and highly profitable.

$ **A government-granted monopoly**, such as a cable-television franchise, which prevents anyone else from entering the same business in your particular territory.

$ **An effective monopoly**, such as Microsoft and Windows operating systems, that is protected by copyrights. Microsoft also has a competitive advantage by its emergence as the *de facto* standard in personal computers, virtually assuring that purchasers of new computers will want Windows.

$ **A great name brand**, such as Jell-O or Oreo cookies, gives a company a prime position in people's minds within that product category. Many small, but long-established businesses also have very strong brand names, such as local restaurants, banks, and bookstores.

$ **Speed** is a powerful competitive advantage. From the days of clipper ships to FedEx jets, customers have always valued speed. Other businesses built with speed as a key competitive advantage include Domino's Pizza, Dell Computer, and any company that uses Web and e-mail applications.

Some businesses have inherently weak competitive advantages. Electronics or appliance retailers, which sell the same products as their competitors, are often forced to compete solely on price and a reputation for service. There are exceptions, however. In New York City, there are thousands of take-out pizzerias, often located within a block or less of each other, yet they all manage to be successful because there is lots of demand for pizza, the stores are easy to operate, and customers usually opt for convenience in choosing which pizzeria to patronize.

Here are the principal strategies you can use with somewhat weaker competitive advantages to make your business profitable:

$ **Lower Your Price.** If you can sell the same products or services as your competitors at a lower price, you will attract customers. However, can you undercut your competitors' prices and still make a profit? You can if your costs are lower than theirs, so the key to this strategy is having an operating plan that makes you more efficient, or able to purchase materials from suppliers or manufacturers at a lower cost than your competitors. This strategy has worked for WalMart, but has failed for the dozens of electronics retailers who have gone out of business because of their inability to match or beat their competitors' prices and still make a profit. Remember my warning—this is a tough strategy to execute.

$ **Provide Great Service.** The differences in service levels are often the deciding factor for customers. A reputation for service will often influence a customer's choice of independent contractors, such as plumbers or electricians. Car dealers make little or no money on new car sales because all dealers of any particular manufacturer sell the same models. They usually end up competing based on postsale services, such as regular maintenance, lending cars to customers during repairs, or offering a pick-up and drop-off service. Dealers often have local reputations that are well known, plus the car manufacturers rate each dealer's service record. Most car buyers would rather pay more for a car from a dealer with a good service reputation, whether they purchase new cars on a regular basis or keep a car for years.

$ **Build a Positive Image and Brand.** Most buyers feel that the brands of the products they buy or the companies they do business with reflect their values, while also sending a message about themselves to friends and associates.

$ **Develop a Good Reputation.** Nothing is more reassuring to a customer than buying from a company or person with a strong reputation. Customers often suffer *buyer's remorse* after making a major purchase, a period of insecurity in which they wonder if the cost was worth the price of ownership. This is when they need the reassurance of knowing they bought the product from a person or company of high reputation or with a strong name brand. A solid reputation is not only a selling point in its own right, but it actually immunizes customers from a bad case of buyer's remorse. Having a strong reputation is a great competitive advantage.

$ **Achieve High Status.** We all know that Rolex, Rolls Royce, and Burberry are status consumer products. For customers who want the status these products impart, there are few competitors and, almost by definition, a higher price to pay.

That's why status is such a desirable competitive advantage. I have a friend who owned a high-status Lexus, which is manufactured by Toyota. When he traded it in a couple of years later, during leaner times, for a Toyota Camry, I asked him what the difference was between the two cars. "Twenty thousand dollars and a lot of status with my friends," was his reply! If your plan includes positioning your product or service as high status, then your business can expect to have higher-than-average profit margins.

Use a SWOT Analysis to Determine the Competitive Advantage of an Existing Business

A good way to begin your research into competitive advantage is with a SWOT analysis, an acronym which stands for strengths, weaknesses, opportunities, and threats. You can even do a SWOT analysis for a startup, if you are brutally frank about where your company will stand relative to existing businesses in your market. Let's look at each of the elements of a SWOT analysis:

   Strengths include the organization's internal capabilities, such as good relationships with key customers, or strong technical skills.

   Weaknesses also include such internal disadvantages as inadequate warehouse facilities or poor sales staff.

   Opportunities relate to external issues such as underserved markets in an adjacent community, or a current competitor who could be bought out.

   Threats are also external to the business and include such problems as an official change in traffic patterns that could make it more difficult for customers to find the store, or a potential increase in sales taxes that could send customers across the border to an adjacent state.

   Your SWOT analysis does not have to be scientific or particularly rigorous, but it will help you organize your thoughts about the strategic position of an existing business. Addressing how you will cope with any problems you uncover in your SWOT analysis will give your business plan credibility. Investors and lenders expect startups, as well as existing businesses, to have weaknesses or threats, but they also expect your plan to indicate how you will manage these potential difficulties and minimize their impact.

Plan Ahead: Anticipate an Exit Strategy

You need to give extensive thought to how you will exit your business—and create profits for yourself and your investors. Some businesses, such as real estate, have assets with clear values that are relatively easy to realize through sales, and can produce quick exits. Other businesses, such as consulting companies, have assets which are based on the owner's expertise and the relationships between staff members and clients, and are much more difficult to value or exit.

Whatever your business, you need to craft an exit strategy in advance and build it into your financial projections. Potential investors are going to ask you about it, because they probably don't see themselves staying with you forever, and are focused on how much they will earn. Lenders want to be sure that any sale of the business will produce enough money to pay them back in full, plus interest.

Matching Your Strategies to Any Type of Industry

Many people believe that only ventures in rapidly growing industries can be successful. In fact, you can build a successful business in any type of industry and in virtually any competitive environment . . . if you use the right strategy. Investors and lenders recognize five categories of industries:

$ Emerging industries

$ Maturing industries

$ Stagnant and declining industries

$ Fragmented industries

$ Industries with dominant leaders

Let's review the nature of these five categories and the specific strategies that are likely to lead to success in each.

Emerging Industries

Emerging industries are the gold-rush opportunities that spring up quickly and attract a great deal of attention and investment in the early phases of their development. Examples include the Internet, over the past decade; housing construction immediately following World War II; and the film industry after the invention of the moving-picture camera. While there was tremendous growth in each of these industries, it was also encumbered by a great deal of competition and uncertainty. Let's look at the pluses and minuses of doing business in an emerging industry:

Pluses of Emerging Industries

$ A rapid rate of growth of new customers

$ Easy entrance to the market, even for people without experience, because no one has experience

$ Lack of established industry leaders who need to be overcome, making the playing field rather level for all competitors

Minuses of Emerging Industries

$ Many of the technologies and standards are unclear and may not be clarified for a long time. If you owned a software company early in the Personal Computer revolution, it was not apparent which operating system would become dominant. If you decided to write your software for an operating system other than Microsoft's, then you probably put yourself out of business. Similar struggles exist today regarding the digital systems for distribution of music, books, and cellular phones.

$ Although the ease of entering the market can be a plus, it can also be a substantial negative if you've established your business first. For example, the low barriers to entry in the website design business have reduced profit margins as new companies and individuals launch their ventures and underprice their services to build revenue and a customer base.

$ Lack of information about your competition can prevent you from making sound business decisions. If you can't figure out who your competitors are, what products they're developing, or how they're advertising and pricing their merchandise or services, you'll be operating in a fog. As a result, you may not realize that your market is too limited and your price too high to attract customers until it's too late and your business fails.

$ Buyers may delay purchasing products in an emerging industry because they want to see if a dominant technology arises or if prices will drop dramatically as manufacturing costs become less expensive. You have probably done this yourself. Maybe you didn't buy a VCR player until you were confident which of the competing systems would capture the market, or you waited until prices were lowered and quality improved. This reluctance on the part of buyers to purchase a new product immediately can spell major problems for entrepreneurs in emerging industries.

$ Necessary resources for emerging industries can be hard to find, and you may have to pay more to procure them. During the California gold rush of 1849, there were reports of prospectors paying more than $100 for a shovel that used to cost only 50 cents. During the peak of the Internet boom, high-school students who could program in HTML, the language used for Websites, were being offered jobs at website design companies for $100,000 per year. It is often better to sell *to* companies in emerging industries than to be one! Otherwise, resources such as financing, components, and raw materials will be expensive, if available at all.

The Best Strategies for Emerging Industries

$ **Create a bold, win-early strategy.** This is the approach that Amazon.com and 3Com, the maker of the Palm Pilot, have used in their emerging industries. Grow as quickly as possible to make yourself the brand name that customers know.

$ **Be the best.** Sony, Hewlett-Packard, and Cisco Systems are companies that established performance standards for their new products, putting distance between themselves and their competitors.

$ **Superserve niche markets.** Define and develop customer groups by geography, application, pricing, or marketing. Computer Associates owns many niche software products, such as computer security and accounting software. It doesn't compete with the big players, but it finds and serves markets that are too small to interest giants like Microsoft.

$ **Pick the winning technology as soon as possible.** If you had owned a company that produced videotapes when the Betamax format was still battling with VHS for dominance, you had to switch to VHS as soon as it became clear that VHS was becoming the market standard. If you didn't act quickly, you would have wasted money on a rapidly disappearing market.

$ **Build brand loyalty, especially with consumer products.** Given all the competition and uncertainty in emerging markets, the quicker you can build a brand that customers can believe in, the sooner you will be constructing some protection from your competitors. Brands are a powerful tool for grabbing and keeping customers.

Businesses in emerging industries need to be prepared for well-financed outsiders to move in aggressively. Microsoft has systematically cornered the word processing, e-mail, spreadsheet, and database software markets, often destroying all competition in its path. Entertainment giants such as AOL Time Warner, Disney, and Viacom had the stability and finances to wait for the cable television industry to develop into a large scale, viable business from thousands of small, local operators and minor programming firms before they set out to absorb them profitably. Today, these companies dominate their industry.

If your business is in an emerging, high-growth industry, you should think about what happens to your venture and your investors when the giants awaken. Will you sell your company to the big guys? Do you have a tactic to withstand their onslaught? Or do you expect to cash in early and be lying by your Olympic-sized swimming pool before this happens? Whatever you expect, you need to cover this issue in your plan.

Maturing Industries

As industries mature, the rate of growth slows. This is happening today in the personal-computer business and the Internet service provider (ISP) industry. It occurred recently in the video rental business and during the 1960s and 1970s in the automobile industry. Here is what typically happens in maturing industries:

$ **Demand slows.** While the industry may still be growing, the rate of demand for the products or services is beginning to diminish. This usually makes competition rougher, because the same number of businesses are fighting over fewer new customers.

$ **Buyers become smarter.** Customers become more sophisticated and demanding as they gain experience with new products or services. Perhaps when you bought your first VCR you didn't know enough to check if it could fast forward without turning the screen blank, but you certainly figured this out by the time you bought your next VCR. If your company is in a maturing industry, expect to see your customers quickly climb the learning curve and want to buy products with better features, or more options that deliver better value. This may make it harder to price your products high enough to be profitable.

$ **Excess supply appears.** As demand slows, it usually takes a while for manufacturers or suppliers to adjust their production. When supply exceeds demand, some suppliers cut prices to push their products out of inventory, which can reduce overall market prices and profit margins.

$ **International competition increases.** For manufactured products especially, foreign competitors who have lower labor costs or higher government subsidies can enter a market during this time and provide tough price competition. After a few years of DVD player sales, a low-cost Chinese manufacturer entered the U.S. market, underpricing the competition by nearly a third.

$ **Profitability suffers.** When competition spurs price cuts, profits suffer. Companies that are weak financially can fail or become takeover targets as soon as their profits decline.

$ **Consolidation follows.** When supply exceeds demand, profit margins diminish, and weaker companies face failure, a maturing industry usually enters a phase of consolidation in which bigger companies buy smaller companies, and some smaller companies combine to form larger ones.

The Best Strategies for Maturing Industries

$ **Reduce cost.** When profits are shrinking from lower prices, companies must strive to maintain profitability by reducing expenses. Ways of doing this include paying closer attention to efficiency, eliminating costly product features, or reducing the product line, so that the company can make fewer products more efficiently. Motorola dominated the cellular telephone industry during its early periods, but when the industry began to mature and Motorola began to lose money, it cut back on its product line, eliminated features that consumers didn't seem to care about, and reduced its operating overhead.

$ **Focus marketing on major customers.** Steady customers with large orders can be serviced more efficiently than small customers who purchase in limited and sporadic quantities. It's also usually easier to maintain price competitiveness with the larger customers.

$ **Expand to new markets.** As existing markets become saturated and it becomes more difficult to remain profitable, you can expand to new markets with less competition and newer, less sophisticated customers.

$ **Purchase rivals.** One way to reduce competition is to purchase your competitors. When many small companies are bought up to form much bigger companies, it is sometimes referred to as a roll-up. This has happened among media businesses, accounting firms, hospitals, and car dealerships.

Think about well-known, recently founded companies and see if their current strategies are a closer match to those companies on the list for maturing industries. As Jeff Bezos discusses in the foreword, Amazon.com executed strategies for emerging industries when it opened for business—namely to get big fast and seize a strong market position. Since then, it has also worked to reduce its costs by focusing on efficiency, expanding its market to include more countries served and more types of products sold, and concentrating on service for bigger customers by using tactics such as free shipping for orders over $100. All of these strategies are effective in maturing industries, even if, in this case, the industry is only a few years old.

Stagnant and Declining Industries

Industries shrinking or experiencing zero growth are called *stagnant* or *declining* industries. The mattress and pillow industries were stagnant for many years until innovative products, such as allergyproof bedding, and new marketing techniques, such as catalog sales, revitalized them. The candle industry suffered decades of decline until recently, when significant numbers of successful, upscale, retail candle stores were established in major cities.

The Best Strategies for Stagnant or Declining Industries

$ **Focus on niches, especially growing niches.** In addition to allergyproof products, the bed and pillow industries have focused on people with back and neck problems, a growing group as the American population has aged and grown heavier. They also target their advertising to magazines, newspapers, and television shows that reach wealthier, older audiences.

$ **Differentiate and innovate.** The candle industry has innovated by creating new designs, such as long-lasting candles, and by adding various aromas, as well as encouraging entrepreneurs to open candle boutiques.

$ **Reduce cost wherever possible.** Cost reduction is always a good strategy, because it allows a company to stay profitable even if it needs to cut prices. In the bedding industry, for example, companies started selling directly to consumers through direct mail catalogs, in addition to supplying their retailers. This reduced costs, and allowed them to target consumers who were too busy to shop in stores and wanted fast delivery of bulky items.

Fragmented Industries

Industries with many competitors, none of which has a large market share, are called *fragmented* industries. They include businesses such as restaurants, lawn-care companies, building contractors, and florists. Fragmented industries are generally easy to enter, because they require only low levels of investment, which accounts for the constant stream of new competitors in these businesses. It's also difficult for fragmented businesses to remain efficient as they grow.

A nonfragmented company, such as General Motors, can make a million cars per year with a lower cost per car than if it made only 1,000 cars annually. However, restaurants, plumbers, florists, and other fragmented industry enterprises, can't benefit from these efficiencies, called *economies of scale*, as they grow. In fact, it can even become more expensive to provide their products or services as they grow.

For example, if a pizzeria owner wants to open an additional restaurant in another neighborhood, he may save a little money on bulk food purchases, but he must hire the same number of waitresses per customer and cooks per meal in order to maintain the excellent service he offers his clientele in the original location. He will also be forced to hire a full-time manager at the new restaurant, since he won't be able to be in two places at the same time. Because of such issues, businesses in fragmented industries tend to focus primarily on local markets.

The Best Strategies for Fragmented Industries

$ **Focus on the local market.** Because of the characteristics of these fragmented industries, one rarely sees regional plumbing companies or regional florists. The successful ones are those that focus on building clientele in their local markets.

$ **Specialize your product or service.** As businesses in fragmented markets specialize, they are able to gain a competitive advantage, maintain strong prices, and become profitable. Bakeries that concentrate on producing elaborate wedding cakes, health clubs that offer expert personal trainers, or lawn-care companies that specialize in sports fields, are all examples of this strategy.

$ **Create formula facilities.** In order to expand, businesses in fragmented industries need to create simple, standardized, no-frills, formula facilities. Examples of companies employing this strategy include Kinko's, McDonald's, Bally's Health Clubs, and Mail Boxes Etc. Formula facilities also open the door to franchising.

$ **Keep costs down.** Fragmented markets are, by definition, very competitive. Only businesses that control their costs can withstand the constant onslaught of new competitors who try to gain a foothold by underpricing the competition.

Industries with Dominant Leaders

Successful industry leaders such as Microsoft, Toyota, or McDonald's, stay on the offensive by constantly striving to improve their operations and efficiency, and by bringing out new, more popular products. They continually promote and advertise to fortify their brands, and only reduce prices as a last resort to maintain their market share. When they do it right, as these three companies have, they are tough competitors.

Not all market leaders do it right. AT&T has withered to a shadow of the untouchable giant it once was through a combination of missteps. It lost its technology edge when management began to focus on stock price through short-term strategies, such as selling divisions, and through regulatory changes that opened up the door to new competitors. Kmart, the successor to the venerable Kresge Department store company, filed for bankruptcy in 2002 because it couldn't keep up with competition from Wal-Mart, Target, Kohls', and others. Its problems included older, smaller stores and weaker management.

This means that you can develop a business strategy to battle the big guys and win.

The Best Strategies for Competing with Dominant Industry Leaders

$ **Focus on the long term.** Large companies tend to focus on their quarterly financial performance, because this is how Wall Street evaluates them. They can miss the long-term trends or be reluctant to invest in long-term projects. The music industry refused to understand the impact of digital recordings until Internet-based services, such as Napster, began to hurt them significantly. Now, traditional music companies are buying digital services to catch up.

$ **Take risks.** Corporate managers are . . . corporate. They can be rather bureaucratic, and reluctant to take risks that might endanger that next big bonus, or a long-awaited promotion. New York Mayor Michael Bloomberg made himself a billionaire by playing the role of David and taking on the Goliaths in the financial-information industry, mainly large banks and brokerage houses. He took a risk and built a better system and now his system has come to dominate much of this industry.

$ **Know the market.** Corporate managers tend to believe that they know the market better than their customers do. In what is probably the worst business decision of all time, Western Union turned down purchasing Alexander Graham Bell's telephone because they didn't think enough people would want it. Pursue your judgment of what will sell. If the big guys don't see it, think of Alexander Graham Bell.

These weaknesses among big companies create what has been rightfully called the *attacker's advantage*. So, if you're a David and want to confront a Goliath, don't despair. With an attacker's advantage based on a long-term focus, your knowledge of the market and your willingness to take risks, you can still compete with the big guys.

It is important to match the strategies you use to reach your business goals to the characteristics of your specific industry. Be sure your strategies are outwardly focused and geared to your best competitive advantage. Make certain that they will impress potential investors and lenders as being the most powerful means to achieve your business goals—and theirs.

4

Action Step Four

Analyze Your Market:

Who will want your product or service?

Identifying your market is one of the great satisfactions of starting your own business. You're thinking about the actual people who will use your product or service, and how pleased they will be buying it as you are selling it.

To determine your targeted market, write down the demographics of the people who will use your product or service. How old are they? What do they do for a living? Will mostly women use your service? Is your product or service attractive to a particular ethnic or economic group? Will only the wealthy be able to afford it? Does your ideal customer live in a certain type of neighborhood, such as a suburb, in order to use your lawn mower? Answering these questions about the demographics of your prime market will help you establish the clear characteristics of the people you need to reach.

If you're selling soap, you may believe that every dirty body needs your product, but you can't start with the entire world as your initial market. Even if you've developed such a ubiquitous item as soap, you need to identify a smaller, more targeted customer group first, such as children under eight, for the bubble-gum scented bubble bath. If your soap only works with pumped well water without fluoride, you must acknowledge that your intended market has geographical limits as well.

If the major benefit of your soap is that it doesn't cause eyes to tear upon contact, your primary customers will probably be children under age eight or, rather, their parents, who do the actual shopping. If your soap contains pumice that will remove car grease, paint, and tile cement without toxic chemicals or fumes, your market will be defined by people who work at specific professions, say, mechanics, house painters, and bathroom contractors. It may be that your product works well on removing garden dirt, too, or that many grownups don't like to cry when they get soap in their eyes, but you want to make sure that you have targeted the best buyers first. The more focused your market, the more convincing your plan will be. You can always branch out later.

Establishing the size of your potential market is important, too. This will be easier once you've completed the demographic analysis. Then you'll be able to research the numbers: How many car mechanics, house painters or bathroom contractors are there in any given community? How many children in the United States are currently under the age of eight? How much soap will they use in a month or a year? How many other soap manufacturers already have a share of the market? How big are your potential competitors? Do any of them make bubble-gum–scented soap? And, where do you find the answers to all of these questions?

There are three aspects of a marketing plan that fall under the heading "more is better." These are research, targeting, and testing. The more of each you do and provide to your potential funders, the better and more convincing your plan will be—and the more likely your business will succeed.

Your marketing strategy begins with a carefully researched, highly specific description of your target market. If you're building welding tools for use in manufacturing and modifying cars, you need to research potential customers and the competitive products they currently use. Based on this, you will be able to create a list of the companies that need your product, as well as the names of the people at each company who make the purchasing decisions. Finally, you can actually test for market acceptance of your product by speaking with people in the industry.

If you're selling poles for pole vaulters, you can research which colleges and universities train pole vaulters and the coaches who decide which poles to buy. From this information, you can create a list of potential customers, and test your concept by speaking with coaches and athletes.

If you're opening a clothing store for teenage girls, you should research this market by collecting industry and consumption pattern data, and by researching the stores that currently sell in the geographic areas you are considering. Based on this research, you will be able to define your potential market by demographic characteristics such as age, geography, income, and race. Finally, you can test your concept by interviewing teenage girls who are in your target group, and actually asking them if they would shop at the kind of store you envision.

The three most important guidelines to follow in defining your target market are:

1. Research your potential market thoroughly. Whether your business plan specifies six potential customers or millions, you must learn a great deal about them. The end of the book lists some helpful sources for consumer data, if you're targeting a broad consumer market. You can also commission or carry out your own research to test consumer reaction to your concept by phone surveys, in-person interviews, or consumer focus groups. This can be very expensive if you hire a professional research company, so try to invest some of your time in speaking directly with members of your target group.

2. Target your market like a bull's eye. The smaller and more tightly defined your target market is, the more likely your plan will grow into a successful business, and attract funding sources. Identifying the most likely purchasers of your product or service will produce the greatest returns on your marketing expenditures, so make the target as specific as possible.

3. Test before you launch. You will increase the effectiveness of your marketing strategy if you actually test your concepts first. A successful test will also greatly increase the confidence potential investors will have in your plan. This test could take the form of a small mailing to potential customers asking them to order your product, putting your product in a few stores and seeing how well it sells, or making sales calls on potential customers and seeing their reactions.

1. Research Your Potential Market Thoroughly

Identifying and defining your target market in the following ways will help you create the most convincing marketing campaign possible.

$ **By geography**, so you can locate your business near specific markets or target your advertising to reach potential customers most efficiently.

$ **By demographics**, so you will understand such customer characteristics as age, gender, and ethnicity in tailoring your advertising messages and focusing your marketing efforts.

$ **By season**, so you can schedule your marketing efforts when buying is most likely.

$ **By purchasing patterns**, so you can identify products or services that tend to be bought at the same time, and match your marketing to those trends.

Understanding your competition and their strategies is key to positioning and promoting your product or service. For each competitor you can:

$ **Collect** their printed promotional materials.

$ **Record** their broadcast advertising to analyze their messages to consumers, and determine their marketing expenditures.

$ **Develop** a profile of their customers based on industry research, interviews with experts, or by simply watching and recording the characteristics of people who enter their stores.

$ **Create** a comprehensive view of their product line, including each product's characteristics and price.

$ **Prepare** a corporate history that details each competitor's business development, including various marketing strategies.

Understanding the history of your industry will help you to see the big trends. For example, the food industry has experienced major changes with the increase of two-income households. With both men and women in the workforce, the demand for traditional food products that require lots of preparation has decreased, while the craving for prepared foods that can be put on the table quickly has increased.

The gradual graying of our population has affected the health-club industry by increasing the demand for low impact exercise equipment that works the cardiovascular system but is gentle on aging joints. Seeing the history and trends in your industry will help you position and market your business effectively. Similarly, gathering financial information such as pricing, profit margins, bank lending practices, and investor interest will be enormously useful in building your financial projections. Much of this information can be obtained from bankers, investors, and industry experts. In my experience, most people will make themselves available and talk candidly with prospective business owners in their industry. Also, as I discuss in the section that follows, and in Chapter 10, much of this information can be obtained in the library or from the RMA database.

Your Field Trip to the Library

Plan on spending at least one entire day in a library, preferably a business library. I have spent thousands of hours in libraries and, although electronic databases have revolutionized the process and speed of research, taking the time to read through material carefully is still the best way to unearth useful information, whether it's on a computer screen, on microfilm, or in a dusty old bound journal.

In the references at the back, I list the databases that I find extremely useful, but the specifics of your industry will largely determine which ones are best for your research. Look at industry-oriented magazines, newsletters, journals, and databases. Use the *Readers' Guide to Periodical Literature* to research products or industries in general business publications. The *Wall Street Journal*, *Forbes*, and *BusinessWeek* cover almost every industry, often profiling specific businesses and interviewing CEOs of both large and fledgling corporations.

Academic journals may not be particularly entertaining to read, but they cover a vast array of subjects. Sometimes an academic journal will publish a study that uses a sample of businesses in your industry to analyze a subject of scholarly interest. Read it, because it may provide statistics and marketing information which will make your business plan even more persuasive and bankable.

Don't forget to talk to the librarians. Most hold advanced degrees in library science, and all are familiar with the tools and organization of their particular facilities. They're experts and are there to help you reduce wasteful research time. Tap their brains and knowledge. They'll be honored and you will be rewarded.

Business Resource Centers

Small Business Development Centers (SBDCs) are local outreach offices of the federal Small Business Administration (SBA). They house useful information about their local markets, data on virtually every industry, and sample business plans. Many state and local governments have business-resource centers to encourage economic development in their areas. Staff members are often very knowledgeable about data sources on the local economy and business environment.

The Web—A Useful Resource, But Caveat Emptor

The good news is that there is a huge amount of information available on the web. The bad news is that you cannot make the web the cornerstone of your research efforts. Many websites exist to generate sales for products, to disseminate information to influence government policy, to sell memberships, or to publicize someone. Sometimes websites sell government data that you can obtain free (as they did).

In addition, the sources of the data are often not stated and even if they are, an independent website may not be playing by the same rules as established, well-respected data sources that you can find in the library. Often, it is hard to tell the good websites from those that are best avoided, and whose agendas can interfere with the objectivity and accuracy of their information. If you take a moment to ask yourself what the website's agenda is, you may come to the conclusion that using its data or opinions as a piece of the foundation of your business could be a big mistake.

In the references, I list the sites I find most useful, including the SBA and census sites. Industry associations may also have useful sites. Beyond that, you are venturing into dangerous internet waters.

Research Relevant Regulation

Every business must function in an environment of government regulation. Think about it: Taxes, employee benefits, construction projects, and contracts—just to name a few areas—are all tightly controlled by regulation. Identifying the key regulatory restrictions that will make an impact on your venture is one of the major tasks in analyzing the market for your proposed business.

If you're opening a restaurant, you will probably need an operating license, and your employees may have to complete mandated training in food handling. There are likely to be regulations controlling noise levels, food delivery times, garbage pickup rules and greasy-kitchen exhaust limits, as well as special licensing fees and taxes to pay, all of which must be included in your proposed budget.

Any business that requires construction will have to cope with zoning regulations, obtaining a certificate of occupancy, and complying with literally hundreds of individual building codes. Although your architect or contractor will be able to handle the specific details, your business plan must address these concerns to make certain that regulations and zoning rules will not interfere with your building design, parking-lot size, or operating hours. There may be upcoming changes in regulations that could affect your product or service, so you will need to speak with government officials, lawyers, politicians, and other business owners.

I know of a restaurant in the Midwest that planned to open on a main road leading into town. The owner didn't check with local officials and, a few weeks after opening his diner, the town changed the traffic patterns and the number of cars passing the restaurant dropped by more than 60 percent. Three months later, the restaurant closed. If the entrepreneur had met with local officials or had attended local town council meetings, this disaster could have been avoided.

Many regulations, perhaps most regulations, are actually good for business. For example, tough licensing standards limit competition. Government granted franchises, such as those for cable television, broadcast stations, taxicabs, or even hot-dog stands, often amount to government-protected monopolies. In many industries, such as education, health, and transportation, mandated government expenditures are the main source of income. Make sure your business plan delineates the way government regulations affect your business—both positively and negatively.

2. Target Your Market Like a Bull's Eye

The more narrowly you can define your target market the more effective—and cost effective—your marketing efforts can be. Suppose your business is Howie's House of Hubcaps, specializing in replacement hubcaps for 1955 to 1960 Chevys. On one hand, you could advertise during the Superbowl to reach half the people in the country, but that would bankrupt you and waste the vast majority of your advertising budget to reach people who don't own 1955 to 1960 Chevys. On the other hand, if your research revealed vintage Chevy clubs that sell ads in their newsletters or would sell you their lists, restorers who specialize in these cars, or annual gatherings of owners of vintage Chevys, you could build an effective marketing program very cheaply. This would make the financials look better and impress your potential investors.

If your plan is to open Bobbie's Sox, a store selling a wide variety of socks, your research might give you information about the age, income, professions, and gender of people who tend to spend the most money on socks. Then you can target your location, store design, inventory choices, and advertising to this segment of the market that purchases the most socks.

Understanding the motivations of your potential customers will help you target customer groups for your marketing strategy. Examples of customer motivation include:

$ Low price

$ Status

$ Quality

$ Speed of delivery

$ Service

$ Design

For example, if you have a glassware-manufacturing business, you need to find out what influences your customers. Do they tend to buy your product when they purchase a second home, or rent a new apartment following a divorce? Is it an item that young couples list on their wedding registries? Or do customers view your glassware as a basic product they buy any time because of function, design, and price? Answers to these questions can help you identify the appropriate target market and incorporate its description into your plan. An executive for IKEA told me that two of their best markets consisted of people buying country homes outside big cities, and people getting divorced who need to set up new homes fast. This knowledge helped IKEA to organize its stores, price its products, and plan its promotions.

I had a Chinese student who was sought out by parents in her neighborhood raising adopted babies from China. They wanted her advice about how to keep their children connected to their Chinese heritage. She thought there might be a business selling Chinese children's books, language lessons, clothing, and other products to this highly targeted market. Within a short time, she had researched the size and characteristics of the market, talked to many parents in her neighborhood, and communicated with friends in China to estimate the costs of purchasing products for children. She built her website herself, which became profitable within a few months. This is more than most dot.com business founders can say about their success. Today www.chinasprout.com continues to grow and thrive by applying strategies to help it move from the initial 100 products sold to its small, original market, to providing more than 3,000 products to a much broader market, including retailers and wholesalers.

3. Test Before You Launch

Remember that your plan is trying to convince readers of the efficacy of your idea. There is a Harvard Business School case study on the startup of *Parenting* magazine, which shows the plan that the founder of the business, Robin Wolaner, used to attract investors. The plan is thorough and sensible, but the most convincing part is the results of the test mailing that Robin made to young parents asking them to subscribe. These results clearly showed that a larger mailing would attract enough subscribers to make the magazine successful, which is exactly what happened. In the *Parenting* magazine case, the mailing was itself a significant expenditure. If your budget doesn't allow for that, there are still many alternatives:

$ **Arrange to put sample products** in stores to see how they sell.

$ **Make sales calls on prospective clients** or customers, and ask them if they will commit to buying as soon as your business is up and running.

$ **Interview potential customers** and industry experts to solicit their opinions of your business idea.

$ **Study the performance of close competitors.** This can include counting the foot traffic into their stores, estimating their revenue from public databases such as Dun and Bradstreet, or private sources such as lawyers, accountants, or past employees.

$ **Run your own research program** with focus groups, consisting of approximately a dozen consumers in your target group, at which you discuss your proposed products or services.

$ **Talk to customers** of a business you are planning to buy to find out how satisfied they are with the products or services they currently receive, and what ideas they have for improvements.

Careful testing will give you useful information about how the market will view your product or service, and it will add considerable credibility to your plan.

CHAPTER | **5**

Action Step Five

Develop a Strong Marketing Campaign:

How will you reach your customers and what will you say to them?

Entrepreneurs, especially inventors, often believe that their business concepts are so spectacular that promoting their product or service won't be necessary—sort of a build-it-and-they-will-come attitude, especially if what you're building is the proverbial better mousetrap. One of the most common flaws I see in plans is the entrepreneur's failure to describe exactly how customers will be reached and how products will be presented to them. Potential investors, staff, and partners won't be convinced that your idea can succeed until you've established well-researched and effective methods of contacting your customers—and the assurance that once you've reached them, you can convince them to buy your product or service. After you have defined, researched, and tested your market as much as you can, you need to develop a plan to reach your potential customers.

Marketing describes how you will position and let your potential customers know about your product or service. *Positioning* means concentrating on the competitive advantages you have identified: will your product or service distinguish itself by its superior quality, its revolutionary features, or its ability to make your customers happier than they've ever been in their lives? Marketing also establishes the best ways to reach your potential customers and precisely what to say to them.

Suppose you're the hypothetical Field Center client who wants to open a financial-services business to advise Wall Street investors who wish to buy stocks in the rubber-sole industry. You've already identified your target market as major New York City-based investors interested in rubber-sole stocks, and your competitive advantage as your unparalleled expertise in rubber-sole stocks.

Some of the questions you'll have to ask yourself before you develop a marketing campaign include: What trade journals and newspapers do your potential clients read? Would ads in these publications be worth the cost of placing them? How could you interest a reporter for one of these periodicals in writing a story about your new advisory firm? Is there an organization of rubber sole company investors that you should join? Are there conventions for investors in rubber sole companies that would be worth attending? Will your knowledge of a related industry, such as flip-flop manufacturing, give you more impressive credentials in finding clients? Will direct mailings to investors or posting information on the Internet be useful outlets?

When you have the right marketing campaign in place, you have an operating plan to gain market share, generate revenue, and bring your financial projections into reality.

I remember several clients coming to the Field Center with various baked goods they wished to market. All of their products were delicious—I know, I tasted them—but the brownie baker opened his store next to a McDonald's, so the existing foot traffic was all wrong for $3.00 chocolate squares. The superb scone maker tried to bake and package and market all on her own—and ended up burning herself out.

The only client who succeeded was the cupcake guy, who plotted his course thoroughly by finding the right spot (an albeit expensive booth in the city's recently refurbished train station), the right price (people didn't think twice about buying a cupcake for $2.00, and came back for more) and the right promotion (he hired a college student part time to hand out samples during the morning and evening rush hours). Within a month, he was clearing enough profit to drop the samples and hire full-time counter help.

The difference between the cupcake guy, the brownie baker, and the scone maker was a well-developed marketing plan.

There are some highly successful companies that were founded on little more than a solid marketing plan. Nike, the shoe and athletic-wear giant, owns no factories and operates very few retail stores. Nike contracts with existing factories around the world to make its products and ship them directly to retailers, such as WalMart or Macy's. Nike owns a few warehouses, but that's it. Instead of owning supermarkets for shoes, Nike is a super marketer of shoes. Nike creates the brands, markets the products to potential customers to create demand, and arranges for distribution to retailers.

I have often thought of real-estate companies such as Century 21 in the same way. They neither build nor own houses. They are contract marketers for people who own houses and want to sell them.

In fact, most retailers are basically marketing organizations. They manufacture little or nothing of what they sell. The key to their success is finding a good location, creating an attractive atmosphere, choosing the right mix of products to sell, pricing their products competitively, and delivering excellent service. These are all marketing functions.

The Four Ps

All marketing campaigns are based on what we call The Four Ps.

1. The **product** or service.
2. The **price** you will charge.
3. The **place** you will sell or distribute your goods or service.
4. The **promotion** and advertising you will use to communicate with potential customers.

Let's review each of The Four Ps.

1. Product

Your business plan must make a compelling case for why customers will want to purchase your product or service. After analyzing thousands of business plans, I have identified the most persuasive reasons:

$ **Convenience.** Domino's Pizza is built entirely on making it easier and faster to eat pizza through a superior delivery service.

$ **New products.** It's rare that a totally new product emerges, but you could be one of the few to do it, like Alexander Graham Bell and his telephone. More recent examples are e-mail, wireless messaging devices, and DVD players.

$ **New applications.** Many people have built successful businesses by finding one more function for a computer during those idle hours when it just sits on someone's desk. Video games, calendar functions, and spreadsheet programs can all be considered new applications for an existing product. The Sony Walkman was developed as a pocket memo and dictation machine for businesspeople, but found a much bigger application and audience playing music.

$ **Improved performance.** A product may be more attractive to customers by being noisier (motorcycle engines), quieter (dishwasher motors), smelling better (deodorant), or not smelling at all (deodorant). Successful marketing is based on improving the performance of a product in the minds of consumers.

$ **Status.** Rolex, Jaguar, Dom Perignon Champagne, Versace, and Sub-Zero refrigerators are all marketed, at least in part, on their status appeal. Think of the Grey Poupon commercials. People buy these items hoping that they will not only run well or taste good, but that their prestige will rub off on the purchaser.

$ **Packaging.** A product's container draws attention on the shelf and sends a message to consumers. Big packages, such as jumbo, plastic laundry detergent jugs, shout *value*. Small packages, such as concentrated laundry detergent in recyclable cardboard boxes, say *convenience* and *environmental responsibility*. Pharmaceutical companies repackage medications in extra-strength formulas, which are really just two pills squeezed into one, creating new life for old products.

$ **Appearance and styling.** The automobile industry has thrived for decades on minor styling changes to create demand for new cars. Flashy fins in the 1960s didn't improve the function of the car—just the appearance. Or at least they made last year's models look dated. Now that computers are commonplace, styling is playing a more important role. Does a see-through computer casing turn you on? Is gel toothpaste a new product or just a styling change?

Remember that you don't need to have a revolutionary product to have a successful business. In fact, it may be quite the contrary. Entrepreneurs with revolutionary business ideas often have trouble recruiting the resources they need. Alexander Graham Bell had a hard time convincing people to invest in his newfangled device, the telephone. Then he had a great deal of difficulty getting businesses and people to adopt it. Sometimes the most compelling business idea is one that takes a widely used and accepted product and just changes it. John D. Rockefeller didn't invent oil; he set up a system to control its manufacturing and distribution. Tom Monaghan, the founder of Domino's, didn't invent pizza; he developed a system that delivers pizza faster.

2. Price

Deciding on a price for your product is key to any bankable business plan. Most of us assume that lower prices are better because we're so conditioned as consumers to look for bargains. Price is an issue that investors, bankers, and partners will carefully scrutinize. However, look before you leap down to a low price for your product because:

- $ It's more difficult to raise prices than to lower them.
- $ Low prices sometimes send a message of low quality.
- $ You need to make a profit.

If you charge too little for your product and can't make a profit, you may not be able to raise prices quickly enough to save your business. Your business plan won't be bankable if you can't turn a profit. Your plan has to demonstrate that you can sell enough widgets at a profit-generating price—not just at a price that will make customers flock to you.

Sometimes companies focus on low price too much. If you have a low-cost means of manufacturing a product that is difficult for others to copy, or you have a patent, copyright, or license that protects your product, your competition may not be able to match your price. In fact, if you focus more on price than your customers do, charging a low price may hurt your ability to be profitable without actually being a major competitive advantage.

I know of several examples of new discount airlines that obviously focused on price as a key element of their strategy. This strategy worked until their larger and better financed competitors took notice and reduced their prices even further, making the upstarts lose customers or lose money on every ticket. Needless to say, the discount airlines didn't last long. They should have focused on something other than just price.

3. Place

If you are opening a store, never forget the rule of "location, location, location." Sometimes a great location—which puts your business right where your customers are—will overcome virtually any weakness. I remember stopping at a gas station at the edge of a desert. This was literally the last gas station for a few hundred miles. The gas was 50 percent more expensive than gas anywhere else in the state, the owner was unfriendly, the service was rude, and the station only accepted payment in cash. None of this made for a happy customer experience, but it probably didn't hurt sales either, because this gas station had the right location!

Place, which also includes how you will manage distribution, is, in my experience, the most overlooked element of many marketing plans. A publishing-industry consultant once said to me "publishing is fundamentally a distribution business." I was shocked. What about great books, glowing reviews, beautiful stores, and word-of-mouth? Well, those are all important, but it means little if there aren't enough books in the stores, or they can't be found by customers, or there are too few bookstores. If too few books are distributed, no one can buy. Too many books, and the store and the publisher end up deeply discounting the title, putting it on the remainder table and losing money. So much for great books!

To avoid these pitfalls, I urge you to answer the following questions:

$ How will the purchaser obtain your product?

$ How do your competitors distribute? Do they use wholesalers or distributors as middlemen?

$ Are there competitors who have locked up all the established distribution channels, making it hard for you to reach your customers?

$ Is there an alternative distribution channel available, such as the Internet, discount retailers, or direct-to-consumer advertising that could give you an advantage?

$ How will you manage the distribution chain so that you know where your products are and what areas are experiencing shortages?

$ How will you focus your distribution? On the most likely markets, within a certain geographic area, or where your competition is weak?

Take a look at the distribution and marketing sections of the business plan for the Zif Medical Devices Company at the back of the book. For this plan, the business owners have chosen to present marketing options, such as using strategic alliances with existing hospital-supply companies. This relieves Zif of the responsibility of developing a means of reaching every potential customer. Existing hospital-supply companies already have the contacts, the distribution system, and the reputation with the hospitals that will help get the Zif products adopted.

Even if you don't make a corporate alliance of this type, you may choose to use distributors, representatives, or wholesalers because they have the ability to reach your potential market with both credibility and quality service.

4. Promotion

Promotion is how your potential customers find out about your product or service. You might place advertisements in trade magazines, drum up news coverage, convince retail stores to display your product, develop a direct-mail solicitation, rely on word-of-mouth from satisfied customers, or any of a dozen other ways to create awareness of, and demand for, your product.

Coupons, free samples, free trial periods, volume purchase incentives, in-store displays, manufacturer's rebates, financial incentives to distributors, contests, and premiums are all examples of sales promotions. AOL has distributed millions of CDs that give new customers thousands of free hours if they just try AOL. Airline bonus miles and coupons for products sold in supermarkets have become standard in their respective industries. Before I review each method of reaching your customers, consider these points in creating an effective promotion plan:

$ **Be specific.** Your promotion plan must be precise and detailed. If you intend to use coupons to publicize your product or service, you must explain the terms of the coupon, decide on how it will be distributed, and determine how many coupons you expect to get back.

$ **State your goals.** Explain what you expect to accomplish and why you are using this means of promotion. Having a product booth at a convention attended by many of your customers is a clear, focused way to reach your market. Many companies that have booths at conventions put on special promotions just for purchases made at the convention to encourage customers to make a purchase before the convention ends.

$ **Establish a system of measurement.** If you expect your newspaper ads to bring people into your clothing store, then you need a way of measuring traffic—before, during, and after the ads appear in the paper. With coupons, you need a way to track how many have been distributed and how many are being redeemed.

$ **Hold your expenses accountable.** By establishing goals and a system of measurement, you can hold your promotional expenses accountable for the results they produce. This will allow you to adjust your strategies and prevent you from wasting money on promotional efforts that fail to produce results. It will also impress the readers of your plan.

There are two basic methods of reaching your customers: through paid advertising or free media. Let's take a look at these approaches so you understand their respective benefits and drawbacks.

Paid advertising. Television, billboards, radio, newspapers, magazines, and even blimps comprise some of the many options for paid advertising and represent a major element of promotion. A great advantage of paid advertising is that it can deliver highly quantified measurements of how many people will see or hear your ad, since professionals who sell space and time slots keep very detailed records of their effectiveness.

Paid advertising is measured in *reach*, the number of different people who will see or hear your ad, and by *frequency*, the average number of times each of those people will see or hear your ad. Reach multiplied by frequency gives you the total number of *impressions* your advertising will make. In my experience, frequency is more important than reach. We are all exposed to dozens or even hundreds of ads daily. Most go in one ear and out the other! The key is to deliver the same message to the same people multiple times to ensure that your message is received.

To plan your advertising campaign, follow these steps.

$ **Research how your competitors advertise.** You have probably already noticed every competitor's ad—much more so than their customers have! Create a table in your plan that lists every competitor, where they advertise, and the message their ads convey, such as price, sales, or special features.

$ **Talk with advertising representatives.** Advertising salespeople from radio stations, magazines, and other media outlets are a great source of information about how your competitors are advertising and what your options are. Meet with them, tell them you're developing a media plan, ask about your competitors' advertising campaigns, and see what the advertising reps suggest. Most will give you specific information about your competitors and good suggestions about how you can develop your own advertising strategy effectively.

$ **Develop a focused and accountable plan.** Take all this information and distill it into the best method of reaching your most important target markets. Your plan should include the reach and frequency data that the advertising reps give you, as well as detailed cost estimates. Describe what you expect to achieve in terms of foot traffic into your store, or calls from potential customers, or name recognition within target markets. Finally, develop your system for tracking results and holding these expenditures accountable.

Free media. Business owners love the idea of attracting all kinds of attention to their products or services without having to spend a penny. A good example of this occurred in 2002 when inventor Dean Kamen unveiled his riding device, Segway, The Human Transporter. It attracted huge amounts of attention on the evening news and in newspapers. Companies, such as Amazon.com and Yahoo, were competing to give one away in exchange for publicizing it. Let me clue you in on one major fact: Free media ain't free.

It's not that NBC was paid to put the story on the evening news. It's that a huge amount of thought, effort, time, and expense went into creating this story. For years, Kamen's company had been building interest in its upcoming product by spreading the word that he was working on a revolutionary item. Keeping it a mystery helped raise interest and expectations, so hype was built far in advance of the product's unveiling.

When the Segway was finally revealed, the company had already produced professional-quality video clips, still photographs, and news releases. Its paid staff members contacted the media and arranged for interviews, demonstrations, and test drives. And, of course, millions were spent to produce this innovative machine. The company continues to generate free media coverage by alerting local newspapers and television stations whenever a city buys Segways for their police force or a major business purchases them for navigating their gigantic warehouses, but this, too, is the result of the efforts of paid professional promoters.

Free media is great, but it takes a huge amount of planning, expense, and effort, and it carries no guarantee of success. If you schedule a grand opening for your new store and your city is hit by a record snowfall, I can assure you, no one will hear of your store, regardless of the blockbuster events you have arranged.

Here are some guidelines for developing the free media element of your business plan:

$ **Write up specific story concepts you think could attract attention.** Maybe you are a former IBM executive who's starting a software company, or you're a retired but beloved ballerina who's opening a dance school. Perhaps your recycling business will be the first to use a new technology. Write the stories and put them in an appendix to your business plan.

$ **Make certain that the stories enhance your business plan.** I once read a story about a former convict who started a security business. Did he actually think that this would bring him customers? Or entice investors?

$ **Plan for the long term.** You can't control whether the media will take to your idea, when they will use it, or how much attention they will give it. Most successful free media efforts put out a steady stream of potential stories. Some get picked up, others don't. Persistence can pay off—eventually. Stating this specifically in your plan and outlining your free media approaches will impress potential investors and lenders.

Every bankable business plan must include an effective marketing strategy in which you describe how you will reach your customers and what you will say to them. As you design your marketing campaign, keep the Four Ps uppermost in your mind: product, price, place, and promotion. This is the portion of the business plan that convinces lenders and investors that you will be able to gain market share, generate revenue, and bring your financial projections to fruition.

CHAPTER 6

Action Step Six

Build a Dynamic Sales Effort:

How will you attract customers?

Potential investors and bankers want to know that you are highly sales oriented. They have all seen entrepreneurs with great ideas go down in flames because they didn't build a strong sales effort.

First, you should be clear about how sales is different from marketing. *Marketing* is the overall way in which you position and promote your product or service. It covers areas such as advertising, market research, distribution, and packaging. *Sales* is the interaction with your customers that produces orders. Sales is the specific process that takes place just prior to the order being written up or the cash register ringing.

The word *sales* covers all the issues related to contacting your actual customers once you've established how to reach them through your marketing campaign. How will you train your sales staff to approach potential customers? Will you divide up your sales staff so some become experts in selling your bubble-gum scented bubble bath to small, independent, retail toy stores? Will other salespeople concentrate on developing relationships with major bubble-gum manufacturers so the bubble bath could be sold in tandem, through their well-established national distribution outlets? Will you have a sales-force expert in buying television slots on Saturday-morning cartoon shows or placing ads on the backs of kid-oriented cereal boxes?

What advertising and promotional efforts will you employ—two-for-the-price-of-one specials or free coupons inside those kid-oriented cereal boxes? Where can you locate lists of the greatest concentrations of children under the age of eight? What will you convey to children about your bubble bath that will convince them to ask their parents to buy it? Will you have to follow federal guidelines that require you to stick warning labels on every bottle to keep children from drinking your delicious-smelling soap?

In planning your sales activities, you will also need to answer questions such as: Is it ethical to contact your colleagues and clients from your former job as a door-to-door soap salesperson to tell them about your new bubble-gum–scented bubble bath? Will you be the only salesperson in the beginning stages of your company? When will you know it's time to hire more sales staff? How do you convince your clients that your sales staff will take care of them as well as you did? What will your basic sales philosophy be—building long-term relationships with a few major clients, or developing a clientele of many short-term customers?

You will also need to consider how you will compensate your sales staff—with a base salary plus a commission, or in bottles of bubble-gum-scented soap? Will you hire full-time staff with full benefits, or part-time staff without benefits? How will you motivate your staff to do the best sales job possible?

Knowledge of your competitive advantage is just as important in designing a dynamic sales effort as it is in developing an effective marketing campaign. You'll need to think about what product or service qualities will be the most compelling to your prospective customers. Then, you'll have to devise convincing language that clearly communicates this competitive advantage to your sales staff who will, in turn, use it when talking to your customers.

In my experience, the most important element of an effective sales effort is having a sales staff that thoroughly understands your business and the needs or your potential customers. Therefore, your sales plan must address the issue of how you will create a sales staff that is as knowledgeable about your business as it is about your potential customers.

Your bankable business plan must demonstrate that you are sales oriented by embracing the following concepts:

Get an Order Today—or Yesterday

The most bankable business plan shows that you already have commitments for orders. In fact, some very successful businesses have started with an order for a product even before there was a means by which to sell it. In 1975, a young entrepreneur discovered that IBM needed an operating system for the new personal computers they were eager to market in competition with an upstart company called Apple. The entrepreneur knew where he could obtain the right program, and made a deal with IBM before he even had the product in hand. His name was Bill Gates and the company he founded on that first sale was Microsoft.

Before you write your business plan, identify key potential customers, talk with them, and obtain commitments from them to buy when you're ready to sell. No other element will make your plan quite as bankable.

Make Sales a Priority for Everyone

Your plan should emphasize the belief that sales is a central function for virtually every employee and every department. You need to assure potential investors and lenders that you'll employ a team selling concept to address any possible questions from prospective customers. For example, if you're starting a software, consulting, or manufacturing company, you should take your technical people, not just your sales staff, to see prospective clients.

I saw a persuasive business plan for a currently successful restaurant that explained how the chef would leave the kitchen at least once a night to ask customers how they liked the food he had prepared. Making sales a priority works in the plan and it works in the business because it communicates to potential lenders and investors that attracting customers and keeping them happy is your top priority.

Never Delegate Yourself Completely out of Sales

Although most entrepreneurs recognize that they must be sales oriented, many don't actually enjoy selling. They may have started their ventures because they preferred to run the show, not sell the tickets, or they were excited about inventing a new computer application, not convincing people to try it. Many became entrepreneurs because they wanted the financial rewards of business ownership, but expected their products to virtually sell themselves. Because of their attitudes, some entrepreneurs structure their firms so that they are far from the front lines of selling. This is not just an organizational mistake, it's a costly error that can displease potential investors.

Many clients want to deal with the founder and head of the business because it boosts their egos to have that level of attention. Others believe they can get the best price and service only from top management. To attract and satisfy these potential customers, your plan must assure investors that you will not delegate all sales responsibility to others. Moreover, if you want to demonstrate throughout your organization (even if you employ only a few people) that sales is a top priority, you need to have contact with potential customers yourself.

Create the Right Ethical Environment

Selling is not about fooling someone into buying from you. Selling is about finding a long-term way to work together for the mutual benefit of both your business and your customers. If your approach to selling hinges on manipulation or being less than truthful, then your plan is built on shaky ground.

I am familiar with a large telecommunications company that enjoyed immediate success because it was well-positioned as a low-cost provider in a rapidly growing market. When growth started to slow, the pressure for increased sales from investors and top management did not. The company's approach was to promise prospective clients the moon, but without a written agreement. This created a truly unethical environment that caused the best, most client-oriented salespeople to leave. When clients caught on to the ruse, they canceled their contracts and spread the word about the company's poor reputation. The company is now struggling to survive.

Your plan should stress that you are committed to developing and maintaining strong relationships with your customers by delivering what you promise and ensuring that everyone within your organization shares these ethical values. Establish this goal through your own example, through professional sales training, by building your relationships with clients on the bedrock of honesty and by developing a strong competitive advantage based on product quality, good pricing, and unequaled service.

Be Highly Organized

By its nature, sales requires keeping track of multiple interactions with many current and potential clients. There are many software sales tracking programs such as ACT! or Goldmine, as well as database systems, such as Access, that can maintain your account lists and client interactions. In many cases, keeping a detailed notebook or a card file is sufficient. Whatever system you use, the key is to be highly organized, so that you provide the proper followup and don't lose your customers in a chaotic mess.

Some systems give management a huge amount of data from the number of sales calls made to the average order size. In my experience, this is useful information to some extent, but managers should not be fooled into believing that these statistics are as important as building long-term, mutually beneficial, client relationships achieved through in-person meetings. Establishing a few dependable and satisfied customers is almost always better than convincing clients to buy your product or service only once.

If your plan has a significant sales component—and most do—it's important to describe your sales system and objectives fully.

Compensate Based on Performance . . . but for the Long Term

Salespeople should earn financial rewards based on performance, but performance should be defined effectively. A commission based solely on sales, may, in fact, encourage staff to overpromise, or pressure clients into buying, or even to write up phony orders. I have worked with organizations that believed they were giving their salespeople the right incentives but, in reality, they were encouraging their staff to concentrate on hard-sell, short-term, unethical techniques that eventually eroded customer trust and satisfaction, as well as future sales. You can assure potential investors and lenders that you understand these problems and can avoid them by stating in your business plan that you will:

$ Pay commissions based on collections, not orders.

$ Set long-term goals and give financial incentives for reaching them, instead of relying on weekly or monthly goals.

$ Give salespeople a fixed financial base, so they're not under tremendous financial pressure to meet short-term quotas.

$ Communicate your goal of building strong relationships with long-term clients.

$ Recruit salespeople who are interested in working collaboratively with clients to help them meet mutually beneficial goals.

$ Train your salespeople to deliver better service based on their understanding of client needs and goals.

Your Sales Force Can Be Your Competitive Advantage

Managing your sales force effectively will provide a major competitive advantage for your business—and it will make your business plan more compelling. Many entrepreneurs view their sales staff as an expensive, hard-to-manage, but necessary, evil. If your sales staff is more client oriented, more knowledgeable about your product, and delivers better service than your competitor, you can build and maintain strong customer relationships. A well designed sales effort can help bring in larger market shares than your competitors can achieve and it will keep business steady even during economic downturns. You can bank on it!

CHAPTER 7

Action Step Seven

Design Your Company:
How will you hire and organize your work force?

You have now defined your venture, its initial needs, targeted markets, and growth objectives. You have also described your marketing and sales strategies. Now, it's time to design the organizational structure that will enable your plan to become a real business. You may hope to run your company as one big happy family—and it may work out that way—but organizations require formal structure and investors will expect to see these issues addressed in your plan.

This portion of your bankable business plan also establishes the staff structure that will be capable of implementing the strategies you have chosen to start your venture. In my opinion, the single greatest determinant of business success is implementation. We have all seen businesses fail because of the entrepreneur's inability to make his dream into a reality.

An example I saw recently was a restaurant owner who failed to establish a chain of command between himself and his on-site manager. The manager was given a strict budget and decided he could only afford to hire poorly trained employees to wait on customers and cook in the kitchen. The new staff produced substandard food and provided mediocre service and the restaurant failed. Surely the owner didn't want this outcome but, by failing to design an organizational structure that created an effective chain of command and decision-making process, the restaurant was doomed. If you structure your business properly and can implement your plan effectively, you can succeed even against tough odds and rough competition.

By the time you've reached this stage of thinking about your potential business concept, you'll probably have a good idea of the number of people you'll need and the skills they'll require to get your enterprise up and running. Keep in mind that your initial plans will undoubtedly change as your business grows. You may need to hire more managers to supervise your expanding staff, or to set up new departments to meet new customer demands. Projected growth and expansion for your company should be mentioned in your business plan, but it's not the primary focus. For now, you want to secure help in getting started and convincing your funding sources that you will become profitable.

Let's imagine that you're a Field Center client who has identified a competitor's ocarina-manufacturing plant to purchase. You have been running your grandfather's ocarina plant since his death, but the operation is still small and old fashioned. Buying the new plant will enable you to bring your manufacturing methods up to date and expand your customer base.

Investors will want to know if you're capable of running the show by yourself after you take over the plant. Do you need to bring in experienced managers right away? Will you keep some of the existing employees or hire all new people? And where do you find these potential employees?

Funding sources will also want to know if any of your partners expect to work alongside you, or if their obligations are only financial. How will you make changes at the new ocarina plant while maintaining the trust and cooperation of the employees you retain from your previous plant and the staff at the newly acquired plant? And how will you reassure both plants' customers that your new ocarinas will be as good as, if not better than, the ocarinas that used to roll off the assembly lines?

Your plan will need to specify the key management jobs and roles. Positions such as president, vice presidents, chief financial officer, and managers of departments should be defined along with stating who reports to whom. Running a manufacturing plant will require you to deal with dozens if not hundreds of employees, but what if you're one of my clients who wants to build a better mousetrap? You will have some of the same issues, such as handling partners who may want to work side by side with you on your venture or convincing investors of your qualifications, but you may be the sole full-time employee for quite some time. How will you find the right consultants to advise you or the best vendors to supply your materials? Will you collect a salary? When will you know you need to hire a staff? What skills must they have? How do you recruit them? How will you structure your company so that the chain of command and quality control are maintained if the company grows dramatically?

And as soon as you have employees, you need to consider how you will handle their salaries and wages, their insurance and retirement benefits, as well as analyzing the extent of your knowledge of tax-related issues. As you think about hiring personnel and organizing your workforce, you must also confront your desire and ability to be a good boss. If you haven't contemplated this aspect of your commitment to owning your own business, now is the time to give it serious consideration.

Options for Structures

There are several basic designs for structuring your business, all of which can be depicted visually by an organization chart. Organization charts have the same two dimensions as maps. The north/south or vertical axis indicates power relationships. The higher up (more to the north) on the chart a position is, the more power that person controls. A person's boss usually appears above him or her on an organization chart. The east/west dimension specifies how tasks are assigned. Questions such as "Who covers Borneo?" or "Which department manages cuttlefish farms?" can be answered by looking horizontally, east to west, on the organization chart.

Organizations are defined by how the first level below the top is structured. Although you can mix and match organizational forms in infinite varieties, most investors and lenders recognize five fundamental structures, which are described on the following page and depicted with their corresponding organization charts:

Functional.   In these organizations, the first level below the top is broken out by functions such as finance, sales, and manufacturing. Smaller organizations in stable businesses with a limited product line and routine technology are typically organized functionally. For example, a real-estate management company would probably be organized functionally, having departments such as accounting, marketing, maintenance, and human resources.

Product.   These organizations have the first level below the top arranged according to products or product lines. Food companies generally organize this way, with each product having its own management team to oversee advertising, distribution, packaging, and promotions. This type of organization allows decision making to be placed at the product manager level.

Geographical.   Many companies, from car dealerships with locations just a few miles apart to airlines with operations on every continent, choose to organize their divisions geographically. This is most appropriate for businesses that need all the functions of the company within each geographical region. While the CEO and his staff in the central office will provide detailed oversight, each geographical division is a self-contained unit that operates independently.

Matrix.   Matrix organizations are generally established in high-technology companies where specialized, technical teams work on solving specific problems related to complex, long-term projects. Matrix organizations tend to have team leaders, while each specialist also reports to the leader of the specialty. Companies that create complex products such as computers or airplanes usually organize this way, so that a manager can be assigned to develop a specific component or solve a particular problem, then pull the needed specialists into the team. The specialist, such as a physicist or meteorologist, reports to the team leader managing the specific task, as well as to the head of his or her specialty (such as physics or meteorology) within the company.

Hybrid.   As its name implies, hybrid organizations combine elements of both functional and product organizations. The chart shows that parts of the organization, such as the finance and distribution departments, are functionally structured, while other divisions, such as metal stamping or oil-drilling rigs, are organized by product. Hybrid structures combine the responsiveness of a product organization with the specialization and efficiency of a functional organization.

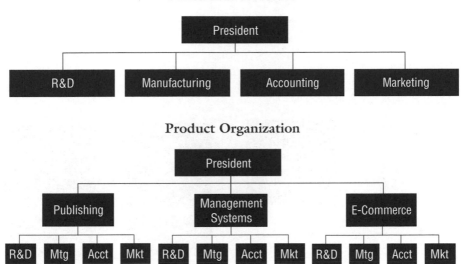

If your business requires an organization of a dozen or more people, it's wise to include a full organization chart along with your plan.

Means of Control

If your plan calls for a sizeable organization, you will need to demonstrate that you will have the means to maintain control of your business. Here are some key means of control you should consider describing in your business plan:

$ **Span of control** is the number of people who report to one boss. This should be stated for organizations with large sales forces, manufacturing operations, or sizeable support departments, such as accounting.

$ **Reporting tools** are ways of keeping management informed of activities. These can be weekly staff meetings, memos, or sales-reporting systems. In manufacturing departments, where cost and efficiency are crucial, tracking systems that report on each employee's production may be needed.

$ **Organizational culture** is the atmosphere of morale and company spirit that exists among the staff. Creating the appropriate organizational culture is an important part of the success of many businesses.

Geographical Structure

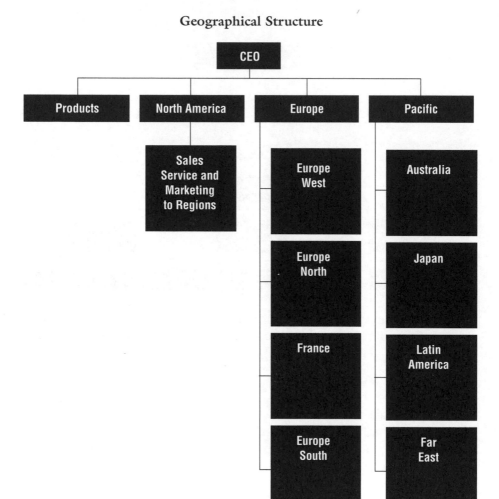

Human Resource Management

Some businesses, such as fast-food restaurants, function best by hiring short-term employees at low wages. Coping with the rapid turnover this policy engenders is part of the business plan. However, if hiring and retaining the right employees for the long term will be crucial to your business's success, you should describe your human resource management approach in your plan. Here are some issues to discuss:

Hybrid Organization

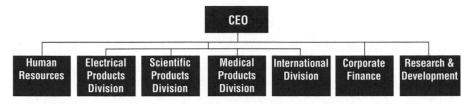

Matrix Organization

	Design Vice-President	Manufacturing Vice-President	Marketing Vice-President	Controller	Procurement Manager
President					
Director of Product Operations					
Product Manager A					
Product Manager B					
Product Manager C					
Product Manager D					

Identify key employees. Business is a team sport and choosing your team-mates may be the most important decision you make. The following template is useful in defining every key position in your organization:

$ Title

$ Job description

$ Required degrees, training, and experience for the person who will fill the position

$ Compensation package, including salary, bonus, stock ownership, and stock incentives

$ Resumes for current and prospective employees

$ Strategies for positions that need to be filled

Design a board of directors or board of advisors.   A significant element of your team can consist of people who are not full-time employees but who offer their expertise, experience, and contacts to support your business. A board of directors is a formal entity with ultimate legal control over the company and, potentially, personal liability for its actions.

A board of advisors is an informal group working to help the company, but without legal authority or any potential personal liability. Showing investors or lenders that you have recruited a high-powered, capable, and contributing group of directors or advisors will make your plan much stronger. For each proposed board member or advisor, I urge you to complete the same template as you would for key employees.

Establish employee compensation and benefit plans.   Your approach to compensation and benefits should fit your overall strategy. If you're opening a fast-food franchise, most of your employees will be young people who want a job, not a career, and see flipping burgers as a way to make money for tuition or a car. For these types of employees, a compensation plan that maximizes their paychecks at the expense of long-term benefits, such as pension plans, is probably best. On the other hand, if you're building a consulting firm and want to keep your employees for the long run because they will maintain strong relationships with your clients, then a plan that stresses long-term benefits, such as health insurance, stock ownership, or pensions, is more attractive and effective.

Employee benefits is a complex, highly regulated, and rapidly changing area. You should consult with a benefits company or financial planner and receive actual proposals for employee benefits to include in your business plan.

Select key suppliers and contractors.   Henry Ford's first automobile plant functioned by funneling coal, iron ore, and other raw materials in one door and rolling finished Model T's off the assembly line and out the other door. When Ford began his business, there were no suppliers of car parts, so his factory had to do it all. In today's world, most companies subcontract out large portions of their essential processes. Dell assembles computers from components it purchases from hundreds of different suppliers. In certain cases, Toyota requires its suppliers to locate their facilities adjacent to the Toyota manufacturing plants so parts can be ordered and delivered within a few hours.

Chances are that your business plan will describe a venture more like Dell or Toyota than Henry Ford's original plant, and you will thus need to identify key suppliers. Here are questions about suppliers that should be addressed in your plan:

$ What materials will they actually be supplying?

$ How long have they been in business?

$ What are their credentials and track records?

$ Why have you selected them? Price? Quality? Ability to supply adequate quantity on time?

$ Have they made a binding offer to supply certain products or services at a definite price?

$ What is your backup plan if they don't do what they promised?

Suppliers with strong track records and excellent reputations will not only contribute quality materials to your business, they will also give your plan a powerful endorsement. If Intel has agreed to supply semiconductors for your product, investors and bankers will definitely take notice.

Legal Structures

Many entrepreneurs find choosing a legal structure for their businesses a daunting prospect and immediately hire a lawyer. A lawyer may be necessary at some point in establishing your venture, but legal services are not an expense you have to assume while preparing your business plan. Whether you hire a lawyer immediately or not, understanding the choices of legal structures is a good idea and, in fact, may not be as complicated as you think.

There are three considerations in choosing a legal structure for your venture:

$ **Tax considerations.** Some types of structure, such as limited partnerships, don't pay taxes directly, but pass profits and losses directly to their owners. The owners then pay taxes based on their own tax situations.

$ **Liability considerations.** Some structures, such as corporations, protect their owners from liability arising from actions of the company or its employees through what is known as the *corporate veil.* You should note that this protection is not perfect and, in cases of fraud or illegal activity, the corporate veil is pierced.

$ **Investor considerations.** The type and number of investors that you anticipate having for your venture is important because some structures, such as S corporations, limit the number of possible investors. Others, such as general partnerships, have only one class of investors, while C corporations allow for many. The option of having more than one class of investors means you can give varying voting or economic power to different groups of investors.

Once you analyze these considerations, you can match your needs with the types of legal entities available and make the best choice, from among these basic options:

$ **Sole proprietorships** have one owner who manages the business and contributes to the investment. There is no liability protection, and profits and losses are passed through directly to the owner's tax return.

$ **General partnerships** can have an unlimited number of partners, all of whom are collectively responsible for managing the business, contributing to the investment, and sharing in the profits. There is no liability protection, and profits and losses pass through directly to the partners' individual tax returns.

$ **Limited partnerships** have two classes of partners. General partners are responsible for the management of the business; limited partners are investors. General partners, however, can also invest as limited partners. Based on the profit-sharing agreement between the classes of partners, profits and losses pass through to the partners' individual tax returns. General partners have no personal-liability protection, but limited partners do.

$ **C corporations** are usually the structure of choice for large companies. They can have an unlimited number of shareholders and an unlimited number of classes of stock. The shareholders have no personal liability. The company is managed by a board of directors, which can be held liable for the company's actions in certain cases. The corporation pays taxes on its profits. The profits then pass through to the shareholders in the form of dividends, which are then taxed again on the individual's tax return.

$ **Limited liability corporations** allow for an unlimited number of investors, called *members*. Profits and losses pass through to the members' individual tax returns. The members cannot be held liable for actions of the company.

$ **Limited liability partnerships and professional corporations** are state-sanctioned forms of organizations that are designed for licensed professionals such as lawyers, accountants, doctors, and dentists. If you are preparing a plan for such a profession, you should ask your attorney about the advantages of using one of these legal structures.

$ **S corporations** are taxed like partnerships, but provide the liability protection of a corporation. This allows profits and losses to pass through to the shareholders. There are some restrictions, for example the number of shareholders must be 75 or fewer, there can be only one class of stock, and all shares must be owned by only certain types of shareholders, such as individuals, trusts, or estates.

Matching the Legal Structure with Your Investors

The number and characteristics of your investors may influence your choice of legal structure. Raising capital from private sources, such as family members, venture capital funds, or individuals is referred to as *private placements*, and will require a lawyer who is a specialist. The key concept here is called the *accredited investor*, which is an institution, such as an insurance company, a pension fund, or an investment firm. An accredited investor may also be an individual with a net worth in excess of $1 million, or an individual income of $200,000, or a joint income of $300,000 or more. When working with accredited investors to raise money for your business, you have much more flexibility than dealing with less wealthy and, therefore (according to the law), less sophisticated investors.

If you're aiming at this market of institutional or wealthy and sophisticated accredited investors, you need to produce a private placement memorandum and file it with the Securities and Exchange Commission (SEC), a process which requires the services of a securities lawyer. To raise money from the broader public, called an *initial public offering*, or IPO, requires a much more expensive and time consuming process of filing a prospectus with the Securities and Exchange Commission. With rare exceptions, this will require an experienced lawyer, if not a law firm, and an investment bank, or a consortium of investment banks, to sell the shares through the public market.

By analyzing the available legal structures, you will be able to choose the most appropriate method of organizing your potential business. This will help convince investors and lenders that you have researched the options, even if you haven't made a final decision or hired a lawyer. In fact, lenders and investors may offer helpful suggestions on choosing a legal structure, once you have established that you have considered this issue in your business plan.

Franchises

Some entrepreneurs believe that buying a franchise eliminates the need to prepare a business plan. The decision to buy a franchise certainly dictates many of the issues that your business plan must include, but it does not remove the necessity of having a plan. The most important issue in a franchise business plan is proving that the location you have chosen will be profitable.

Franchisors should provide potential franchisees with the basic business model for the franchise, including detailed cost estimates, average revenue for existing franchises, and typical financing structures. The plan for your specific franchise should cover:

$ **A detailed analysis** of local competition from other franchises for the same company, as well as for other competitive businesses.

$ **A line-by-line comparison** of the expenses that the franchisor projects with the local costs for your franchise. For example, if the franchisor gives you projections that include rent at $50 per square foot, you will need to demonstrate that you can obtain space at or below that amount.

$ **An analysis of the franchise agreement** that shows you have sufficient protections to ensure that no other franchises will be sold directly in your vicinity. Also, you should show that the franchisor is capable of fulfilling all promises, such as national advertising, or new product development, to keep your business viable.

$ **Interviews with existing franchisees** (who were *not* suggested by the franchisor) to substantiate the claims made by the franchisor, and to further demonstrate business viability.

The Key Question about Franchises

The key question to ask yourself about purchasing a franchise is "Do I need to buy a franchise to be in this business?" Many people buy franchises because they like the idea of having a proven model for a business that comes with a template for operation. Many others believe that a franchise has a greater chance of success than a nonfranchise business. I don't believe that the evidence supports this. The major negative to franchises is cost. First, there is the price of purchasing the franchise. Second, there are the fees calculated from revenues that go directly to the franchisor.

It is not unusual for a franchise to pay 10 percent or more of its revenue to the franchisor in fees and mandated contributions to collective advertising. Think about how much of your profit is represented by these fees. The price of a great name brand franchise may make these costs a bargain, but your plan still needs to address what you're getting from being a franchise relative to what you are paying.

Get a Franchise Lawyer on Your Team

The franchise area is a legal speciality unto itself. There are a surfeit of laws governing franchises, including many local regulations. You need to have a lawyer who is highly experienced in this area, and who can contribute advice as well as help you negotiate the terms of various agreements, including the franchise contract and leases. Place the lawyer and his or her credentials prominently in your plan.

Use the RMA Database

The RMA data will give you important insights into a proposed franchise, and improve the quality of your plan. First, you can compare the franchisor's data with the RMA figures for similar nonfranchise businesses. This research will help you analyze the profitability of buying a franchise, as opposed to starting your own business. Second, just as in any business, a comparison with industry averages for margins, financing, and operating costs is important in proving the reasonableness of your projections. Read Chapter 10 for a more detailed description as to how to use the RMA database in creating a bankable business plan.

Action Step Eight

Target Your Funding Sources:
Where will you find your financing?

As your business concept begins to take shape, you can begin to home in on the most likely financing sources. Issues such as the size of your business, the industry it is in, whether you are starting a new business or buying an existing one, and whether you can provide collateral to a lender, are among the issues that must be considered in creating a target list of funding sources. Banks and other funding sources don't lend money because people with interesting business ideas are nice. They follow specific guidelines, such as the RMA database, which are designed to insure that they will make money by investing in or lending to your business.

For the vast majority of entrepreneurs, well-known, high-profile means of raising money, such as from venture capital or by going public, are not viable options. Your own credit, credit rating, and business history are key factors in obtaining financing for your business through Small Business Administration (SBA) guaranteed loans and other bank credit options. Remember, the bank is essentially lending to you, not your business plan. Your ability to tap into your personal network of friends, family, and professional contacts is crucial to raising money beyond what your own personal funds or credit can provide. In all these cases, there are important considerations, such as the potential impact on relationships when family and friends become investors.

When you have completed this process of identifying the best potential funding sources for your business, you will be able to write a bankable business plan that addresses their issues and answers their questions, even before they ask them! Remember that a strong plan must meet the needs of financial supporters, whether they are bankers interested in prompt loan payments, investors who are looking for long-term profits, or family members who simply want you to have the chance to pursue your dream.

There are two main types of funding:

Debt.   Debt is an agreement to borrow money and pay it back with interest. Types of debt include loans, mortgages, lines of credit, and leases. The bank, credit company, or individual lending the money usually requires collateral to cover the loan in case the borrower can't meet the payments. Common examples of collateral include real estate, equipment, and stocks. Debt with collateral is called *secured debt*. Debt is ranked by the order in which it is paid in the event of a default, liquidation, or bankruptcy. Senior debt is reimbursed first. Junior or subordinated debt is paid only after senior debt has been fully discharged.

Equity.   Equity is ownership in a business. It can take the form of stock in a corporation or shares in a partnership. When you sell equity you are promising to give your investors a share of the profits from business operations or from an eventual sale of the business. Some equity investors require control of the companies they invest in and will want at least 51 percent of the stock, while others are content to be minority shareholders without ultimate control. In either case, stock sales in private companies usually involve a contract specifying the precise terms of the investment and the rights of the shareholders. These rights can vary greatly, but often include an option to buy more shares or force the company to buy the stock back within a certain time at a preset price. Creating such a shareholders' agreement requires an experienced lawyer who specializes in this area.

Potential Sources of Financing

The sad fact is that you will probably have fewer options than you hoped for in financing your business, especially if you're planning a small, startup company. As options become more limited, your ability to finance your business becomes more important. Let's look at the potential sources for funding:

You.   The truth is that about 90 percent of businesses start with the financial support of the entrepreneur. You should be prepared to make an investment by providing collateral, using your credit cards, or taking out personal loans to bring your idea to reality. Putting your own money into your business, or personally signing on loans that will require you to pay them back if the business cannot, is a huge step that you need to consider carefully. I have no doubt that you have a great deal of confidence in the likelihood of your venture's success, but the reality is that most new businesses fail. You have to decide in the most objective way whether you are prepared to sell your house, give up your retirement account, or even file for personal bankruptcy, if the worst happens.

Family and friends.   Business and family are so tightly intertwined it is hard to separate them. More than two-thirds of all businesses involve two or more family members, have a manager who is a member of the family, and are majority-owned by family members. Next only to the entrepreneur, the family is the leading source of financial resources to start or grow a business. Relatives and close friends are a common source of financing for businesses because their agendas are more personal than business oriented—they want to help you succeed. Of course, they would like to share in your success, and they may see investing in your business as an opportunity to get in on the ground floor, but in my experience, these goals are secondary. Family and friends make good investors because they are accessible and you can usually use your personal relationship to encourage their investment. The negative is that if the business fails, you will still be seeing them often!

I know of a fellow who started a moving company with investments from family members, including his parents and his father-in-law. The business failed despite his good efforts, because the city in which he had established his company experienced a sudden downturn in the economy. His parents treated the investment as a gift to their son. They told him they thought he did the best job possible, and they said they would invest again if he wanted to start another business in the future. His father-in-law, however, could never come to terms with his financial loss and raises it every time he sees his son-in-law.

There are several important lessons here. First, be selective about whom you ask for money, avoiding friends or relatives whose relationship with you might suffer too much if your business fails. Second, be sure to warn your investors of the real financial risk they are taking and give them every opportunity to say "no." Third, be prepared for the long-term negative consequences from some individuals, no matter how thoroughly they were warned, if your business *does* fail.

All these *caveats* not withstanding, family and friends represent strong potential funding sources for most entrepreneurs.

Angels.   Angels are wealthy individuals who invest directly in businesses. Although there are numerous web-based matching services linking entrepreneurs and potential angels, in my experience you are more likely to find an angel investor through an established personal or business relationship with an accountant, perhaps, or a lawyer who handles your business dealings. Angel investors tend to focus on industries they know through their direct experience or previous success. Most angels know exactly how much risk they are taking by investing in a startup or relatively new business, so they expect to earn high returns on their stake if the business becomes successful. Some will ask for a seat on your board of directors or for an option to purchase enough stock to control the company.

Making a deal with an angel is a bit like getting married, and requires careful thought before the actual commitment is made. Angel investors who are experienced in your industry will have strong ideas about how your business should be run. Unless these ideas closely match your own, you may be in for a long struggle. Many angel investors are also very tough negotiators when it comes to making a deal. They know how important obtaining financing is for you, because many have been in exactly the same position before, so be prepared for long and complex negotiations.

Venture capital firms.   Venture capital firms are generally large, professionally managed funds. Many are organized as Small Business Investment Corporations (SBICs) which enables them to obtain SBA guarantees on part of their investment. Venture capital firms attract investment from pension funds, large corporations, and wealthy individuals. Many entrepreneurs think that venture capital is a serious option for them, but, in reality, venture capital is a relatively small and highly specialized source of funding. Even in peak years, the venture capital industry makes fewer than 10,000 investments. In most cases, they are looking for large private companies with a strong probability of growth, in which they can invest several million dollars or more. They prefer to invest in companies that will provide a clear and profitable exit within a few years, such as going public or a merger with a larger company. Despite having invested in startups during the dot-com boom, venture capital firms rarely invest in new businesses. Generally, venture capital firms want to control the companies in which they invest.

Corporations.   Occasionally, corporations will make direct investments in outside ventures. This is most often seen in technology industries, in which a large company, such as Intel, will invest in a small company that is developing a product Intel would eventually like to own. This type of investment is rare, and almost always carries an agreement to sell to the corporate investor at some point in the future if the investor wants to buy your product. It makes sense to look for this type of investor if you have personal contacts at a specific company, know your product would be very useful to them, and you feel comfortable becoming a division of the corporation in the future if you are successful.

Going public.   To be blunt, for most businesses this is the equivalent of winning the lottery. Just look at the numbers. There are more than 10 million businesses in the United States, but only about 17,000 public companies. It is true that, during the dot-com boom, many companies with little more than a cute logo were sold to the public. However, that period was an aberration and is now as faint a memory as most of the money that was invested in those companies. A company usually needs to have at least $20 million in annual revenue to be a candidate for a public offering.

Banks.   In the next section, I discuss how banks decide on making loans to businesses. Most of their decisions focus on the financial record and strength of the individual entrepreneur. Banks almost always want the owner of the business to stand behind the loans by signing a personal guarantee or putting up some personal assets, such as a home, as collateral to be used to pay the loan if the business fails. If the company has a very strong record of profitability (and, therefore, the ability to pay interest and principal) or if the assets of the business are more than enough to secure the loan, this personal risk can sometimes be avoided. Most banks prefer making large loans over small loans, often with $50,000 as the cut-off point. This varies by bank, but the rule of thumb here is that the smaller your request, the *less* likely it is to be viewed favorably at most banks.

How Banks Decide on Loans

Every time they make a loan, banks assume the risk that they may not be paid back. They manage this gamble by several means: lending to low-risk people, whom they call *creditworthy*, lending less than the customer is requesting, obtaining collateral or a guarantee from a third party whom they judge to be creditworthy, charging higher interest rates and fees to compensate for accepting risk, obtaining collateral that they can seize and sell if the loan is not paid back, and, most often, by not lending at all. Banks judge their loan decisions by looking at personal factors such as:

$ **Your credit history.** In this electronic age, lending sources can instantly evaluate how quickly and thoroughly you have paid your obligations to banks and other financial companies. Late payments, delinquent loans, bankruptcies, how much credit you have been extended by banks, credit card companies, department stores, and credit bureaus are all readily available to potential financial sources at the touch of a few computer keys.

$ **Your character.** Ultimately, the loan decision often comes down to a personal evaluation made by one or more loan officers. I've witnessed loans granted to entrepreneurs with bankruptcies in their past, and loans denied to people with stellar credit histories because the loan officers' sixth sense was triggered. This is so common that banks have a term for loans made to people without enough credit worthiness to sustain a loan. They're called *character loans.*

$ **Your collateral.** Nothing makes a banker happier than collateral to back up a loan. Mortgages are collateralized by the houses they finance. Leases are collateralized by the equipment that is being leased. Having collateral is a way for a bank to be repaid if the loan is forfeited. Most lending sources require existing collateral, such as an entrepreneur's home, securities, or other assets, before they grant small-business loans.

$ **Your personal guarantee.** Lending sources want to make the entrepreneur generally liable for the loan, not just the business she's starting. A personal guarantee provides this assurance without necessarily specifying the particular collateral. If you have few assets, a personal guarantee may not mean much, but if you have a home with significant equity value, or a large savings or investment account, giving the bank a personal guarantee will make the officers very happy, just as it should make you very nervous.

$ **Government loan guarantees.** Federal agencies, such as the Small Business Administration, and various state programs help banks say *yes* to loans, essentially by agreeing to guarantee repayment of some portion of the loan, ranging from 50 percent to 90 percent. While these government loan guarantees carry a paperwork burden for both entrepreneur and lender, they encourage lenders to feel more comfortable approving loans. The presence of a government guarantee rarely stops a lender from asking for—and usually receiving—other collateral or personal guarantees, for the loan. This gives bankers more than 100 percent in collateral and guarantees, and is rather like wearing both a belt and suspenders—unnecessary and unattractive, but it certainly keeps your pants up.

$ **Your credit score.** Some credit research firms, most notably Fair, Isaac and Company, calculate a single figure into what they call a *credit score*. Factors such as your payment history, the amount of borrowing relative to your credit lines, recent inquiries by other financial institutions, and the types of credit you use, are put into a computer model that produces a single number, which is scored on a scale from a low of 400, representing poor credit, to a high of 900, representing strong credit.

The best loan for any banker is one in which the business generates enough money to comfortably make the interest payments and, ultimately, return the entire amount of the bank's money. Government guarantees, personal guarantees, and collateral are just fallback positions in case the business fails, and the entrepreneur defaults on the loan. Collecting from a guarantor or taking and selling collateral generates a huge amount of work and aggravation for the bank, and invariably marks the end of its business relationship with the borrower.

When a business performs as anticipated, meets its obligations, and grows to the point that its credit needs increase, the bank, the loan officers, and the entrepreneur have a win-win situation in which they can build a long-term, mutually beneficial, business relationship. This partnership must begin with financial projections the bankers find credible and then, throughout the relationship with the bank, *prove* to be credible. Of course, you want to have a strong credit score, show yourself to be of good character, and be able to offer as much in collateral or guarantees as are needed so the bank makes the loan, but, in the long run, financial performance and credibility are what truly matter.

CHAPTER 9

Action Step Nine

Explain Your Financial Data:

How will you convince others to invest in your endeavor?

The accuracy of your financial figures and projections is absolutely critical in convincing investors, loan sources, and partners that your business concept is worthy of support. The data must also be scrupulously honest and extremely clear. Since banks and many other funding sources will compare your projections to industry averages in the Risk Management Association (RMA) data, your numbers will be more credible if they compare reasonably to the industry averages. If they don't closely match the RMA data, you should address this divergence thoroughly in your business plan. Chapter 10 explains how to complete this comparison, step by step.

The actual number-crunching portion of your business plan is not the place to talk about your pie-in-the-sky hopes for opening an ocarina plant in every country around the globe, or for convincing the U.S. Army that your squid-flavored pancakes should become standard fare in all military mess halls. It is the place to discuss how and why you need certain equipment, time, or talent; how much these items will cost; when you expect to turn a profit; and how much return and other benefits your investors will receive.

More new businesses fail because they simply run out of cash reserves than for any other reason. Investors lose confidence in the entrepreneur and the business and become reluctant to invest more when projections are not met. Had the projections been less optimistic and the investors asked to invest more in the beginning, they probably would have done so. In most cases, proper planning and more accurate projections could have prevented this problem completely.

Start analyzing your financial information by going back to the section "Identify Your Company's Initial Needs," in Chapter 2. Study your list of the tangibles and intangibles required to start your company and the costs you have estimated. Your business plan should clearly state the financing you need, how soon you require it, and how long before you start repaying investors. You should also explain what type of financing you hope to acquire, either *equity* (such as the sale of ownership shares in your company) or *debt* (such as loans to the company), and if you require capital expenditures to buy an automated pancake maker or working capital to pay for mousetrap design and market research.

If you're planning to buy an existing business, or already own a business you would like to improve or expand, you will also need to provide a detailed historical financial summary of how well—or poorly—the business has done in the past. This analysis should also include a comparison of this venture's financial performance compared to the industry standards presented in the RMA database. Just as with your projections, the bank will likely perform a similar historical analysis anyway. If you do the comparison first, you show yourself to be diligent and savvy—and you can explain any differences between the company's performance and the RMA data in a way that reflects positively on your plans.

You should identify whatever miscalculations you believe the previous owner might have made. Perhaps she put a great deal of money into producing gold-plated ocarinas that nobody wanted to buy. This is also the section of your business plan in which you should provide detailed figures on expected income, cash flow estimates, balance sheets, and future reasonable forecasts for your business. Do you hope to be producing 1,000 ocarinas a week in five years? Will you be able to lower the price of your better mousetraps once you can buy titanium by the ton? Are you planning to open three additional restaurants featuring squid-flavored pancakes?

By the time you've pulled together all the important financial data, you'll have a clearer picture of how much money you'll need to borrow, how much of your own funds you'll be able to commit, and the amount of investments you'll have to secure. This is also a good time to take a crash course in accounting principles or learning how to create spread sheets on a computer program. No matter what business you intend to start, you will need to know how to analyze not only projected profits and losses, but actual profits and losses as soon as your first customer walks through your pancake house door or buys a bottle of your bubble-gum scented bubble bath.

The Essential Financial Statements

With the presentation of your financial data you are addressing the fundamental reason why virtually all businesses exist: to earn money. Your financial data must include the following elements, from income statements all the way through schedules of investment. Specific examples of these documents are located at the back of the book in the two sample business plans and, at the end of this chapter, you'll find guidance as to how to produce them.

Income statements are summaries of an existing company's performance over a period of time. They are usually prepared using the *accrual system*, which recognizes revenues when they are earned and expenses at the time goods or services are consumed—not when the revenue is received or the expenses are paid. *Projected income statements* are called *pro forma income statements* and are an absolute requirement for any business plan.

Balance sheets are statements that present the financial status of an existing or projected business at a particular point in time. An overview of a company's capital position, such as how much debt it owes and the value of its assets, is located on the balance sheet.

Cash flow projections are income statements revised to show the anticipated actual inflows and outflows of money. A company's cash flow can differ significantly from that which the income statement shows; because keeping adequate cash reserves is necessary for the company to continue to operate, the cash flow projections are essential. Generally, cash flow statements differ from income statements in the following ways:

$ **Revenue** shows up on the cash flow statements when payment is received, which, for most businesses, is between 30 and 90 days after bills are sent out.

$ **Expenses** are recorded on cash flow statements when they are actually paid, not when the product or service is billed, which is usually 30 or 60 days after the bill is received.

$ **Depreciation**, which is recorded as an expense on the income statement, but not a cash item, is not included on the cash flow statement.

$ **Principal payments** on loans or purchases of stock from shareholders are included as a use of cash on the cash flow statement, but are not seen on the income statement.

Operating cash flow is the cash flow from the operations of the business such as manufacturing hats or building tree houses. *Net cash flow*, which is what one sees on the *sources and uses statement*, includes other sources or uses of cash, such as sales or purchases of assets and investment performance.

Statements of sources and uses show the actual sources and the uses of money by combining information from the *profit and loss statement* and balance sheet. Sources of funds typically include investment, increases in loans, and profits. Uses include items such as investment in equipment, loan repayments, dividends, and operating losses.

Debt-management schedules are projections that indicate your company's ability to pay interest and principal in accordance with your loan agreements. It is absolutely critical that the projections show that the company's obligations to its lenders will be met. Failure to do so will result in the company's credit being reduced, and can eventually lead to foreclosure and bankruptcy. An essential financial projection is a separate statement or table that shows the interest payment and principal repayment schedule and the company's ability to pay them. Since payments are made from cash flow, the cash flow statements must show what percentage of cash flow is going to make payments and how much cash the company still has after paying its debt obligations.

Returns analysis is a statement that shows the projected financial returns on the investment in your company. Potential investors need to see how much their investment will earn for them, through current payments, such as dividends, or by distributions from the sale of stock or the company as a whole. Whatever your particular strategy for producing returns for your investors is, the plan needs to show it and calculate what the returns will be.

"How much money will I make?" is the single most important question that potential investors will ask you. The answer is found in the returns analysis, which shows potential investors how much they will earn expressed both in dollars and in the percentage terms. As the returns analysis attached to the Zif Medical Devices plan shows, for each year of the projection, you add profit distributions and the value of the equity in the business and compare it to the investment made. Thus, $1 million invested in year one, earns 50 percent annually if it is worth $2 million in year three (two years later). A returns analysis requires that estimates of the value of the company be completed.

If your plan is to sell the business in a few years, the returns will largely be a function of the value of the company at the time it is sold. If, on the other hand, your plan is to own your business for a long time, the returns will largely be a function of profit distributions over time to the shareholders.

Schedules of investment and capital expenditures are lists of the amounts of money that need to be spent on items with long usable lives. The initial startup of your business, either by purchasing an existing company or founding a new one entirely from scratch, requires investment. A schedule that details this initial investment, including items such as legal expenses, equipment, banking fees, and rent deposits, is essential. Every year of operation results in further capital expenditures for new equipment, buildings, or product development. This should also be presented in the schedules of investments and capital expenditures, the total of which is then carried over to the cash flow statement.

Break-even analysis answers several key questions, including how much revenue your business will need to break even, what your fixed costs are, and how much the business will earn on every dollar of sales after breaking even. Not only are these figures extremely useful for your own understanding of your business, but you can expect potential lenders and investors to ask you these questions as well.

The key to preparing a break-even analysis is separating your costs into fixed costs and variable costs. Fixed costs remain the same, regardless of your revenue. These include items such as salaries, rent, interest payments, and insurance. Variable costs go up with greater revenue and include items such as costs of raw materials, royalties, shipping, and costs of returns. Basic introductory accounting books will take you through this process in greater detail. I suggest a few at the end of the book in the references.

The Six Key Financial Assumptions

The six key financial assumptions provide the foundation of projections, and should be clearly listed along with them. The test of complete financials is whether someone can read them and fully understand them without having to ask you questions. In my experience, you can pass this test if you take the time to fully explain your assumptions. Of course, you need to be careful about all your financial estimates. Mistakes undermine the confidence of anyone who reads your plan. These key financial assumptions are critical—mistakes here will not just erode confidence, but will probably doom your efforts:

Assumption number one: Up-front-costs.   No matter how profitable a business you expect to have, if you overpay to start it, it just won't work. I've seen this problem every day on both a large and small scale. Daimler-Benz's purchase of Chrysler and Hewlett-Packard's purchase of Compaq, are examples of this on a big scale. On a smaller scale, you can probably recall patronizing a restaurant that failed after overspending on renovations. The famous Russian Tea Room next to Carnegie Hall in New York City flourished for decades through good and bad economic times. After purchasing the restaurant for a high price, the new owners spent millions on a lavish renovation. Within a year after its grand reopening, the Russian Tea Room closed its ornate doors forever.

The components of up-front costs include:

$ Acquisition price of buying an existing business.

$ Capital investment in land, building, renovations, and equipment prior to starting operations.

$ Operating losses during the startup phase, which usually arise prior to achieving sales goals and heavy, initial marketing expenses.

Assumption number two: Sales and revenue numbers.   All the entrepreneurs I have advised believed that their biggest problem would be handling the volume their businesses would generate, with customers beating a path to their doors. Reality is quite different, as most experienced entrepreneurs will attest. Generating first-time orders is one of the toughest assignments in business, and building and expanding a list of customers is a close second. The great difficulty with revenue projections is that for many people they are pulled out of thin air. The solution to this is twofold:

$ **Anchor revenue projections** to reality by using techniques such as supplying lists of potential customers, pretesting your products or services through surveys or focus groups, comparing your product's features and price to the existing competition, and by comparing your revenue projections to industry averages or to similar businesses that you know.

$ **Be conservative in the extreme.** After you have created projections that you are certain approximate reality, cut them mercilessly. Based on what I have seen, when revenue projections seem ludicrously low to the entrepreneur, they are approaching reality!

Assumption number three: Operating costs estimation. Calculating potential expenses after startup requires a tremendous amount of work. To make certain you have covered each item, use the following as a checklist:

$ **Estimate every cost** from fixed costs, such as rent, utilities, advertising, employees, and employees' benefits, to variable costs, such as raw materials, shipping your products, and commissions to your salespeople. These are used in the Break-Even Analysis which was discussed earlier in this chapter.

$ **Set up your statements of costs** with as many categories as you can imagine and provide an explanation of how each estimate was determined so that people who question your numbers can follow your process. Providing this backup to your numbers helps establish you as a thorough manager who will inspire confidence in funders and investors.

$ **Build in contingencies** for issues such as additional advertising, legal expenses, traveling to meet with customers, and terminating employees who don't work out. After making these provisions, add a general contingency number of at least 5 percent to your total estimated expenses.

Assumption number four: Borrowing estimation. You need to speak with lenders about their particular guidelines for lending to your specific type of business, which is covered in Chapter 8. One of the great mistakes that entrepreneurs often make is assuming that they will get a bank to lend them more than it usually does. Banks have precise guidelines and rarely deviate from them. The RMA data is a great source to determine how much, on average, banks lend to businesses such as yours. Your financial projections need to show how much more cash flow the company will have than interest costs and how much more cash reserves it will have than are required for principal payments.

Assumption number five: Estimation of equity returns.   The amount of investment you are seeking in the form of stock or partnership shares requires that you project credible returns to investors. Because equity investors earn money from company profits and from the increase in the company's value, these figures must be calculated based on how much investors will put in and how much they will get back. Following these calculations, a return on investment can be determined and shown. If the return looks like a number you might earn from a bank savings account, you need to rethink the deal.

Assumption number six: Company value.   Tracking your company's estimated worth should appear throughout the entire period of your projections. Investors and lenders want to know where they stand, and you need to know where you stand if the company has to be closed at any given point. Calculating the company's value depends a great deal on the industry. Some businesses, such as restaurants, sell for the value of their real estate (or leases) and fixed assets. Technology companies, such as manufacturers of high-tech medical products, will sell as a multiple of their revenue, while media companies, such as magazines, will sell for a multiple of annual cash flow. Of course, some businesses, such as a one-person consulting firm, will sell for little, because there is no assurance that clients will move to the new owner.

Typical financial methods of calculating a company's value include estimating profits for the next ten or fifteen years and then calculating the *net present value* (current cash equivalent) of this stream of profits. Lenders will often ask businesses to calculate *book value*, which is assets less liabilities. You need to do the research in your industry to come up with a company valuation to use in your financial projections.

How to Create Statements

Many people are intimidated by the prospect of producing financial projections. However, if you manage the process by breaking it down into its components, doing what you can do best, finding resources to make other parts easier, and bringing in professionals to help with the remaining pieces, it can actually be a great way to learn a huge amount about the financial aspects of your business.

Build the Structure of Your Statements. By now, you should have copies of financial statements from companies that are in your industry. You may have obtained these from your lawyer, accountant, industry trade group, industry reference book, such as those listed in references to Chapter 4, or from a company in the industry. If you have not been able to obtain such sample statements, you can use standard statement formats from an accounting book, from one of the websites listed in the references, or by following the statement formats in the sample plans at the end of this book.

Start Filling in the Blanks. Now, do the best you can to fill in the blanks. In my experience, most people are able to do very well creating a statement of estimated start-up costs, income statements, cash flow projections, and debt-management schedules. The key technical accounting issues are the differences in the timing of expenses and revenue between the income statement and the cash flow statement. The income statement recognizes income based on an accrual system, which is when the income is earned or expenses incurred, and the *Cash flow statement* recognizes income when it is received and expenses when they are paid.

Statements of sources and uses and balance sheets have more technical accounting issues to manage. If you cannot complete the statements yourself, take advantage of the resources listed at the back of the book, or get professional help.

Use Some Outside Help. If you are not experienced enough to prepare statements yourself, I suggest you consider one of the following options:

$ **Use a template** similar to those available on the websites listed at the end of the book. Quicken and Quickbooks also offer statement templates.

$ **Obtain technical assistance** from a small business develop-ment center or other type of entrepreneurship center. Once you have researched good estimates and produced statements as well as you can, the rest will not be a big job for an experi-enced professional.

$ **Ask your accountant for help.** Finishing the statements is not a daunting task for a professional accountant, but you probably want to keep the expenses down, so I suggest this as a last re-sort. Do as much as you can yourself before seeing the accoun-tant, and get a fixed price from the accountant to finish the statements before you agree to use her services.

10

Action Step Ten

Use the RMA Database:
Check your answers against the answer key.

Now that you've learned how to create a credible, thoughtful, detailed, conservative, and properly presented bankable business plan, you're prepared to apply the advantage of the Risk Management Association (RMA) database. Most potential lenders and investors will compare your projections with the data supplied by the RMA, an association of more than 3,100 banks and other financial institutions that pool their business clients' financial data.

As the name of the association implies, its purpose is to help its members limit risk by avoiding loans to businesses whose numbers are inaccurate or unrealistic. The RMA database serves as an answer key against which bankers can double-check the financial projections of any business plan. If you compare your figures to the RMA database *before* you submit your business plan to potential lenders or investors, you will improve your chances of achieving the financial support you need to start your business.

No matter how high your credit score, or how many government guarantees you can produce, or how much collateral you can offer, there is no replacement for credible, accurate projections. Some bankers will simply pass on making a business loan if the projections are not convincing. Others will decline to make a business loan, but will offer to make a personal loan if your collateral or guarantees are strong enough. Neither of these options should be as attractive to you and your business as obtaining a business loan, which reduces your personal risk, and builds your business's credit.

While virtually all banks and many other funding sources use the RMA data, hardly any entrepreneurs take advantage of this significant resource, but you can, and I strongly urge you to do so. The RMA data may seem intimidating at first, because their publication looks like the Manhattan telephone directory, but it's actually quite straightforward and easy to decipher. I will guide you through the process of finding the right data for your business plan and using it to your advantage.

Obtain the RMA Data

Most libraries with some focus on business and virtually all Small Business Development Centers have the RMA data book. Since you will need copies of only a few pages, it is not difficult to obtain the data you need this way, and the cost is minimal. The RMA also sells their data over their website, one category at a time, for a cost of $60 by going to http://www.rmahq.com/Online_Prods/asstOL.html#single. The RMA site is not particularly friendly to entrepreneurs, so using their book is probably best.

Locate the page that pertains to your business. While the RMA book may be thick, there is only one page that pertains to you and your business. For example, suppose you're planning to open a florist shop. You find that page by looking through the table of contents to locate the section on retail businesses, then read down the list of retail businesses until you find *florists*. The RMA book is actually organized by government codes for business types, called *SIC codes* (for Standard Industrial Classification), so you can find the SIC code from the SBA website first. But it is simpler just to look down the list. SIC codes are being replaced by updated codes called *NAICS*, which are discussed in more detail at the end of this chapter.

Find the column that matches your business size. There are two pages for florists. One page sorts the florists by the amount of assets reported on the florists' financial Balance Sheets. Ignore that page for now, because it is easier to look at the next page which sorts the florists based on their annual revenue. Find the column that most closely matches the sales you project. This column of numbers is all you will need for your comparison.

Place your numbers next to the RMA numbers.   In Chapter 9, I explain which pieces of financial information are most important to a banker or investor. You will see that I've organized these items so that they match the items in the RMA data. Now, your projections and the RMA data can be easily compared. All the numbers and ratios that you will need to compare to the RMA data can be created from the financial projections you prepared earlier. Clearly, startups will have to present forecasted numbers without financial history.

Explain the differences between your data and the RMA data, or adjust your projections.   If your projections closely match the RMA data or are more conservative than the RMA data, you have nothing more to do, other than to point this out proudly to your potential funders. If your projections are more optimistic than the RMA data, you need to explain this discrepancy in the text of your plan.

Put It All into Action

Suppose you want to open a florist shop, and have written a plan that includes detailed financial projections. You look in the RMA data for florists and find the category for sales that covers your own projections. Let's say that you're projecting $1.5 million in annual sales. This will guide you to the data for florists with between $1 million and $3 million in sales. The RMA reports that florists of this size have an average margin on sales of 56 percent, which means they sell flowers for about twice what they pay for them. If you project that you will sell flowers for three times what you pay for them, you need to explain this discrepancy. Perhaps you'll sell only fancy floral displays, and the margin is higher for those than it is on cut flowers sold by the bunch. If, on the other hand, there is no explanation, you will need to take a new look at your projections and revise them.

The RMA data includes information that relates business profits to the amount of interest that florists pay. The average florist in the RMA database has three times as much in operating profits (called *EBIT*, or

Earnings Before Interest and Taxes) as interest costs. I would say that if you are projecting less than two times as much operating profit, or EBIT, as interest you should revisit your projections and revise the amount of funding you expect to receive.

Once you perform the same comparison for the other key figures explained here, you'll be in great shape to present your numbers to the bank.

The Primary RMA Data

Although the size of the RMA book is as thick as the Manhattan telephone directory, there is only one column of 81 numbers that will be of importance to you. On the page that presents your industry, this is the column that has data from businesses of a size similar to that which you are planning. Of these 81 numbers, you probably need to compare only 14 to see whether your numbers will pass the bankers' test. All of the following numbers can be created from the financial sheets and projections you created earlier in the book. Here are the most significant numbers you should compare to projections:

Receivables.   This figure represents how much your business is owed by its customers, with a reasonable allowance for accounts that will never pay. Some industries, such as fast-food restaurants, have almost no receivables, while other industries, such as contractors who sell to government agencies, have huge receivables. If your assumption is more optimistic than the industry norm, you may find yourself running short of cash. And running short of cash closes more businesses than anything else.

Debt.   This number appears in liabilities as notes payable and long-term debt. Notes payable generally have a term of one year or less, and long-term debt has a term longer than one year. Since a bank's loans are usually made in the form of long-term debt, the banker will be very attentive to your projections here.

Income and profit margin.   The group of numbers labeled *income data* starts with *net sales*, which are gross sales less returns and discounts. *Gross profit* is net sales minus the cost of the items or services you sold. *Operating expenses* includes all selling, administrative, and depreciation costs (but not interest expense). *Operating profit* is gross profit minus the operating expenses. The category *all other expenses* covers interest and miscellaneous expenses not included in operating expenses. *Profit before taxes* is the business's profit after all expenses, including interest, is calculated.

Financial ratios.   These calculations are used to evaluate business performance. The RMA data presents three numbers for each ratio: the average of the top quartile of businesses, the median ratio for the entire sample, and the average for the bottom quartile. Presenting the numbers this way gives you a sense of the *average* (median) and the range for each ratio. All ratios are used as indicators of potential problems. When a ratio seems too far from the norm, it usually signals the need for further analysis. The key ratios are:

$ **Current ratio** is current assets (generally the company's cash, receivables, and inventory) divided by current liabilities (generally short-term loans and upcoming loan payments, payables, and taxes currently owed) and is a rough indication of a company's ability to pay its current obligations. The higher the ratio, the stronger it is, but the quality of the assets and liabilities must be measured as well.

$ **Quick ratio**, or acid test, is cash and equivalents (such as money market accounts the company may have) plus receivables minus allowances for nonpaying accounts divided by current liabilities. This is a similar, but stricter, measure of a company's ability to pay its bills.

$ **Sales divided by receivables** (invoices that your company has sent out but has not yet been paid) gives a measure of turnover or how many days on average it takes for your customers to pay. The higher this number, the fewer days on average for your customers to pay.

$ **Cost of sales divided by inventory** (items held by the company waiting to be sold) measures how often your inventory turns over in a year. A fruit store turns over its inventory every week or less. An antique store turns over its inventory a few times per year. A high ratio can mean efficient use of inventory or it might mean that a company starved for cash has cut its inventory to the bone.

$ **Cost of sales divided by payables** (bills received but not paid) shows how quickly a business pays its bills. A high ratio means that bills are being paid promptly. A low ratio may indicate a company that is experiencing a cash shortage is paying its suppliers too slowly.

$ **Coverage ratios** indicate a company's ability to pay its debt obligations. Earnings before interest and taxes divided by interest shows the ability to pay interest. It is unusual to see this ratio below two for small businesses. The ratio of net profit plus depreciation and amortization divided by the current portion of long-term debt shows the same coverage, but for scheduled principal repayments. Depreciation is a noncash item that is usually calculated by your accountant to reflect how your company's long-term assets are used over time. *Amortization* is the payment of the principal part of your company's loans.

$ **Leverage ratios** show how much debt a company has in comparison to its value. The RMA data has two such measures: net fixed assets divided by *tangible net worth*. Both these figures show what percentage of the long-term assets, such as a manufacturing plant and equipment, have been paid for by the owners' investment. The lower the ratio, the more it appears that the owners have invested in their company for the long term. Total liabilities divided by tangible net worth shows the relationship between the owners' and the lenders' capital. The higher the ratio, the less the owners have put in the company relative to the lenders.

$ **Operating ratios** are calculated by dividing sales or profits by investment in the business or the values of its assets. Operating ratios give some measure of management's performance. The higher your profit relative to your investment, the better your company looks. Your industry may already have an operating ratio that it uses, which is the one you should choose. For most small businesses, these ratios are rarely used.

$ **Expense to sales ratio** is presented towards the bottom of the column. This ratio tends to vary greatly by industry. Before you calculate this ratio, talk to other business owners to find out if your industry typically uses this as a means of comparison, or check with accountants who specialize in your industry.

$ **Owners', officers', and directors' compensation as a percentage of sales** indicates whether their compensations are in line with industry standards.

SIC and NAICS Codes

The RMA data is organized by a government system called *SIC*, or *Standard Industrial Classification*, that categorizes all businesses. There are two complications that you need to know about. The first is that a new system, called *NAICS, North American Industrial Classification System*, is replacing SIC, which has become out of date. The SBA and OSHA websites can take you through the process of finding the right code for your business, or helping you find the new NAICS code if you already know the SIC code. The simplest and fastest way to find the right code is to look through the table of contents of the RMA book.

The second complication is that it might not be obvious which code is best for your business. For example, if your business is a retail bakery with a line of prepackaged baking products that are sold in other stores, you could choose the SIC for retail bakery or the one for bakery products manufacturing. In these cases, you may want to present both sets of RMA data for comparison purposes. Or you can choose the RMA data that by comparison shows your business in the best light.

How you choose to categorize your business may have an impact on lenders. For example, if the bank has told you that they are less inclined to lend to retailers than to manufacturers, then choose the category that will appeal to them the most.

It Really Is That Simple

Producing a meticulous set of financial projections and comparing them to the RMA data, along with either explaining or reducing the differences, will result in a banker or investor who says "Your numbers look good." This is the best possible reaction, and one you can achieve by plugging the RMA numbers into your spreadsheets and using the definitions above to explain the numbers like an expert!

Explanation of Contractor-Percentage of Completion Basis of Accounting Balance Sheet and Income Data

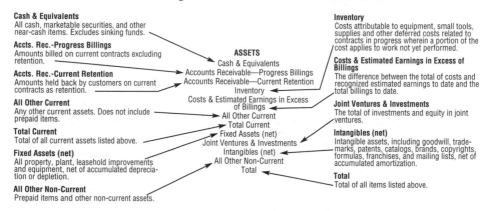

Cash & Equivalents
All cash, marketable securities, and other near-cash items. Excludes sinking funds.

Accts. Rec.-Progress Billings
Amounts billed on current contracts excluding retention.

Accts. Rec.-Current Retention
Amounts held back by customers on current contracts as retention.

All Other Current
Any other current assets. Does not include prepaid items.

Total Current
Total of all current assets listed above.

Fixed Assets (net)
All property, plant, leasehold improvements and equipment, net of accumulated depreciation or depletion.

All Other Non-Current
Prepaid items and other non-current assets.

ASSETS
Cash & Equivalents
Accounts Receivable—Progress Billings
Accounts Receivable—Current Retention
Inventory
Costs & Estimated Earnings in Excess of Billings
All Other Current
Total Current
Fixed Assets (net)
Joint Ventures & Investments
Intangibles (net)
All Other Non-Current
Total

Inventory
Costs attributable to equipment, small tools, supplies and other deferred costs related to contracts in progress wherein a portion of the cost applies to work not yet performed.

Costs & Estimated Earnings in Excess of Billings
The difference between the total of costs and recognized estimated earnings to date and the total billings to date.

Joint Ventures & Investments
The total of investments and equity in joint ventures.

Intangibles (net)
Intangible assets, including goodwill, trademarks, patents, catalogs, brands, copyrights, formulas, franchises, and mailing lists, net of accumulated amortization.

Total
Total of all items listed above.

Notes Payable—Short Term
All short term note obligations, including bank and commercial paper. Does not include trade notes payable.

Accounts Payable—Trade
Open accounts and note obligations due to the trade.

Accounts Payable—Retention
Amounts held back as retention in payments to subcontractors on current contracts.

Long Term Debt
All senior debt, including bonds, debentures, bank debt, mortgages, deferred portions of long term debt, and capital lease obligations.

Deferred Taxes
Total of all deferred taxes.

All Other Non-Current
Any other non-current liabilities, including subordinated debt, and liability reserves.

LIABILITIES
Notes Payable—Short Term
Accounts Payable—Trade
Accounts Payable—Retention
Billings in Excess of Costs & Estimated Earnings
Income Taxes Payable
Current Maturities—LTD
All Other Current
Total Current
Long Term Debt
Deferred Taxes
All Other Non-Current
Net Worth
Total Liabilities & Net Worth

Billings in Excess of Costs & Est. Earn.
The difference between the total billings to date and the total of costs and recognized estimated earnings to date.

Income Taxes Payable
Income taxes including current portion of deferred taxes.

Current Maturities—LTD
That portion of long term obligations that is due within the next fiscal year.

All Other Current
Any other current liabilities, including bank overdrafts and accrued expenses.

Total Current
Total of all current liabilities listed above.

Net Worth
Difference between total assets and total liabilities. Minority interest is included here.

Total Liabilities & Net Worth
Total of all items listed above.

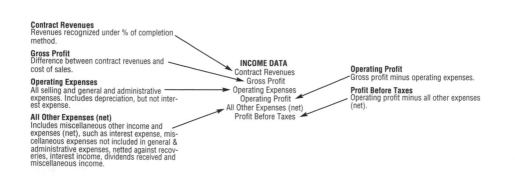

Contract Revenues
Revenues recognized under % of completion method.

Gross Profit
Difference between contract revenues and cost of sales.

Operating Expenses
All selling and general and administrative expenses. Includes depreciation, but not interest expense.

All Other Expenses (net)
Includes miscellaneous other income and expenses (net), such as interest expense, miscellaneous expenses not included in general & administrative expenses, netted against recoveries, interest income, dividends received and miscellaneous income.

INCOME DATA
Contract Revenues
Gross Profit
Operating Expenses
Operating Profit
All Other Expenses (net)
Profit Before Taxes

Operating Profit
Gross profit minus operating expenses.

Profit Before Taxes
Operating profit minus all other expenses (net).

Explanation of Noncontractor Balance Sheet and Income Data

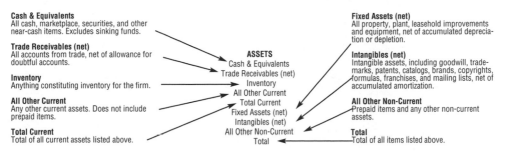

Cash & Equivalents
All cash, marketplace, securities, and other near-cash items. Excludes sinking funds.

Trade Receivables (net)
All accounts from trade, net of allowance for doubtful accounts.

Inventory
Anything constituting inventory for the firm.

All Other Current
Any other current assets. Does not include prepaid items.

Total Current
Total of all current assets listed above.

ASSETS
Cash & Equivalents
Trade Receivables (net)
Inventory
All Other Current
Total Current
Fixed Assets (net)
Intangibles (net)
All Other Non-Current
Total

Fixed Assets (net)
All property, plant, leasehold improvements and equipment, net of accumulated depreciation or depletion.

Intangibles (net)
Intangible assets, including goodwill, trademarks, patents, catalogs, brands, copyrights, formulas, franchises, and mailing lists, net of accumulated amortization.

All Other Non-Current
Prepaid items and any other non-current assets.

Total
Total of all items listed above.

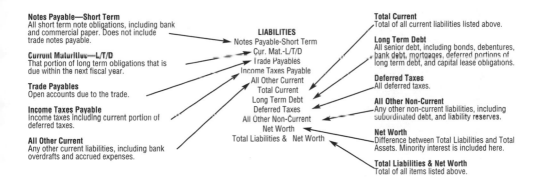

Notes Payable—Short Term
All short term note obligations, including bank and commercial paper. Does not include trade notes payable.

Current Maturities—L/T/D
That portion of long term obligations that is due within the next fiscal year.

Trade Payables
Open accounts due to the trade.

Income Taxes Payable
Income taxes including current portion of deferred taxes.

All Other Current
Any other current liabilities, including bank overdrafts and accrued expenses.

LIABILITIES
Notes Payable-Short Term
Cur. Mat.-L/T/D
Trade Payables
Income Taxes Payable
All Other Current
Total Current
Long Term Debt
Deferred Taxes
All Other Non-Current
Net Worth
Total Liabilities & Net Worth

Total Current
Total of all current liabilities listed above.

Long Term Debt
All senior debt, including bonds, debentures, bank debt, mortgages, deferred portions of long term debt, and capital lease obligations.

Deferred Taxes
All deferred taxes.

All Other Non-Current
Any other non-current liabilities, including subordinated debt, and liability reserves.

Net Worth
Difference between Total Liabilities and Total Assets. Minority interest is included here.

Total Liabilities & Net Worth
Total of all items listed above.

Net Sales
Gross sales, net of returns and discounts allowed, if any.

Gross Profit
Net sales minus cost of sales.

Operating Expenses
All selling and general & administrative expenses. Includes depreciation, but not interest expense.

INCOME DATA
Net Sales
Gross Profit
Operating Expenses
Operating Profit
All Other Expenses (net)
Profit Before Taxes

Operating Profit
Gross profit minus operating expenses.

All Other Expenses (net)
Includes miscellaneous other income and expenses (net), such as interest expense, miscellaneous expenses not included in general & administrative expenses, netted against recoveries, interest income, dividends received and miscellaneous income.

Profit Before Taxes
Operating profit minus all other expenses (net).

Retail Florists SIC # 5992 (NAICS 45311)

Current Data Sorted By Assets

	0-500M	500M-2MM	2-10MM	10-50MM	50-100MM	100-250MM		4/1/97-3/31/98 ALL	4/1/98-3/31/99 ALL
Type of Statement		(4/1-9/30/01)		(10/1/01-3/31/02)				*Comparative Historical Data*	
Unqualified									
Reviewed									
Compiled	15	31	2					84	2
Tax Returns	18	7	1			1		91	33
Other	53	1	1					34 / 14 / 14	21 / 16 / 16
		22	2	38		1			
NUMBER OF STATEMENTS	38	14	5	2		1		79	86

	0-500M %	500M-2MM %	2-10MM %	10-50MM %	50-100MM %	100-250MM %	4/1/97-3/31/98 ALL %	4/1/98-3/31/99 ALL %
ASSETS								
Cash & Equivalents	9.4	9.8					12.5	12.0
Trade Receivables (net)	20.5	17.0					17.9	16.3
Inventory	20.4	28.4					27.7	24.3
All Other Current	1.3	3.2					1.0	2.0
Total Current	51.6	58.4					59.1	54.6
Fixed Assets (net)	35.4	35.4					32.2	35.7
Intangibles (net)	6.3	1.0					2.7	3.8
All Other Non-Current	6.6	5.2					6.0	5.9
Total	100.0	100.0					100.0	100.0
LIABILITIES								
Notes Payable-Short Term	7.5	9.7					10.5	6.7
Cur. Mat.-L/T/D	7.4	7.2					2.7	4.9
Trade Payables	23.0	17.2					16.9	17.7
Income Taxes Payable		.7					.4	.3
All Other Current	21.8	7.1					8.4	14.0
Total Current	59.8	41.9					38.8	43.5
Long Term Debt	41.7	22.3					20.0	29.7
Deferred Taxes	.2	.4					.1	.2
All Other Non-Current	2.1	4.5					2.5	3.9
Net Worth	-3.8	31.0					38.5	22.7
Total Liabilities & Net Worth	100.0	100.0					100.0	100.0
INCOME DATA								
Net Sales	100.0	100.0					100.0	100.0
Gross Profit	53.7	50.4					54.7	52.6
Operating Expenses	52.4	48.5					50.2	49.8
Operating Profit	1.3	2.0					4.4	2.8
All Other Expenses (net)	1.0	.4					.7	.0
Profit Before Taxes	.3	1.6					3.7	2.7
RATIOS								
Current	2.0	2.6					2.9	2.5
	1.2	1.5					1.7	1.5
	.6	.9					1.0	1.0
Quick	1.3	1.7					1.6	1.6
	.8 (13)	.6					.7	.7
	.4	.4					.4	.3

Sales/Receivables	12 29.5 17 21.6 26 13.9	7 50.0 17 20.9 30 12.3				9 39.6 17 21.5 31 11.9	8 48.3 15 25.0 22 16.3	
Cost of Sales/Inventory	18 20.0 34 10.7 51 7.2	39 9.3 67 5.5 90 4.1				28 12.9 68 5.4 114 3.2	22 16.9 47 7.8 81 4.5	
Cost of Sales/Payables	6 58.2 33 11.2 64 5.7	23 16.1 29 12.4 67 5.5				22 16.7 37 9.8 58 6.3	22 16.9 34 10.8 51 7.1	
Sales/Working Capital	13.2 53.9 -54.4	5.8 19.7 -61.6				6.8 15.2 UND	8.4 17.3 -133.8	
EBIT/Interest	(32) 5.1 2.0 -.2	(13) 4.0 2.0 1.1				(70) 5.1 2.2 .8	(79) 6.7 2.8 1.3	
Net Profit + Depr., Dep., Amort./Cur. Mat. L./T/D						(18) 2.8 2.1 1.0	(20) 5.3 2.1 1.4	
Fixed/Worth	.5 5.8 -1.0	.5 1.1 NM				.3 .8 3.0	.4 1.0 19.7	
Debt/Worth	1.5 13.0 -3.9	.8 1.2 NM				.7 1.6 5.2	.8 1.9 30.2	
% Profit Before Taxes/Tangible Net Worth	(23) 89.5 17.8 -4.3	(11) 25.3 6.6 -.3				(65) 37.1 13.2 1.9	(66) 50.3 21.1 4.6	
% Profit Before Taxes/Total Assets	17.9 3.0 -3.0	12.2 1.8 -.2				14.4 3.6 -.7	15.6 7.1 1.0	
Sales/Net Fixed Assets	34.2 17.8 8.1	13.7 8.6 6.3				25.7 12.8 5.7	24.1 10.6 5.3	
Sales/Total Assets	7.0 4.8 2.4	4.0 3.3 1.9				4.3 3.0 2.1	4.5 3.3 2.2	
% Depr., Dep., Amort./Sales	(37) .9 1.7 3.0	(13) 1.6 2.2 2.9				(69) 1.2 2.0 2.8	(77) 1.2 1.8 3.1	
% Officers', Directors', Owners' Comp/Sales	(25) 4.4 6.2 9.1					(40) 3.2 6.3 -3.4	(50) 3.9 6.6 9.9	
Net Sales ($)	26815M	33885M	52015M	162474M	192519M	834795M	744653M	
Total Assets ($)	7118M	11344M	20692M	49545M	146687M	523373M	400950M	

M = $thousand   MM = $million

©RMA 2002

103

Retail Florists SIC # 5992 (NAICS 45311) *(Continued)*

	Comparative Historical Data			Current Data Sorted By Sales					
Type of Statement	4/1/99-3/31/00	4/1/00-3/31/01	4/1/01-3/31/02	0-1MM	1-3MM	3-5MM	5-10MM	10-25MM	25MM & OVER
	ALL	ALL	ALL		22 (4/1-9/30/01)			38 (10/1/01-3/31/02)	
Unqualified									
Reviewed		12	4						
Compiled	28	27	24	10	31	4	1	1	2
Tax Returns	16	20	20	17	9	1	1	1	1
Other	23	17	10	43	2				
NUMBER OF STATEMENTS	74	69	60	31	17	5	2	2	3
	%	%	%	%	%	%	%	%	%
ASSETS									
Cash & Equivalents	9.6	14.0	10.9	9.1	10.2				
Trade Receivables (net)	19.1	17.0	18.8	19.6	18.7				
Inventory	24.4	23.4	22.3	21.0	26.4				
All Other Current	1.8	2.1	3.1	1.4	2.1				
Total Current	54.9	56.5	55.1	51.1	57.4				
Fixed Assets (net)	33.9	32.7	33.2	34.6	37.2				
Intangibles (net)	4.9	4.6	5.2	7.7	.2				
All Other Non-Current	6.4	6.2	6.4	6.5	5.2				
Total	100.0	100.0	100.0	100.0	100.0				
LIABILITIES									
Notes Payable-Short Term	8.0	6.0	8.6	8.2	6.7				
Cur. Mat.-L/T/D	4.5	5.2	6.5	7.9	5.3				
Trade Payables	16.7	21.2	20.8	25.3	16.8				
Income Taxes Payable	.5	.2	.2	.0	.5				
All Other Current	13.4	19.5	16.8	23.2	10.0				
Total Current	43.1	52.2	52.9	64.7	39.3				
Long Term Debt	35.0	28.9	34.4	46.3	21.7				
Deferred Taxes	.2	.3	.3	.1	.7				
All Other Non-Current	5.1	6.4	2.9	2.0	4.9				
Net Worth	16.5	12.2	9.5	-13.1	33.4				
Total Liabilities & Net Worth	100.0	100.0	100.0	100.0	100.0				
INCOME DATA									
Net Sales	100.0	100.0	100.0	100.0	100.0				
Gross Profit	53.5	52.8	52.5	54.7	50.0				
Operating Expenses	50.3	51.9	50.9	53.0	48.7				
Operating Profit	3.1	.8	1.6	1.6	1.3				
All Other Expenses (net)	.1	.1	.9	1.2	.8				
Profit Before Taxes	3.0	.7	.7	.4	.5				
RATIOS									
Current	2.2	2.2	2.5	2.0	2.2				
	1.4	1.3	1.4	1.2	1.7				
	1.0	1.0	.8	.6	1.0				
		(59)		(16)					
Quick	1.3	1.3	1.5	1.3	1.4				
	.7	.7	.8	.8	.7				
	.4	.4	.4	.4	.5				

	C1	C2	C3	C4	C5	C6	C7	C8	C9
Sales/Receivables	7 55.9 / 18 20.4 / 29 12.8	7 54.4 / 17 21.0 / 27 13.4	11 33.1 / 18 20.3 / 28 13.3	13 28.1 / 18 20.4 / 25 14.5	7 52.3 / 18 20.2 / 28 13.0				
Cost of Sales/Inventory	26 14.0 / 52 7.1 / 85 4.3	23 15.9 / 45 8.1 / 82 4.5	27 13.7 / 42 8.7 / 75 4.9	26 14.1 / 37 9.7 / 67 5.4	34 10.7 / 53 6.8 / 79 4.6				
Cost of Sales/Payables	18 20.0 / 32 11.3 / 52 7.0	21 17.7 / 28 13.0 / 48 7.6	16 23.3 / 31 11.7 / 66 5.6	14 25.2 / 40 9.1 / 68 5.4	14 27.0 / 30 12.3 / 55 6.6				
Sales/Working Capital	9.4 / 20.8 / 240.1	11.4 / 24.3 / -397.7	8.6 / 34.2 / -66.3	11.7 / 57.0 / -22.7	5.6 / 24.8 / NM				
EBIT/Interest	(65) 6.1 / 2.4 / .8	(60) 4.0 / 1.8 / .0	(51) 4.8 / 2.5 / .9	(37) 5.1 / 2.5 / .7	(14) 3.3 / 1.3 / .2				
Net Profit + Depr., Dep., Amort./Cur. Mat. L/T/D	(12) 8.0 / 3.2 / 1.9	(14) 3.5 / 1.6 / .4	(12) 3.8 / 1.9 / 1.1						
Fixed/Worth	.4 / 1.2 / -2.7	.4 / 1.3 / -11.4	.5 / 1.4 / -2.2	.7 / 7.5 / -.9	.5 / 1.1 / 36.8				
Debt/Worth	.8 / 1.9 / -7.1	.9 / 2.7 / -25.7	1.1 / 2.3 / -6.0	1.6 / 18.7 / -3.6	.8 / 1.2 / 99.1				
% Profit Before Taxes/Tangible Net Worth	(51) 48.0 / 19.3 / 4.2	(48) 31.7 / 9.8 / -2.8	(40) 49.0 / 10.5 / -.2	(18) 104.1 / 28.9 / -1.2	(14) 23.6 / 2.8 / -2.8				
% Profit Before Taxes/Total Assets	20.1 / 6.4 / -.6	13.4 / 2.7 / -3.2	14.4 / 2.5 / -1.1	17.8 / 3.7 / -1.8	5.5 / .9 / -2.2				
Sales/Net Fixed Assets	25.2 / 12.0 / 6.0	23.5 / 12.7 / 7.4	31.2 / 13.3 / 7.1	38.9 / 20.2 / 6.8	14.0 / 9.3 / 6.8				
Sales/Total Assets	5.0 / 3.5 / 2.1	4.8 / 3.5 / 2.5	5.3 / 3.5 / 2.2	6.0 / 3.8 / 2.2	4.8 / 3.8 / 2.1				
% Depr., Dep., Amort./Sales	(65) 1.1 / 1.8 / 3.1	(61) 1.1 / 2.0 / 3.1	(56) 1.0 / 1.7 / 2.8	(22) .8 / 1.6 / 3.1	(15) 1.7 / 2.5 / 2.9				
% Officers', Directors', Owners' Comp/Sales	(40) 4.3 / 5.7 / 9.4	(37) 3.6 / 6.7 / 9.6	(38) 3.1 / 5.6 / 7.7	4.1 / 6.3 / 10.3					
Net Sales ($)	217449M	1895585M	467708M	16053M	30151M	19405M	12114M	34992M	354993M
Total Assets ($)	64909M	500708M	235386M	5092M	10260M	6395M	4889M	12518M	196232M

M = $ thousand   MM = $ million

PART II

Putting It All Together

11

What a Business Plan Should Look Like

Congratulations! Now that you've thoroughly considered the basics of your business, you're ready to write your plan. Remember that your business plan represents who you are. You want it to be professional, organized, and persuasive. The text should demonstrate how completely you have researched your business concept. It must also reflect your commitment to seeing the project through to a successful completion.

The first physical impression your plan makes when it arrives on a reader's desk is crucial. If it has been folded into a thin paper envelope, it will arrive dog-eared and creased. If you've used a paper clip to hold it together, the sheets will separate as soon as the reader tries to flip through the pages. If you've used flimsy paper, your plan will look old and worn out by the time it's passed along to the next reader.

To help you understand the importance of the physical presentation of your business plan, let's examine exactly how it should look.

The Physical Qualities

The look of your business plan will create an indelible first impression, negative or positive. I'm shocked to see how often my clients at the Field Center for Entrepreneurship make the mistake of creating a presentation that overshadows the content of the plan. Many entrepreneurs commit a great deal of effort and expense to designing an eye-catching written presentation. I've seen several that were true works of art—slickly produced with fanciful graphics and expensive, glossy paper. Other clients have cobbled together a sloppy business plan mixed with both original and photocopied pages generated by different computers and printed in mismatching fonts.

In all of these cases, even the most persuasive text was completely eclipsed by the physical presentation. Such artfully or poorly produced business plans give the impression that these entrepreneurs either have more flash than polish or are too disorganized and incompetent to start their own businesses. The physical qualities of your plan should demonstrate that you took exceptional care to produce it and that you are a competent, meticulous, enthusiastic, and knowledgeable professional.

Neatness counts. If your business plan represents you, think about the impression you would make entering a potential investor's office with your shoelace flopping and your tie splattered with the pea soup you had for lunch, or with your slip showing and your silk blouse missing a beautifully embossed button. A disheveled appearance sends an instantly negative, and often unalterable, message about you to the other person.

So, too, does a messy business plan. I have seen plans that looked as if they had been pecked out on 1937 Underwood typewriters by major holders of White-Out stock. I once reviewed a plan for a financial-consulting venture in which words in the typed text were crossed out, with handwritten changes squeezed between the single spaced lines. The columns of numbers in the fiscal sections weren't lined up properly, so the subtotals and totals weren't clear. The content of the plan was actually rather impressive, but as I thumbed through the messy, amateurish pages, all I could think was, "What kind of work will these people be able to produce for their customers?"

One of my clients submitted a meticulous and persuasive plan, but left off a contact name, address, and telephone number. Another failed to include a heading with the name of her company and page numbers on each sheet. Both omissions could spell disaster if the order of the pages became jumbled, or the investors wanted to call to arrange a meeting.

Speaking of spelling disaster, misspellings, incorrect financial numbers, inconsistent text fonts, or pages that fall out easily, all reflect badly on you. Your plan must be neat, accurate, well proofread, and generated on a computer, so that changes and updates can be made easily. If you know how to use a spreadsheet program, do so, but a clean, clear list of financial figures produced on a quality printer will work well, too.

Color printing is nice, but not essential. Have your plan spiral-bound at your local copy store, with a clear top sheet and an opaque back sheet to further protect it during what you hope will be extensive reading and handling. Spiral binding also keeps the pages in order and allows your plan to be opened flat for easy reading. With a neat, accurate presentation, you will greatly increase your chances of convincing investors not only to read about your potential business, but to support it as well.

Decent paper is proper. Be sure the quality of paper you choose for printing is good enough so it stands up to multiple readings, but not too contrived or elaborate that you actually send the wrong message to your investors. I once saw a plan for a Christmas tree ornament store that was printed on alternating red and green paper. Not only was this idea terribly precious, it also rendered the text extremely difficult to read.

Another client presented a business plan to me that was done entirely on glossy card stock. This, too, was hard to read under any artificial lighting conditions and made flipping back and forth between the pages virtually impossible. Using stock that is difficult to read, or inordinately expensive, may indicate that you're not very serious about your business plan or that you're a spendthrift who enjoys squandering money. Needless to say, none of these qualities will encourage potential investors to support your endeavor. Standard 20 lb. paper that is used in a copy machine or printer is the safest choice.

Excessive length equals longwindedness. Coming to the point quickly and effectively is important in both speaking and writing. Do not be fooled into believing that the longer and more detailed your plan, the more impressive it will appear to potential investors. Being excessively wordy implies that you do not value the small amount of precious time readers have to evaluate your written business plan. Take a look at the four sentence executive summary for Bug-Be-Gone later in this chapter. Four sentences should not necessarily be your goal, but if you strive for a statement this distilled, you should be able to cover all ten action steps with very few words.

The same is true for the text of your business plan. Although this section should detail each of the ten action steps, you want to keep your statements clear, pithy, and highly readable. William Strunk, Jr. and E.B. White, in their famous 1,300 word book *The Elements of Style*, emphasize rule 13: "Omit needless words." As the authors explain, "This requires not that the writer make all his sentences short, or that he avoid all detail, but that every word tell." Chances are your first business plan draft will have many needless words. Find them and eliminate them.

Additional media is not a must.   In this era of Palm Pilots, PowerPoint projections, and other innovative communication techniques, it's tempting to employ cutting-edge technology in presenting your business plan. Some technology can be eyecatching and make a memorable impression on your readers, but it should only supplement your written plan, not replace it or overshadow it. In fact, many of those who read your plan will never meet you, see an in-person presentation, or look at supplemental material such as videos or DVDs. They will base their decision solely on the written plan, which must achieve your purpose on its own.

I once saw a plan for a commercial fishing venture that was presented as a slick videotape showing boats, large catches of fish, and happy consumers enjoying elaborate seafood dinners. It was quite impressive, but I suppose the authors of this plan mistakenly thought it was too mundane to include a few pieces of paper outlining their capabilities or projected returns to their potential investors.

The Actual Layout

Banks, loan institutions and professional investors review dozens of business plans every day. They want to grasp the business concept easily and evaluate the numbers quickly. To make sure their staff time is spent effectively, most financial institutions and investors prefer that all business plans conform to a particular format. Although there may be individual variations from one firm to another, which you must determine in advance, most formats are fairly standard and include the following five components in this order:

$ **A cover page** that is cleanly designed and contains all the right information

$ **A table of contents** that is short and to the point

$ **An executive summary** that is concise, but touches on all ten action steps in one paragraph

$ **A complete text** that is well edited and describes the ten action steps in detail

$ **An appendix** that contains a complete set of exhibits

When your business plan is complete, have it spiralbound with firm plastic backing and a clear protective cover sheet.

The cover page is the first impression of your business plan that reviewers will receive. Remember that old saw, "First impressions count"? It's true. The cover page must be neat and legible, and contain all the basic information so reviewers can contact you quickly and easily—that is, if they want to schedule an in-person meeting. Readers don't want to thumb through the entire plan to find your name, the title of your company, or its purpose.

The cover page should display the following:

$ **The name of your company** in large type near the top of the page

$ **A single phrase** describing what your company does, directly beneath the company name

$ **The names of the founder or partners** involved, half-way down the page

$ **The name of the primary contact person**, near the bottom of the page

$ **The contact information for reaching this person**, including telephone number, fax number, e-mail address, and mailing address, directly beneath the contact person's name

Here's an example of a clear, clean cover page:

Bug-Be-Gone
A Company that Manufactures
Nontoxic, Fruit-scented
Bug Spray

Roger Roach
Founder and Chief Executive Officer

Contact: Roger Roach

telephone: 888-BUG-BEGONE (212-284-2343)
fax: 888-284-1245
e-mail: bugbegone@aol.com
Mailing address: Roger Roach
           Bug-Be-Gone
           123 Silver Fish Lane
           Insect, Indiana 12345

The table of contents is helpful, even if your plan is fairly brief, and necessary if your plan is still lengthy after numerous edits. Place the table of contents directly after the cover page, so investors can turn to any specific section quickly. You may also consider attaching identifying tabs to each of the sections, so readers can locate them more readily.

The executive summary is ideally a one-page (or shorter!) overview of your plan, with a compelling argument for the success of your business concept. More than a simple explanation of your idea, the executive summary is the hook that must grab and hold the attention of the funding sources evaluating your plan. If potential investors don't like what they see in the executive summary, they rarely read any further, and your beautifully crafted plan will be tossed onto the already sky-high reject pile. Most bankers and venture capital firms see hundreds of plans every year. If your executive summary doesn't immediately assert that your plan merits attention, you're history.

An executive summary should briefly cover the ten action steps outlined in Part I, which are:

1. **Define your company:** *What will you accomplish for others and yourself?*

2. **Identify your company's initial needs:** *What will you require to get started?*

3. **Choose a winning strategy:** *How will you distinguish your product or service from others?*

4. **Analyze your market:** *Who will want your product or service?*

5. **Develop a strong marketing campaign:** *How will you reach your customers and what will you say to them?*

6. **Build a dynamic sales effort:** *How will you attract customers?*

7. **Design your company:** *How will you hire and organize your work force?*

8. **Target your funding sources:** *Where will you find your financing?*

9. **Explain your financial data:** *How will you convince others to invest in your endeavor?*

10. **Use the RMA database:** *Check your answers against the answer key.*

The following example of an executive summary is only four sentences long, but mentions all ten action steps clearly and succinctly:

Bug-Be-Gone Corporation is seeking to raise $10 million in equity capital from individuals who will invest at least $1 million each (2, 8) to develop and market a unique line of fruit-scented insecticides that are nontoxic to humans and pets (1, 3, 4, 5). Bug-Be-Gone is owned and managed by Roger Roach, whose 20 years of experience in the insect extermination business will enable him to hire the most knowledgeable entomologists and the most precise bug sprayers in the industry (7). The company has already received preliminary orders from the three major firms that supply 80 percent of the California market, which consumes 50 percent of all insecticides in the United States (4, 5, 6). The financial projections show the company achieving higher than average profit margins (10) and that equity investors will receive returns in excess of 35 percent annually by the third year of operation (1, 9).

If your venture is more complex than Bug-Be-Gone's, you may need two or three paragraphs, but polish and trim until you have the most highly distilled executive summary possible. Here are a few more examples:

SUNNY CITY BUDGET MOTEL

There is no budget hotel within the Sunny City market. Relative to standard measures of hotel/motel rooms, for the volume of travelers on the adjacent interstate highway, the city population, and jobs in the market, the Sunny City hotel/motel market is underbuilt and represents an opportunity for new hotels and motels. I have identified a location adjacent to the interstate highway, within two miles of downtown, that can be purchased for the construction of a hotel or motel. The XYZ national budget hotel chain is willing to sell a franchise for this location. The cost numbers for the land and construction are below the franchisor's national averages, while room rates are projected to be at or above their figures. Financial projections show that $2 million in equity investment will earn 21 percent returns, and $8 million in debt can be repaid in eight years.

THE LAWNRIDER COMPANY

The riding-lawnmower industry has grown threefold in the last 15 years. The trends show the market is very sensitive to price and features. The LawnRider Company is being formed to become a major player in this market. A line of LawnRiders has been designed that adds features to midpriced riding lawnmowers that previously have only been seen in high-end machines. LawnRider has negotiated a contract with a Korean factory to manufacture the machines and give LawnRider the lowcost advantage in this market. The largest home-center company in the U.S. market has agreed to carry LawnRider exclusively in its 1,200 stores. Both agreements are negotiated. The key remaining elements for LawnRider's success is for the company to market the product. Towards that end, a detailed marketing plan has been created. LawnRider is seeking $4 million in investment, which is projected to earn 32 percent average annual return over the next three years.

MOM'S RESTAURANT

Mom's has been a successful restaurant with more than $2.5 million in annual revenue, and profits of more than $80,000 annually for the last nine years. The building, land, and contents are appraised at $425,000. Janet Wise, the founder and manager of Mom's, is looking to sell. My Restaurant Corp. is a company managed by Bob Wyler, who has been the head chef at Mom's for six years, and his wife Sylvia Wyler, who has been a manager at Mom's for four years. My Restaurant has negotiated the purchase of Mom's restaurant, including the land on which the restaurant and parking lot stand, for $350,000. The Wylers are investing $100,000 and are looking to obtain a bank loan for the balance of $250,000 to be secured by an SBA guarantee, the building, and the land. The restaurant performs within industry standards as reflected in the RMA data for restaurants. The Wylers have an excellent personal-credit record. There are no outstanding claims or liabilities against Mom's. The economy of the neighborhood, based on employment, housing prices, and new construction, is strong.

These are four compelling business-plan summaries. When you write your executive summary, keep in mind that it is a document with a purpose. The Sunny City plan is written for investors and lenders; the LawnRider for investors; and the Mom's Restaurant plan for a bank. Ask yourself what is missing from your plan or research that could keep your plan from accomplishing its purpose. If you find nothing, then you are ready to put the entire plan together.

The text presents a more detailed version of the ten action steps. Remember to check these points in designing the layout of the text:

$ **Don't forget to paginate** and put a heading on *each* page of your plan so that, if the pages get separated from each other, your readers can reconstruct your plan.

$ **Design your text** with boldface, underlining, and enough white space to make the different subjects and paragraphs stand out visually. This will enable your readers to find particular points more readily.

$ **Double-check your table of contents** against the text to make certain you have included all the right heads and subheads. It's astonishing how many business plan writers forget to compare the table of contents to the text!

$ **Use crisp, clear language.** A business plan is not the place to impress people with your extensive knowledge of your industry's arcane jargon, which may make a potential investor believe that you're not capable of explaining your plan clearly in terms everyone can understand. You may be perceived as a person who is unable to work well with employees or suppliers who might not speak your lingo.

$ **Include a time line**, which helps show your prospective investors when you expect to accomplish key milestones. This is discussed in greater detail in Chapter 12.

The appendix of exhibits should consist of detailed information that would break up the flow of the text, such as market studies or copies of the partners' resumes, or data you may wish to be kept confidential to a small audience of readers, such as cash flow projections and partnership agreements. Interleaving these documents into the actual text of your business plan will only slow the reader down. It's better to footnote the text with a phrase such as "detailed market studies are available on request," or "see appendix for partners' resumes."

If you have information that you will be giving only to certain readers, it's important to bind your appendix of exhibits separately from the main body of your text, so that you can provide it on an as-needed basis to your readers. The cover page of the appendix should mirror the cover page of the plan with the word *Appendix* clearly displayed.

Remember that all tables and exhibits must be completely self-explanatory. You must spell out what the information is, where it comes from, and any underlying assumptions you have made in projections. Think about someone reading your plan on an airplane or in the middle of the night. They can't reach you to ask their questions, so the plan needs to supply all the answers.

Have Outsiders Read It

When you have finished writing your plan, ask friends or colleagues with business experience to read it and offer brutally honest comments about its clarity and persuasiveness. You may eventually want to follow their advice about tearing down the restaurant you want to buy and putting up a car wash in its place, but at this point, you primarily need to know if your plan is clear and complete.

Make the Time to Give It a Rest

It's extremely helpful to put your business plan in a drawer for any period of time you can afford before you reread it. This bit of perspective can reveal flaws or weaknesses that you hadn't initially noticed. A final polish is always worth the effort.

Reread and Revise

Many of my Field Center clients have asked me how long it should take to write a plan and how many pages a plan should be. It's a little like Abraham Lincoln's response to the person who needled him about his own excessive height. "How long should a man's legs be?" he was asked. He answered, "Long enough to reach the ground."

I have seen persuasive and thorough plans that were only five pages long, and equally strong plans that exceeded 100 pages. Most plans require about 20 to 30 pages to cover the 10 Action Steps, including appendices and financial projections, but a plan needs only to be long enough to convince potential funders that they should invest in your endeavor.

Most entrepreneurs work on their plans from initial concept to polished final version over a period of several weeks. It's rare for someone to research and write a quality plan in less than a week, unless most of the background work and financial projections have already been done. However, after I've watched people work on plans for months, I begin to think that they would rather write plans than start a business. At the other extreme are the equally unconvincing clients who download a plan from a website and run a few find-and-replace functions to insert their names and the names of their businesses in place of those in the sample plan. Would you want to invest your money with a person who put so little time and effort into a business plan?

If you aim for a 20- to 30-page document, and budget a few weeks' time, you will be in the average range of most of my clients.

CHAPTER 12

How to Create
a Time Line

A time line is an extremely useful tool in designing and presenting your business plan. Depending on the complexity of your plan, your time line could be a simple list of the key dates of expected events arranged in chronological order. If you're planning a restaurant, a time line will estimate when you expect to rent your store front, begin your renovations, order your tables and chairs, hire your cook and waitresses, and open your doors for business. If your venture is very complicated, such as a business that manufactures major appliances or develops complex software, your time line may list thousands of steps, all linked in a sophisticated computer program.

Here are the main ingredients of a time line, along with the reasons for including a time line in your business plan:

$ **Develop a realistic schedule.** A time line will force you to allot a length of time for each step in your business plan. The total time required will give your potential investors and lenders a reasonably accurate estimate of how long it will take you to establish your business, and make it profitable. I have advised many entrepreneurs who tend to gloss over these details in what I call the *build-it-and-they-will-come phenomenon*. It may be true that customers will come when you're open for business, but getting to that point may involve many time-consuming steps, such as obtaining zoning approvals, licenses, and financing. Unless you'll be working from a corner of your living room, opening an office requires, at a minimum, negotiating a lease, ordering and delivering furniture, and having phones installed.

$ **Create an accurate budget.** The process of creating the time line will help you produce a detailed and accurate budget. Since budgets and financial projections all have time dimensions, a time line will indicate when items need to be ordered, employees hired, and fees paid. On the revenue side, the time line can indicate when you estimate receiving any outside funding, and when you will begin to turn a profit. It will also be helpful to establish the extent of the initial profit and when you expect it to increase in the future.

$ **Focus on the critical path.** In any project that has many steps, such as starting a business or even writing a business plan, there is a *critical path* of events that will determine whether you complete your project on time. The first example that follows demonstrates this for a business that sells cotton candy at a fair. Any delay in completing tasks along the critical path delays the completion of the entire project. Delays in tasks that are not on the critical path can be tolerated, because they will *not* delay completion of the entire project. Therefore, you should focus on those events that comprise this critical path, and work hard to make sure they stay on schedule.

$ **Establish a system of accountability.** Once you have created your time line, you have benchmarks against which to compare your actual operation and performance. The time line will keep you constantly apprised of what you need to focus on next, or what steps might be holding up your progress. No business creation follows its plan precisely. With a time line in place, you can easily check your progress, and revise your plans as needed.

$ **Demonstrate your professionalism.** In Chapters 13 and 15, I discuss how the plan has to demonstrate your qualifications and professionalism. Providing a detailed and realistic time line clearly shows potential investors and lenders that you know how to build your business, that you are reasonably optimistic about your venture, and that you have projected far enough into the future to accurately assess both your business needs and goals.

$ **Give feedback to your investors.** Just as the time line works for you as a planning tool, it will work for your investors in judging your performance. You will be asked many times, "How are you doing compared to your plan?" The time line gives you a simple, presentable method to show your investors, bankers, employees, and suppliers precisely how well you are doing compared to your written plan.

Examples of Time Lines

The simplest time line is a list of activities along with their projected dates and key expenditures. Here is a time line for an entrepreneur who wants to set up a business selling cotton candy at the county fair.

Activity	Dates	Expenditures Required
File with county-fair manager to get permit/location	October 23	$50 fee
Obtain permit	December 15	—
Order trailer and cotton candy maker	December 16	$3,000 deposit required
Delivery of trailer and cotton candy maker	March 1	$5,000 payment required
Take trailer for painting	March 10	$750 deposit required
Pick up painted trailer	March 22	$2,000 payment required
Order candy-making supplies	April 20	$600 payment
Supplies delivered	May 1	—
Test weekend at Little League games	May 15-17	$300 for workers
Set up at county fair	June 3	—
Fair week	June 6-13	$1,200 for workers

Gantt Charts

Gantt charts (named for their developer) are similar to the cotton candy business time line, but with a graphic presentation of each activity. The major advantage of the Gantt Chart is that it is easy to see whether the various activities listed are running sequentially, parallel to each other, or overlap. Gantt charts can be created using word-processing programs, spreadsheet programs, such as Lotus or Excel, or specialized programs, such as Microsoft Project.

Gantt charts offer several advantages over a list format, such as:

$ You can fill in or color over the lines that represent each task as the task is completed.

$ You can draw a line across all the branches of the chart to see how many tasks are running longer than projected.

$ You can create subtask lists that show all the underlying components of any single task on the chart. This can happen automatically if you use project management software.

Gantt Chart for Opening a Florist Shop

Activities	January	February	March	April	May	June
Write plan						
Search for location						
Obtain financing						
Renovate shop						
Development of major accounts						
Search for and sign up with suppliers						
Grand opening prep and week						

PERT Charts

The most sophisticated time line system is the PERT chart or Program Evaluation and Review Technique. PERT charts make it possible to determine the Critical Path of a project, which is the precise sequence of activities that must be completed on time in order to avoid delays. PERT charts are most useful for projects that are highly complex with many interdependent steps, or where the cost of delay can be crippling. Large-scale construction projects, for example, often use PERT charts.

Similar to the simple time line, or Gantt chart, a PERT chart is produced by creating a list of all the activities that must be accomplished to bring your plan to fruition, along with an estimate of how long that process will take. For each activity on the time line, you should also list its immediate prerequisites. For example, you can't sign the contract to construct the factory until the bank loan is approved and the zoning variances are granted. Once you have listed all the activities and their immediate prerequisites, you can create a time line similar to the PERT example.

To determine which activities are on the critical path, you can look backward from completion to find the shortest path. You can also follow a procedure outlined in the reference material and estimate the earliest and latest completion times for each activity and then find the shortest path. For complex projects, you can also employ software that does this calculation automatically along with charting and updating.

I believe that your basic time line should include no more than 20 activities. Over 20 and it will be hard to fit the time line on one page and you're better off using a software package such as Microsoft Project.

Task	Antecedent	Description of Activity	Time-Duration
A	—	File w/ county manager for permit (Feb 8)	1
B	A	Obtain permit (Feb 18)	10
C	B	Order trailer and cotton candy maker (Feb 19)	1
D	C	Delivery of trailer and cotton candy maker (Mar 1)	10
E	D	Take trailer for painting (March 10)	1
F	E	Pick up painted trailer (March 22)	12
G	B	Call county manager for mailing to review site and details (March 25)	1
H	G	Meet with fair manager to confirm location at fair (April 1)	7
I	B	Place ad for jobs (April 15)	1
J	F, H	Order candy supplies (April 20)	1
K	I	Review applicants (May 1)	15
L	J	Candy supplies delivered (May 1)	10
M	K	Meet with applicants (May 3-10)	7
N	M	Offer jobs to two applicants (May 10)	1
O	N	Confirm applicants for jobs (May 14)	4
P	O, L	Test weekend at Little League games (May 15-17)	3
Q	P	Set up at county fair (June 3)	1
R	Q	Fair week (June 6-13)	8

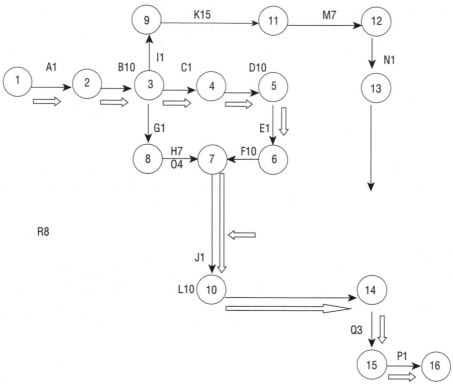

Key

⟹ = Critical Path
Letter + number = tasks and time to complete
Numbers in circles = steps
⟶ = antecedents

CHAPTER 13

Your Plan Is an Extension of You

Many entrepreneurs treat their business plans simply as a foot in the door, designed to elicit interest so the door opens wider. They assume that the plan will produce questions about issues not covered in the document, so reviewers will want to place a phone call or request an in-person meeting to get the answers. In my experience, this attitude is simply the rationalization of someone who is unwilling or unable to produce a quality plan.

Your plan is an extension of you and speaks for you. If the plan is inadequate or unfocused, then people will assume that you are inadequate and unfocused. If your written plan inspires more questions than positive comments during the initial reading by an executive or at a group discussion of your business concept, you can expect it to be added to the towering pile of rejects.

I am familiar with a midsized technology firm I'll call Duke's Photon Farm, that worked hard over more than a decade to raise capital and grow. The company's history indicated that it was successful at raising funds during periods when technology-oriented firms attracted more money than there were places to invest it. When the love affair between the financial community and technology cooled, there were more deals than money to fund them. At this point Duke's Photon Farm began to have trouble raising capital.

Duke's sent out a so-called business plan to potential investors that consisted only of a marketing section asserting that new financing would cause sales to grow rapidly. Investors considered this document inadequate. Investors view increased sales as only a step toward generating profit, and profit as a necessary step toward generating returns— and returns are the investors' *primary* concern. Duke's plan never went beyond increased sales, and Duke's never received any callbacks. Duke's plan was inadequate, and investors assumed that Duke's Photon Farm was equally inadequate.

Your plan must project who you are both explicitly and implicitly. By stating your background and qualifications, you are providing convincing reasons for others to consider your plan. By presenting a plan that is well organized, complete, easy to read, and persuasive, you are implying that you're the person who can make this business concept a success.

The Six Immutable Points

You can make certain that your business plan communicates your strengths by stressing what I call the *six immutable points*. When these six points are stated clearly and forcefully in your business plan, your best qualities will be transmitted to the reader. The six immutable points are that:

1. You are profit oriented.
2. You are honest.
3. You are qualified.
4. You are thorough.
5. You are committed to meeting everyone's needs.
6. You are flexible.

Let's look at each of the six immutable points in greater detail, so that you can make your business plan as bankable as possible:

1. You are profit oriented.   Perhaps it sounds absurd to stress this goal. Isn't everyone profit oriented in the business world? Well, frankly, no. People have many reasons for wanting to start, buy, or build businesses, and profit is not always the most important goal. An entrepreneur may be driven by the desire to be her own boss, or to bring a needed product to the market. Entrepreneurs are also good at attracting people who will participate in the venture for reasons other than profit, such as to get needed experience when starting a new career. However, fundamentally, profit is what drives business and you need to make it clear that profit is your focus.

There are many examples of people who start medical-research companies to find cures for diseases that afflict a family member or, as in my earlier example, a beloved pet. Investors would certainly be skeptical of a business plan for such a venture, wondering if profit were truly the founder's main motive. Funding sources may also be concerned that if the initial goal is met—a cure for the featherless parakeet—that the founder's commitment to continue with the business and realize a profit will be negligible.

2. You are honest.   If people participate in your plan by investing money, selling you raw materials, extending you credit, or becoming your employees, they need to know that you are honest. I have seen plans corrode people's reputations by leaving out key facts that are eventually uncovered, such as owning a previous business that failed, or by misrepresenting their credentials, such as claiming executive positions they held at a company when they really worked as mail sorters.

Lies are a particularly dangerous trap. I saw a business plan for a media company that listed the schools one of the partners attended and the degrees he earned. The only problem was that they were all fabrications. When one potential investor checked, as he did routinely, he discovered the lie and the plan quickly went into the trash.

Be candid and truthful about the information you present in your plan. Everyone has experienced some sort of failure, whether it's being fired from a job, training extensively for a profession you never entered, or starting a business that went belly up. Being honest about these issues and explaining how you learned an important lesson about yourself or running a business, almost always raises the esteem in which others will hold you.

3. You are qualified.   The plan must demonstrate that you are qualified to undertake whatever the proposal requires. Many people feel that they need to possess all the qualifications themselves, but the business plan only needs to demonstrate that you are capable of identifying colleagues or becoming partners with others who have the technical knowledge you may lack. If you've been an airline pilot all your life, and have never run a pancake house that features squid-flavored dishes, explain how you will compensate for this lack of experience, preferably by hiring a manager who has run a successful restaurant, even if he lacks your extensive knowledge of squid.

If your team is already in place, mention their qualifications along with yours. This should be presented briefly in your executive summary, more comprehensively in your business plan text, and completely in your appendix, which should feature every resume, including your own.

4. You are thorough.   The plan must be comprehensive in your approach to your venture. You can't skip any steps. All ten action steps must be covered in detail. Make a copy of the ten action steps and keep them next to your computer as you write your proposal. Read your executive summary and indicate, for your own edification, which of the ten action steps are covered in each sentence.

I recall seeing a plan for a chain of gyms that failed to mention how the owner would acquire the physical facilities in each community. When I asked about this missing piece, the entrepreneur said that he figured he'd go to a real estate agent in each town after he had raised his millions and was ready to open his facilities. Bad answer! Obtaining accurate real-estate projections on both space availability and rental costs are critical steps in creating an effective business plan for a chain of gyms. This entrepreneur's omission may have been a sign of his inability to understand all the requirements of running a profitable business.

5. You are committed to meeting everyone's needs.   Entrepreneurs have moral, ethical, legal, and self-interested reasons to treat everyone who participates in their enterprise fairly. There are contracts with the capital sources, as well as numerous legal requirements regarding the treatment of investors and employees. These include providing timely and complete financial statements, keeping the company current in all its taxes, and, of course, sharing profits according to the company's shareholder agreements. The plan must demonstrate that you are aware of these responsibilities, that you take them seriously, and will dispatch them fully.

I am familiar with the owner of an entertainment company, I'll call him Mr. Prince, who was brilliant, but scattered and disorganized. Mr. Prince raised a great deal of money because his plans made great sense and he was very smart. However, he never raised capital from the same source twice. Mr. Prince's disorganization prevented him from meeting the deadlines for providing financial statements to his investors and lenders, who liked his business, but refused to work with a company that didn't meet these basic requirements.

6. You are flexible. One of the fundamental challenges in writing a business plan is stating a short, compelling argument for your business concept in the executive summary while, at the same time, providing all the necessary details in your business plan text. In writing a business plan, you need to present yourself almost as a two-headed talent. Establishing and managing an enterprise are two very different tasks. You want to create an image of yourself as a founder who sees the mission of the organization in clear, simple terms and who will not be deterred from reaching any goal. On the other hand, you must impress those evaluating your plan that you are also a boss who can carefully manage the day-to-day minutiae of running a business. You must demonstrate that you are flexible enough to adapt to any task that might come your way.

Since your ultimate success will depend more on your ability to manage the daily operations of your business, you must address this issue directly. Nothing speaks to these points more powerfully than previous experience. Even if you have never started your own ocarina-manufacturing company before, you may be an ocarina virtuoso who understands the instrument in all its manifest quirks, which would prepare you to judge manufacturing results. Or perhaps you were the leader of an internationally acclaimed ocarina orchestra, which demonstrates your ability to work with a number of colleagues, including finicky ocarina tuners as well as temperamental performing artists.

There is another reason to impress those reading your plan with your flexibility.

The sad truth is that as soon as your business plan is written, it's probably already out of date. No matter what your industry is, your plan exists in a rapidly changing world and market. New competitors are emerging and old competitors are disappearing. Financial assumptions such as rents, raw materials, telecommunications services, and locations are all likely to change before your plan has been read by a potential investor. Even your own thinking may change regarding how your business should be positioned in the market once you have considered all the issues and completed your plan. You can deal with these changes by:

$ Frequently updating and revising your plan.

$ Keeping track of revisions by placing the date of each version on the cover page and the page headers.

$ Welcoming the chance to revise, because each time you refine your thinking and change the plan, you are making it better.

Flexibility is often the key to business success. Bill Gates didn't start out to build a company that sold computer operating systems. He responded to a need that IBM expressed for a personal-computer operating system. John D. Rockefeller didn't plan to be an oil tycoon. He worked as a bookkeeper with a food wholesaler, then started his own food wholesaling firm. He saw a good opportunity in trading and the rest, as they say, is history. I am familiar with a logistics software company that began as a one-man trucking company, but that one man knew how to find opportunities and take advantage of them. Like these people, you—through your plan—must present yourself as someone who is flexible enough to respond to good opportunities.

14

Demonstrate That You Can Manage Conflicting Goals

There are inherent contradictions that you should take into consideration when writing your business plan. These conflicts involve your strategy, your view of your competition, your vision, and your presentation. Most entrepreneurs I advise struggle with these contradictions, but, if you identify them in advance and learn how to manage them, they will not undermine your business plan.

The four main contradictions to keep in mind as you prepare your business plan are:

Keep It Simple . . . Yet Detailed

Your plan needs to make a simple, compelling case as to why your business concept represents a strong investment opportunity. As in our example of the Bug-Be-Gone Corporation in Chapter 11, a few sentences can cover all ten action steps clearly. You may feel that this is enough and, for some people it may, in fact, be enough to decide to invest. However, not for most funders. They want to see the detail behind your conclusions, such as financial figures, analysis of your competition, lists of potential customers, and market research. Your task in writing the plan is to give everyone the specific information they demand without burying the clear and simple message of why your business idea is a smart investment.

Remember that a business plan is a document written for a purpose. Most often, that purpose is to convince people to contribute resources to your venture. You must answer all readers' particular questions to their complete satisfaction. Issues that are important to some readers will be irrelevant to others. Your dilemma is to give all the answers to all the questions without losing your readers in a morass of detail.

Don't despair! You can resolve this conflict and create an extremely well-organized, balanced business plan by employing three basic tools: a complete table of contents, eye-catching headings, and a clearly labeled appendix of exhibits. This allows readers to locate the topics that are important to them while skipping over the less relevant sections.

A table of contents serves the purpose of giving your reader an overview of your plan and help in finding topics. For example, a potential investor will probably want to study your projected returns in detail. The table of contents will guide this reader to the section on financial projections, with a subheading for projected returns. This particular section, however, will be less important to future suppliers, who will be more eager to read about your market and sales projections.

I have seen plans that are solid blocks of type, rather like densely written college papers. Faced with this format, the investor must either commit to reading every word, or risk missing parts that she believes are important. Headings should appear every time you change the subject and should be complete enough to clarify what topic is covered in each section. I have tried to use headings in this book to help you locate subjects of importance to you and sincerely hope I have succeeded!

An appendix is a section of specific documents bound separately from your written business plan. It supplies information too detailed or specialized to be included in the body of the text, such as lists of potential customers, copies of materials from your competitors, industry reports, or the resumes of your company principals. I have seen plans that place the financial projections in the appendix, but this sends the wrong message to readers who may assume that profits are not central to the plan, when they *always* are.

Employing these tools will help you create a plan that is focused and simple, yet complete and easy for readers to follow and analyze. You will show that profits are important (immutable point number one), that you are a thorough researcher (immutable point number four), and that you can address every reader's issues (immutable point number five). Striking a balance in your written plan between stating a simple goal and providing complete information will also demonstrate that you'll be a flexible manager who can focus on the details while still maintaining the course toward your company's overall objectives (immutable point number six). After reading your plan, people will see that you are honest and qualified (immutable points number two and number three).

Focus on Growth . . . Even in Mature Industries

Investors generally prefer to see business plans for companies with high growth potential. Growth of revenue usually translates into increased profits and business value. This growth fuels returns for investors, generates more cash to pay interest, and creates new opportunities for employees, suppliers, and business partners. As an entrepreneur, you should also prefer to plan for business growth, because any increased profits and business value directly accrue to your benefit. You have probably witnessed growth opportunities in your industry since you first hatched your idea, such as an overlooked consumer group, a better product that will attract more customers, or a rapidly growing market.

If your business is in an industry that is experiencing high growth, most investors will assume that your company will grow right along with this rapidly expanding field. Of course, this is not always the case, because certain fast-growing industries, such as e-commerce, attracted investors faster than they attracted new customers. The Internet and e-commerce businesses that succeeded over the last decade are exceptions. The reality is that the vast majority of industries grow at the same modest pace of the overall economy, which is about 2 to 3 percent per year.

The conflict here is this: Everyone wants to see dynamic growth projections in your business plan, but most industries are growing slowly. You cannot resolve these two seemingly contradictory statements, but you can make this conflict work to strengthen your written plan by doing the following:

$ **Acknowledge** the conflict.

$ **Explain the benefits** of owning a business in this slow-growing industry now, such as stability and fewer new competitors.

$ **Present** opportunities in this industry, such as being able to purchase competitors at low prices, and propose doing so if it fits your plan.

$ **Offer a strategy** that takes customers away from existing competitors rather than simply capturing a share of new customers.

$ **Detail your operations** to explain how you will attract and retain these customers.

I have seen many plans for mature industries that have very ambitious growth objectives. Most plans fail to explain how this growth will be achieved. Others simply state that their management is so superior to their competitors' teams that they will far exceed industry expectations and standards. That simply doesn't work, and it's usually simply wrong. Strong management is essential for successful ventures, but bankers, investors, and partners want to know *specifically* what management will do to create growth. If you discuss your business benefits, opportunities, strategies, and operations in detail, you will be able to demonstrate strong growth potential even in a slow-growing, mature industry.

Reassure Investors . . . Even with Competition All Around

Here is an executive summary for a business that will definitely reassure investors:

> I have obtained, at no cost, the exclusive license to collect tolls on the Golden Gate Bridge. The California Bridge Authority will continue to maintain the bridge at taxpayer expense. I need to raise $10,000 for the purchase of bags to carry the money to the bank. For every $1,000 invested, investors can expect to receive 1 percent of future profits, or about $1 million per year.

If only it were so easy! Since the demise of colonial rule, America hasn't seen such good deals. Just think for a minute about what makes this deal so reassuring to investors: You have no competitors. Aside from a few ferries or the alternative of a 50-mile drive, there is no other way to get from San Francisco to Marin County. There is no competition nor is there any prospect of new competitors.

Many bankers and investors—often without coming out and saying it—are looking for competition-free businesses, such as the exclusive Golden Gate Bridge franchise. Here are examples of the excuses investors may use to avoid supporting a nonexclusive business:

$ There is too much competition in your industry for us to feel comfortable. Just opening the *Yellow Pages* under your business category and seeing so many competitors scares us away from this industry.

$ What's to keep a copycat business from opening up next door to you?

$ The barriers to entry are just too low for us.

The fact is that virtually *every* business has competition. The point of your business plan is to analyze the market, the competition, and your company's position, not to try fruitlessly to find a business that has no competition. Your business plan must make clear that you, like all entrepreneurs, function in a competitive market and will succeed by identifying and serving your customers while managing your business profitably. By focusing your business plan on these issues, you will address the conflict about competition head on, and weaken its potential to derail your goal of gaining the support you need to start your venture.

Commit to Your Plan . . . But Be Willing to Pursue Other Good Opportunities

Many investors believe that for a business to be successful it needs a driving force or visionary who is committed to winning at any cost. They want to see a John Wayne or Sylvester Stallone type who will fight any foe to bring the plan to fruition. Many investors screen business plans looking for this brand of unwavering leadership and, to some extent, they're right.

There are limits to this ideal which can create yet another baffling conflict. The business plan you write, and are committed to now, may require adjustment in the future. Market conditions, competition, economic factors, and technology—just to name a few issues—can change drastically and will force your plan to change as well. Those movie studios that remained committed to producing silent movies after talkies were invented, were soon silenced forever by bankruptcies. Electronics manufacturers who were slow to adopt the transistors that replaced vacuum tubes were soon expiring in an economic vacuum.

Your plan should present you as both committed and highly motivated, but also capable of looking for new opportunities and better ways to operate your business. Investors need reassurance that once you attain your goal, like the entrepreneur who hoped to find a cure for feather loss in parakeets, you will remain determined to make your venture profitable. People who start businesses with personal agendas, such as getting revenge on a former employer or finding a cure for a disease that afflicts someone they love, often meet resistance from investors.

To resolve this conflict, I suggest that you include a section in the plan that speculates about some of the directions in which you may want the business to go in the long term. For example, you can discuss changes in technology that you might adopt in the future to improve service, reduce costs, or expand your market. A plan for the Squid Pancake Restaurant could discuss possible developments in the squid-farming industry and the opportunities they present, such as expanding your menu to include all-you-can-eat squid dinners, or adding chicken dishes if squid proves to be less popular than anticipated.

Your plan should demonstrate how well you're attuned to the market and its shifts and how willing you are to make adaptive changes, while still believing that your concept is the best possible course for today's conditions.

Present Yourself in the Best Light

The talents, experience, and enthusiasm you bring to your enterprise are unique. They provide some of the most compelling reasons for others to finance your concept. Keep in mind that investors invest in people more than ideas. Even if your potential business has many competitors, or is not on the cutting edge of an industry, the qualifications and commitment you demonstrate in your plan can convince others to proffer their support.

Your resume will be included in the separate appendix of exhibits at the end of the plan, so this is not the place to list every job you've ever had or the fact that you were an art history major in college, especially if these experiences have no direct bearing on your ability to start your own business. It *is* the place to emphasize qualifying skills that may not be readily apparent from your resume. Therefore, it is critical to convince potential funders that you are highly qualified to establish and run your venture.

Say you are the Field Center client who wants to open the restaurant featuring squid-flavored pancakes. Investors won't be initially impressed by your long and successful career as a commercial airline pilot.

They may be much more swayed by the fact that from the age of eight to eighteen, you worked after school and weekends in your father's delicatessen. This information has probably never appeared on your professional resume, which stresses the number of flying hours you have logged, your outstanding safety record, and the citations you received for the most ontime flights. However, having worked for so long and intimately in a family-owned retail food business indicates that you know how to supervise cooks, run a cash register, and order perishable foodstuffs in bulk. You are probably even an expert in the Heimlich maneuver which, with squid-flavored pancakes, may come in handy.

Perhaps before you embarked on your flying career, you joined the Peace Corps and worked in a country that happened to be the world's largest squid harvester. The knowledge you've acquired about the squid business and the contacts you have maintained in your Peace Corps country will enable you to purchase tons of high-quality squid more cheaply and rapidly than any of your competitors.

Don't overlook the impact being a pilot may have on your ability to run a restaurant, especially if those skills are not apparent to your potential investors. You should stress that you know how to supervise a crew of people working together to make a group experience, if not comfortable, at least safe. You have undoubtedly handled dissatisfied or enraged customers. Even that B. A. in art history may enable you to teach cooks how to make their dishes more appealing to the eye.

If you have partners or staff, you must cover the same issues for them, especially if they bring skills to the venture you don't have. Perhaps one is an expert in state-of-the-art handheld computers that waiters can use to send orders immediately to the kitchen or to tally bills or approve credit card purchases within seconds. Another may be a champion napkin folder who can create caricatures of customers as soon as they sit down at their tables.

Your unique qualifications will separate you from all the other people who have sought venture capital for squid-flavored pancake restaurants. Boasting about these skills is not hubris; it indicates that you have highly honed business savvy.

The body of your text and your attached resume must state who you are, what you have done, what you can do, and what you will do. Think of these elements of your business plan as a personal sales pitch about your qualifications to start your business and guide it to success.

You should demonstrate that *you* are as bankable as your business plan. Your qualifications assure financial supporters that your goals are reasonable and attainable. They are just as important as developing the right marketing strategy or establishing your competitive advantage, because *you* must implement these ideas and make them profitable. Prices don't select themselves and customer service doesn't evolve without strong leadership from an exacting manager. Your marketing strategy, competitive advantage, and sales efforts are useless without *you* and your qualifications.

Stressing your enthusiasm is not the most effective way to indicate to potential investors and lenders that you have the skills, savvy and determination to be successful. Focus on your accomplishments and experience that apply to starting the company. You must also convince funders that your partners or the employees you are planning to hire for their particular experience or skills are equally qualified.

The text of your business plan that stresses your credentials has the same purpose as the resume you attach to your appendix, but each is achieved through quite different means. A resume should be short and easy to read, so potential supporters can see a quick overview of the experience, training, and education you bring to your venture. The text is where you can elaborate on the skills you brought to each of your previous positions and the areas of expertise that you developed on each job. The resume provides the bare bones of your experience; the text supplies the muscle. Both need to be strong.

Let's take a more detailed look at how the text of the plan and your resume can help create a convincing case that you are the best person to start and run your business.

The Text of Your Business Plan

The body of your business plan is where you can elaborate on talents and skills that are not obvious from the work record listed on your resume. Remember the earlier example of the commercial airline pilot who wanted to open the restaurant featuring squid-flavored pancakes? His resume will show that he enlisted in the Peace Corps, but it will not indicate that the country he served in is the largest harvester of squid in the world or that the contacts he made there will enable him to buy and export squid efficiently.

His resume will mention his professional citations for the best safety and on-time records, which indicate that he is goal oriented and takes pride in the service he provides his customers. Only in the text can he explain how having been a pilot will enable him to train his staff to maintain their composure when a grease fire starts in the kitchen, and they need to reassure diners to remain calm.

The pilot's experience in the Peace Corps may have honed his problem-solving skills and his ability to inspire others to be good workers. His years in his father's delicatessen would never appear on his professional pilot's resume, but this expertise will be invaluable in assuring investors and lenders that he knows how to buy food in bulk and run a cash register.

The information you provide in the text of your business plan will help you expand on your resume and convince others that you have acquired particularly useful skills that will make your business a success.

Here are some additional points to follow in describing your experience:

Style.   Most business plans use the third person in discussing the qualifications of the entrepreneur seeking financial support. The pilot will probably refer to himself throughout his plan by his last name only, after introducing his full name near the beginning of the text. Employing the first person *I* in the body of the text is, however, a growing trend. The advantage is that it reinforces your role as the key person in your venture's success. However, if you have an equal partner in the business, stick to the third person, which indicates that neither owner will dominate, and that your relationship with each other will be balanced and well defined.

Placement.   Since presenting yourself in the best light is so important, it must be mentioned briefly in your executive summary, as well as in the text. Work to keep your executive summary description of your skills and experience as concise as possible, but make certain it reflects the basic thrust of your sales pitch about yourself in the text as well as the information in your resume. Place each of these side by side, and read them one after the other to make certain the accomplishments you stress in the executive summary are reinforced in the text and in your resume.

Honesty.   Be honest about your skills, but don't oversell or undersell yourself. You are not boasting when you claim particular talents or expertise. Stressing your strengths reassures potential funders that you have the ability and experience to succeed, but if you go overboard, you will raise serious doubts about your honesty. Even if you began a business that failed, it is far better to mention it in your plan in a positive light than to hide the fact and have it emerge later. Many successful entrepreneurs have failed in earlier attempts to start a business, but learned from their experiences. Milton Hershey, of chocolate bar fame, founded several candy companies that went belly up before he adopted a Swiss candy maker's process of combining milk with chocolate. Emphasize what you learned about running a business, hiring employees, attracting funding sources, being a boss or figuring out the right recipe. If your new venture builds on what you've learned, negative experiences won't appear negative at all.

Amplification.   The text is the place to expand on the basic information you outline in your resume. Investors and lenders may not understand your background well enough to grasp the additional expertise you learned from a particular job. Remember the entrepreneur who wanted to buy a larger, more modern ocarina factory? Merely listing the fact that she played in an ocarina concert band on her resume won't explain all the skills she acquired. Investors and lenders unfamiliar with the instrument may not understand how much she learned about dealing with artistic temperaments, or working as part of a team to achieve a cohesive musical presentation, or what qualities other ocarina performers admired and preferred in their instruments. This is the kind of resume amplification you need to provide in the text of your business plan.

Your Resume

Your resume should be organized to emphasize your skills, experience, education, and training. Do not slip your standard professional resume into the appendix of your business plan. Write a new one from scratch that stresses the credentials that make you absolutely the best person to start and grow your business.

Creating an effective resume is an art. Like your overall business plan, your resume must be neat, well designed, and free of spelling errors. It should have enough white space to make it easy to read and it should employ bullets, boldface, and underlining to emphasize important elements, such as the names of your previous employers and your job titles.

This is not the place for you to list every job you've ever had, or to proclaim unrelated professional or personal skills. You may have had the best baseball-card collection in your neighborhood or bowled 300 twenty times in your league last year, but if these accomplishments have no bearing on your ability to start and expand a business, leave them out. If you have an interest that may not have appeared on a previous resume, but adds to the case you're making about your qualifications, include it now.

The airline pilot with the pancake restaurant may have earned money towards his college tuition by waiting tables in the school cafeteria, in addition to working in his father's deli during the summer. He might also want to include the leadership-training workshop he completed on his own. These experiences have no place on his pilot's resume, but they certainly indicate that he knows the food industry from the ground up, and that he's committed to polishing his managerial skills.

Here are some finer points of resume creation:

Be simple.   Keep it to one page. This is a quick overview to remind readers of your basic skills and experience. Even if you feel compelled to list every one of the 155 weddings that your band played at to establish your ability to start your band and DJ service, don't do it here. Name a couple of the famous brides and grooms and list the total number, but, if potential investors want a more complete list, attach it to your appendix, or mail it to them later. Don't try to be slick or snazzy by using special paper or fancy fonts. A resume should impress people with its content, neatness and readability, not by multicolored headings or a typeface that looks like calligraphy.

Be clear.   Choose the right format for your resume that expresses your experience in the most powerful way possible. The organization of your skills and expertise must emphasize the qualities you wish to highlight for your readers. There are three basic formats to follow:

$ **The chronological format** lists your work experience from the most recent job, placed first, back to your first job, which is placed last. It also includes the specific lengths of time you worked at each position. This is the most common type of resume, but it may not stress the skills you wish to emphasize to potential funders. It's a good exercise to create a resume in this format, so you can scan your complete employment history on one page and choose which experiences you want to highlight in a more effective version.

$ **The functional format** organizes your experience and employment under particular headings according to the type of positions you held. This format allows you to group related skills, even if they were acquired during part-time jobs or from purely personal interests. Dates are not usually included in this format. Compiling your background by function enables you to present your skills in a more interesting and compelling manner.

$ **The targeted format** focuses even more closely on the specific skills needed for your particular venture. If all your past experience has been in the same field, each position has moved you higher on the professional ladder, and starting your own business is simply a culmination of your entire career, you probably won't need either the chronological or the functional format; the targeted design will work best for you.

Be consistent. Keep the style similar to the tone and language of your business-plan text. Use parallel construction in verbs, so that you describe your duties in each of your jobs with similar tenses. If you use the past tense under one position, such as "coordinated travel schedules for a touring ocarina concert band," don't employ the present tense in another job description, unless you are still in that position, such as "analyze customer-service staff effectiveness." However, when you mention in your resume that business you founded that failed, all you have to do is list the information without discussing the outcome.

Be animated. Use action verbs and an active voice to describe your duties at each of your jobs. Words such as *achieved, devised,* or *pioneered* express power and accomplishment. Phrases should be short and to the point. Avoid complete sentences or paragraphs. Omit professional abbreviations or jargon that potential funders might not recognize. Never use the first person to discuss your skills and accomplishments.

Be careful. Check your grammar, spelling, indents, and layout. Then check them again, then one more time. Give your resume to someone else, preferably an English teacher or a professional editor, to make sure you haven't committed some terrible error that will ruin your credibility in an instant—or in a punctuation mark.

Be honest.   Your resume should be scrupulously honest. It is standard practice for many funding sources to check statements made on resumes. Don't say "Vice President" if you were Assistant Vice President, or "supervised staff of 12," when it was actually 10. I know of several aspiring entrepreneurs who had their deals derailed by this kind of inaccuracy, including a lawyer who claimed he graduated from Princeton when he had not. His funders, who were ready to write a check, liked him, his idea, and his references. Nothing on his resume would have changed their minds—except a lie.

Remember that you are selling potential investors and lenders on you and your abilities, not just on your business idea. You must impress people you want to support your venture that you—and your team— are uniquely qualified to establish this company and make it profitable. This is not gloating or boasting; this is the way to reassure funders that you have the background, talent, and enthusiasm to make your enterprise successful.

CHAPTER 16

Make a Great In-Person Presentation

In spite of all the electronic communication methods available today, nothing is more effective than an in-person meeting. In fact, it is unlikely that you will raise funds from investors or a bank without meeting your potential supporters in person. An in-person meeting gives you the chance to reinforce key points of your plan, respond to questions, and discover more about the potential funder's goals, learn what did not come across well in the plan, and demonstrate the personal characteristics that lenders and investors want to see in an entrepreneur before writing a check.

As you prepare for an in-person presentation, keep in mind that there are three aspects of a business meeting that you will need to understand and manage: the *context*, the *content*, and the *code*.

The Context

The most productive meetings occur when the atmosphere, or context, is conducive to having an open, honest discussion about mutually beneficial goals. Your attitude, your ability to listen, and your understanding of the physical setting, will help you create an effective context for your presentations.

Attitude.   Your own individual perspective, or point of view, that you bring to every meeting is an important factor in establishing a productive context. You need to be thoroughly prepared and know that you are thoroughly prepared. You must be confident that the plan you're presenting is strong and can benefit the people listening to your presentation. You must be open to answering questions—and to asking questions—so you can understand the funders' or investors' goals.

Listening.   A critical element of creating a successful context revolves around thoughtful and attentive listening. By being a good listener, you allow the other people in the meeting to feel comfortable about sharing information openly. This enables you to uncover their professional concerns more readily and respond to them effectively. The presentation of a business plan is not a one-sided performance; it's a meeting to determine if you and the potential investors or funders want to work together to produce a mutually beneficial venture.

Setting.   You will have minimal control over your physical surroundings, since you'll probably be meeting in the bankers' or investors' offices. There are ways you can enhance the setting. First of all, arrive on time. No matter how pleasant the office may be, the meeting can not proceed comfortably if you're late. If you're too early, don't hang around the waiting room looking like a person with nothing else to do. Go sit in your car or a nearby coffee shop. When you're ushered into the meeting, try to choose a seat which gives you the best angle for making eye contact with all the others in the room without pivoting your head too much. Take out your cell phone, turn it off, and place it on the table to indicate your willingness to concentrate solely on the matters at hand.

When you have the right attitude, listen fully, and create the most effective setting possible, you are establishing a strong context and demonstrating that you're worthy of the other people's time and attention.

The Content

The content, or subject matter, of your presentation should always be focused on the topics that are most crucial to the other people in the room. Whether you're meeting with a potential investor or banker, you must address their measurable goals in your presentation. This includes such subjects as being able to pay back a loan within a certain time period, or projecting the return on an investor's stake, in other words, how your business will make money for them. Many entrepreneurs waste the opportunities intrinsic to an in-person presentation by concentrating solely on their own goals rather than focusing on the investor's or lender's objectives.

Start strong and end strong.   Research shows that people tend to form opinions based on what they hear at the beginning and the end of any meting. These tendencies, called the *primacy* and *recency* effects, are powerful tools. Be sure to put what you believe is your strongest point first in a presentation and to conclude with the same point, or with an equally strong message.

Customize your presentation.   Don't waste bankers' time detailing the equity returns that your investors will earn, or bore your potential investors by describing your employees' stock options. These points may merit quick summaries in every presentation, but tailor the information for each group or individual. Make a list of the issues that are most important to your specific audience before your meeting and focus on those topics.

Don't create a Broadway Production.   People seem to think that the proverbial dog-and-pony show needs a high level of production values in order to appear professional and credible. This may be true for the weak presenter who has little to say if the slide projector goes dim, but for someone who has created a quality bankable business plan, there are several significant reasons to avoid dependence on these devices:

• The slide show or PowerPoint presentation can't be changed easily on the fly. It does not allow you to alter your presentation to incorporate new issues or a particular focus that might emerge through discussions with bankers or investors.

• Using visual presentation tools discourages people from talking, because they know that you're essentially following a script. You are, therefore, stifling one of the greatest assets of the in-person meeting— the opportunity to elicit productive discussion and address any questions that may arise.

• Many people don't pay attention to presentations that aren't interactive. Dim the lights, turn on the projector, and most people will tune out. An interactive presentation can only occur if your audience is involved, not passively watching a performance.

Keep the exposition of your plan simple and flexible. PowerPoint slides or projections can work only if you're prepared to adjust the order of your material, or skip some parts entirely as you're making your presentation. Maximize the value of your in-person time with bankers or investors by encouraging them to focus on their important issues.

The Code

Nonverbal means of communication, such as body language and facial expressions, that occur during any in-person meeting, comprise the code. During your presentation you will be sending and receiving innumerable code transactions. Misinterpreting this unspoken dialogue can lead to feelings of rejection that can interfere with your ability to make an effective presentation. And broadcasting the wrong unspoken statement can be equally disastrous.

Seeing is not always believing.   Many presentations are derailed because the presenters become unnerved by how their audiences behave and not by what they say. People coming and going, looking bored or angry, or taking a challenging tone when asking questions can make presenters feel that they have already failed before they've even begun to talk. However, interpreting body language alone is not always an accurate guide to determining the other person's interest or intentions. I once attended a 20-minute sales presentation to a buyer who never once looked up from a game of solitaire on his computer. The presenter plugged along, befuddled by the buyer's rude and strange behavior. Much to the presenter's astonishment, the buyer agreed to the purchase at the end of the presentation.

Don't be prejudiced.   A similar problem occurs if you prejudge your audience. You may make a presentation to a group of young, arrogant MBAs, who annoy you by the disdainful tone of their comments. The question you need to ask yourself is, "Would it be okay if these people liked my business plan and gave me the resources I need to create this business?" If the answer is *yes*, as I assume it would be, that you would be happy for their participation, then you need to work on understanding and controlling your prejudices.

Your mother was right: first impressions count.   When you mother said "You only get one chance to make a good first impression," she was absolutely right. Research shows that within the first minute of meeting someone, people form an enduring opinion.

In studying the interviewing process, University of Toledo psychologist Professor Frank Bernieri documented the extraordinarily rapid pace at which people form first impressions. Bernieri discovered that people who watched video clips of job applicants simply enter a room and shake hands with the interviewer reached virtually the same conclusions about that person as the trained and experienced interviewer did after a 15-minute interview.

The impact of this on presenting your plan is tremendous. That initial impression made in less than the first minute will largely determine what the other person thinks of you. You need to use that first 60 seconds to every advantage. You might be the most organized person in the world but, if you're late to an appointment because of unforeseen traffic and are forced to climb seven flights of stairs because the elevator is broken, you will walk into the other person's office sweaty and out of breath, creating a long lasting impression of being disorganized.

To improve that crucial first impression you make, be aware of it. Many people have no idea how they come across to others, and often impress people quite differently than they intended. People may feel they present themselves as aggressive or ambitious, but actually appear soft spoken and timid to others.

Ask some people who will be candid to the point of pain to participate in a exercise with you. Schedule meetings either at their offices or homes and ask them to describe your manner, your clothes, your posture, and your speech *one minute after your arrival.* An even more helpful demonstration is to videotape yourself in a similar business practice session so you can draw your own conclusions about the impression you make. And, if necessary, fix it!

Practice.   If you are not too experienced in giving presentations, or you are worried about being nervous, or just want to be as well-prepared as possible, be sure to practice in front of friends, colleagues, the mirror, or that video camera you used for testing the first impression you made. This will help you master the flow and facts of your presentation, and you'll be able to focus on addressing the specific needs and interests of your audience. It is generally a good idea to keep an outline and a copy of your full plan in front of you so you don't skip any important points or can find your place if you get lost.

Just be yourself.   Many entrepreneurs believe that, in order to convince others to invest in their ventures, they must be forceful and manipulative, even if those qualities are not part of their personalities. However, there is absolutely no reason to be anyone other than yourself while making an in-person presentation. You have probably written your plan with yourself in mind as the founder and president of the business, and the plan already has a section explaining your (and your team's) qualifications to run this business.

During the presentation you should project that level of experience, knowledge, and professionalism. You don't need to be a Nobel Prize-winning scientist, an Olympic gold medalist, or the global entrepreneur of the year. You don't even have to be a bulldozing salesperson, you just have to be yourself.

I have seen too many entrepreneurs try to be formal when they are usually relaxed, funny when they are essentially serious, or pushy when they are really quite unassuming. All they achieved was a level of discomfort in the role they were playing, which interfered with their ability to communicate their enthusiasm for their ventures.

You simply need to demonstrate that you embody the six immutable points (covered in Chapter 13) and that, therefore, you are the right person to start your business.

Leave something behind . . . the right something.   Handing a copy of your plan, financial projections, or background materials to the people who just heard your presentation is an effective, and often expected, tool, but it's better to leave nothing than to leave a pile of relatively unimportant or even inaccurate documents. You can always mail or drop off the right materials later.

Let's suppose you're presenting your plan to a bank for a loan. If you have prepared your financial projections under the assumption that the bank will lend 80 percent of your fixed asset valuation, but in the meeting, you learn that they'll actually lend 90 percent, it's better to revise your projections after the meeting and deliver the new documents a few days later. Having the wrong projections in your file may hurt your chances of receiving the best loan coverage. So, leave only those documents behind on the banker's or investor's desk that accurately reflect your in-person presentation. Handing out a business card will do quite nicely until you can deliver your strongest materials.

Establish a schedule for follow up. Take out your calendar at the end of your presentation so you can arrange a date by which you will hear the investors' or funders' decision about supporting your venture. As the meeting winds down, state clearly when you will deliver any revised financial projections, and confirm which materials you need from the investors or lenders, such as their sample contracts or agreements, references of people in whom they have invested, and feedback on your financial projections. Then establish what will happen next.

In my experience, it's more important to get a commitment on a fixed date than it is to get an early date. What is most important is to establish that you're waiting for a response. Having a specific deadline gives you a valid reason to call and say, "When we met, you promised an answer by this date. Do you still expect to make a decision by that date?"

Making an effective in-person presentation is your last chance to convince others to support your venture. It should follow the same logical organization of your business plan by moving from the general to the specific. Be aware of the Three C's of any meeting—the context, the content, and the code—so that you maintain as much control as possible over the impact of your presentation. Allow enough time for questions, but don't misinterpret the tone of voice or body language of your audience. Being enthusiastic and knowledgeable about your plan and your presentation will convey your determination to bring success to your business, as well as to your lenders and investors.

PART | III

Business Plan Outlines and Sample Plans

A plan can be short, sweet, and very effective. I have seen many compelling plans comprised of only four or five pages of text, followed by an appendix with a few financial projections. A simple plan is usually better if you can cover all the important issues in a few pages. It's easier to read, and can take less time to write.

On the other hand, if you want to start a business which will have lengthy developmental phases, or various products sold in numerous markets, or a complicated manufacturing system protected by several patents, you will probably require a much longer, complex plan.

Remember, as you read through the following plans and outlines, these are examples, not templates. The outlines for a simple business and a complex business do not correspond directly to either of the actual plans. These are samples to read and analyze, not formulas to copy. Your bankable business plan must be *your* unique plan.

The example of a simple business plan, that of S & J Advertising, is strong because, in a very few pages, it covers all ten action steps in a manner that a banker would be hard pressed to turn down. I adapted it from a similar plan created by a group of advertising executives lead by Neal Newman and Bill Parshall, two veteran broadcasters. They never executed this plan because other opportunities developed for them, but they passed it on to a group in another city that adapted it to build a successful agency.

The example of a complex business plan, Zif Medical Devices, was written by two Indiana University MBA students, David Bean and Joseph Schroeder, under the supervision of Professor Arnold Cooper. The plan won competitions at Indiana University, Purdue University, the University of Nebraska, and competed in the prestigious MOOT CORP competition at the University of Texas at Austin. The authors did a splendid job of clearly presenting complicated issues such as government licensing, patents, distribution, and estimates of success for various strategic options. Their plan culminates in complete, persuasive, and understandable financial projections.

The authors of the Zif Medical Devices plan decided that potential legal struggles over patents and certain marketing battles with well-financed competitors, would make pursuing their idea too risky at this stage in their careers. To my way of thinking, if this plan helped its authors realize the risks of their idea and make an informed decision about whether to take those risks, it served a very valuable purpose. In addition, the authors are now experienced and eloquent business-plan writers who will be able to produce an equally compelling plan for another venture in the future.

Your own plan will probably fall somewhere between these two in both length and complexity. By the time you've completed all the steps described in the previous chapters, the best length for your outline and business plan should be apparent. Although most quality plans tend to be in the 20- to 30-page range, this is only a guideline, not a rule. Remember to write your executive summary last, and make sure it covers all ten action steps.

Outline for a Simple Business Plan

Here is an outline for a simple business plan. Remember that the exact headings of the subjects, and even whether these subjects should exist in your outline, depend on the specifics of your business and the purpose of your plan.

Cover Sheet

- Name of your company
- Month and year
- One sentence statement about your company
- Your name and any partners' names
- Contact name
- Contact information including telephone, fax, e-mail address, and mailing address

Table of Contents

Executive Summary (less than 1 page)

- Statement of business opportunity
- Statement of what you require in loans or investment
- Purpose of plan
- Major reasons opportunity exists
- Expected financial results
- Compare against Ten Action Steps to make certain all issues are covered

Description of the Business

- Product/service description and strengths
- For existing business, give history and financial performance
- Organization of the business, including information on management and ownership
- Legal structure

Market Overview

- Describe target market by geography, income, and demographics
- Competitive products, current buying patterns, and trends of the market

Industry Overview
- Competitors' history, products, and financial performance
- Trends, such as product changes, technology adoption, or consolidation
- Projections for the future
- Regulatory issues

Business Opportunity
- Business strategy
- Product/service strengths
- Marketing and sales strategies
- Research to support projections
- Time line for business plan

Financial Projections
- Historical financial statements if business exists
- Projected financial statements:
  - Income Statements
  - Balance Sheets
  - Cash Flow Statements
  - Debt-Service Projections
  - Comparisons to industry standards
  - Returns Analysis
- Assumptions page

Appendices
- Newspaper, magazine, industry trade reports
- Resumes of key managers
- Leases and other key contracts
- Historical financials for existing businesses only
- Research done to support projections

A Simple Business Plan:
S & J Advertising Agency

Executive Summary

The purpose of this plan is to establish a strategy for the creation of
S & J Advertising, a new agency that will be based in Toledo, Ohio.
Sonica Smith and Sally Jones are the co-founders of S & J who, between them, bring 19 years of experience in the Toledo advertising
market to this venture. Their relationships with current advertisers will
result in at least five clients coming to the firm at its inception. These
five clients have given S & J letters stating this intent.

The co-founders' experience as professional and proven advertising executives will insure that their current clients will be satisfied, and
that additional clients will join the S & J roster. Moreover, recent
changes in the Toledo media market have created the need among advertisers for a firm of this caliber and expertise.

S & J expects to be profitable within its first year of operation, but
seeks $50,000 in bank debt, for working capital and the construction of
production facilities. The owners expect to personally guarantee this
debt and to put in $50,000 of their own capital. The projections show
that the company's cash flow will exceed debt service by a ratio of more
than five to one in the first year and that the debt can be repaid within
five years.

The Market

Toledo is an economically healthy and diverse market of more than 600,000 people located in northeastern Ohio. Major employers include Daimler Chrysler, Libbey Glass, Dana Corporation, and General Motors. There are more than 50,000 students enrolled in local institutions of higher learning, including Bowling Green College, the University of Toledo, and Owens Community College. For the last five years, unemployment has been consistently below 5 percent. Toledo has an opera company, a symphony orchestra, an art museum, a zoological society, a minor-league baseball team, and a regional airport.

The Advertising Market

The local advertising market has more than $150 million in annual revenue, and includes seven television stations, one local newspaper, and 20 radio stations. According to the 2001 *Duncan Radio Market Guide*, the market revenues break down as follows:

Radio	$ 29 million
Television	56 million
Newspaper	54 million
Outdoor Advertising	7 million
Cable Television	4 million
TOTAL	**$150 million**

Advertising Agency Competition

There are currently three advertising agencies in the Toledo area.

Bob Williams Advertising is a one-man shop that has been in business for 12 years and has three clients: a large local bakery, a car dealer, and a local bank.

Global Agency has been in business for five years, has six employees, and about 15 clients, including two car dealerships, a few restaurants, and a local college. They have video-production capacity.

The Kryzyki Group has been in business for eight years, has three employees and 10 clients, who mostly require copywriting services and print-ad production. Clients are generally nonprofits and educational establishments, including the opera company, the symphony orchestra, the zoo, and a chain of day-care centers.

The Current Opportunity

Various changes in the local media market have left local advertisers underserved.

Radio Consolidation. Over the last six years, the radio industry has gone through a major consolidation. As a result, two companies now have more than 90 percent of the radio revenue, each owning eight stations. To make this consolidation work, the radio companies have cut back on their production staffs and advertising reps. The remaining reps no longer have enough time to work with local advertisers on the creative and media planning aspects of their advertising expenditures. Production is more rushed, and sometimes is even issued from remote, centralized facilities which slows down the process and results in frequent mistakes, such as the mispronunciation of local proper names.

Media Service Reductions. In addition to this reduction in service from radio stations, local television, newspaper, and cable companies have all reduced the level of service to local advertisers, apparently as they push for higher profitability or respond to weak national trends in advertising.

The Rise of the Internet. While the Internet has not proven itself as a mass advertising force, nonetheless, many businesses have websites and e-commerce strategies. Generally, local businesses rely upon computer-oriented people to build these web pages and do a poor job of integrating their Internet strategy with their overall advertising.

The opportunity that Smith and Jones have identified is the existence of many local advertisers who need and want higher levels of service, including the development and implementation of Internet strategies.

The Management Team

Sonica Smith holds a degree in advertising from Ohio State University and worked as an account representative for a local radio station for five years before becoming Sales Manager, a position she has held for the past four years.

Sally Jones was a local radio personality in Findlay, Ohio for seven years, which included responsibility for producing advertisements. She moved to Toledo 10 years ago, and became the advertising manager for a local bank. In that capacity, she dealt with all the local media, developed the bank's website and completed courses in computer science and programming at the University of Toledo.

Smith and Jones are prepared to invest $25,000 each in the agency and to work at minimal salaries to keep the agency's break-even point low until the agency produces adequate profits to compensate them additionally.

Sales and Marketing Strategies

The sales and marketing strategies have already been established by commitments from five sizeable advertisers to engage S & J as their agency. These clients include the bank at which Sally Jones currently works, a local nightclub, two car dealerships, and a large outlet store. In the previous 12 months, these five businesses spent $1.1 million on advertising, not including website expenditures.

Smith and Jones have a target list of 23 additional advertisers that they know personally and believe will sign on as clients. They are currently meeting with each of these potential customers to tell them their plans, and try to obtain a commitment to join their roster of clients. In addition, Smith and Jones have identified an additional 135 potential clients in Toledo with annual advertising expenditures of $75,000 or more.

Company Structure

S & J will be an LLC, so income will pass through to the two owners without being taxed at the company level, and to afford personal liability protection to both owners. Smith and Jones are currently working with a lawyer to draft the papers for the organization of the company, including an agreement between each of them to cover all contingencies in case one wishes to leave, or in the unlikely event that their working relationship deteriorates.

Capital Requirements

The appendix details the projected expenditures, including estimates from vendors, but Smith and Jones foresee the following basic capital requirements:

Computer hardware	$ 7,500
Computer software	1,500
Audio production studio	12,500
Video editing equipment	8,000
Office furniture	5,000
TOTAL	$34,500

Financing Requirements

Smith and Jones are seeking $50,000 in bank debt as working capital and to help build offices and production studios. They are willing to personally guarantee this loan. The attached tables show that the company will be profitable in the first year, and capable of handling this amount of debt.

Financial Projections

The attached projected financial statements make conservative assumptions for both revenue and expenses. They show S & J having an income of $23,485 in year one, and $32,325 and $65,040 in years two and three. The revenue projections assume that the company adds a net of eight new clients in year two and ten in year three. Given that five clients have already signed on, and that the company has a prime target list of 23 clients and an additional target list of 135 clients, this is also conservative. If, for any reason, the company does not meet its Cash Flow and Profit targets, the principals are prepared to reduce their salaries.

The Operating Cash Flow projections show that the company ends it first year of operation with a cash balance of $72,951, which is nearly six months of operating expense. The projections also show that the company will comfortably service debt, including repaying $10,000 in loan principal, at the end of year one. The Ratio Analysis and Comparison with RMA data shows that the company is within the range for the average advertising agency, with the exception of having more cash than the average. It also has fewer short term liabilities than the average agency. This is likely due to the fact that the typical agency does much more expensive production than S & J expects to handle. S & J plans to focus more on time buying, which will result in a positive cash flow because time will not be ordered until S & J has received payment from the client. This focus also results in lower fixed-asset percentages than the average agency. The quick test ratio comprised of cash and net receivables divided by current liabilities similarly shows S & J to be more financially secure than the average agency.

The projections show that the S & J Advertising will be able to repay the loan in its fifth year.

S & J Advertising: Projected Profit and Loss

	Year 1	Year 2	Year 3
Revenue	150,000	270,000	405,000

Operation Expenses

Salaries & Related expenses:

Founders' payroll	60,000	80,000	120,000
Employees' payroll	0	55,000	82,500
Benefits and employee taxes	21,000	47,250	70,875
Total Salary and Related Expenses	**81,000**	**182,250**	**273,375**

Office Expenses:

Rent	12,000	14,400	16,800
Communication	7,200	8,400	9,600
Advertising and website	5,400	7,200	12,000
Subscriptions	840	1,200	1,560
Misc. office expenses	1,200	2,400	2,400
Insurance and legal fees	4,800	4,800	4,800
Depreciation	3,075	5,225	7,425
Utilities	1,200	1,800	1,800
Other	4,800	6,000	7,200
Total Office Expenses	40,515	51,425	63,585
Total Operating Expenses	**121,515**	**233,675**	**336,960**

Income From Operations	**28,485**	**36,325**	**68,040**
Interest Expenses	5,000	4,000	3,000
Income	**23,485**	**32,325**	**65,040**

Assumptions
1. The company earns 15% commission on advertising it places.
2. First year company commissions are $150,000 from 5 clients already committed.
3. The company projects that its advertising contracts volume will increase
   —in 2nd year by 80% by adding 8 new clients
   —in 3rd year by 60% by adding 10 new clients
4. Company pays bills in 35 days and receives payment in 45 days.
5. Income and Expenses are spread evenly through the year.
6. Owners purchase $50,000 in Common Stock and guarantee $50,000 loan.
7. Because S&J is LLC, taxes are paid by owners on personal tax filings.

S & J Advertising: Operation Expenses Detail

Salaries & Related Expenses:

	Year 1	Year 2	Year 3
Smith	30,000	40,000	60,000
Jones	30,000	40,000	60,000
Secretarial	0	20,000	30,000
Salesperson	0	35,000	52,500
Salary total	60,000	135,000	202,500
Benefits and payroll taxes @35%	21,000	47,250	70,875
Total Personnel Expenses	**81,000**	**182,250**	**273,375**

Office & General Expenses:	*Monthly Expenses*		
Rent	1,000	1,200	1,400
Communication: wireless, wireline & mail	600	700	800
Advertising and website	450	600	1,000
Subscriptions	70	100	130
Office expenses	100	200	200
Insurance & legal Fees	400	400	400
Utilities	100	150	150
Other	400	500	600
Total monthly office expenses	3,120	3,850	4,680
Total Yearly Office Expenses	**37,440**	**46,200**	**56,160**

Interest Expenses

	Year 1	Year 2	Year 3
Bank loan outstanding	50,000	40,000	30,000
Principal repaid	10,000	10,000	10,000
Principal remaining at year end	40,000	30,000	20,000
Interest @10%	5,000	4,000	3,000

S & J Advertising: Projected Balance Sheet as of Year End

	Year 1	Year 2	Year 3
ASSETS			
Current Assets:			
Cash & cash equivalents	72,951	107,185	180,790
Accounts receivable	26,719	35,438	37,969
Other short-term assets	8,000	8,000	8,000
Total current assets	*107,670*	*150,623*	*226,759*
Fixed assets:			
Furniture & equipment cost	34,500	46,000	57,000
Less accumulated depreciation	3,075	8,300	15,725
Total fixed assets	31,425	37,700	41,275
Other assets:			
Other assets and miscellaneous investments	1,000	1,000	1,000
Total Other assets	1,000	1,000	1,000
TOTAL ASSETS	**140,095**	**189,323**	**269,034**
LIABILITIES & STOCKHOLDERS' EQUITY			
Current liabilities:			
Accounts payable	26,610	53,513	78,184
Short-term bank borrowing	0	0	0
Other short-term liabilities	0	0	0
Total current liabilities	*26,610*	*53,513*	*78,184*
Noncurrent liabilities:			
Long-term debt	40,000	30,000	20,000
Total non current liabilities	40,000	30,000	20,000
Stockholders' equity:			
Common stock	50,000	50,000	50,000
Retained earning	0	23,485	55,810
Income	23,485	32,325	65,040
Total stockholders' equity	*73,485*	*105,810*	*170,850*
TOTAL LIABILITIES & STOCKHOLDERS' EQUITY	**140,095**	**189,323**	**269,034**

S & J Adversting: Cash Flow Statement

	Year 1	Year 2	Year 3
Net Profit	23,485	32,325	65,040
Plus:			
Depreciation	3,075	5,225	7,425
Change in accounts payable	26,610	26,903	24,671
Increase (decrease) other liabilities	0	0	0
Increase (decrease) long-term borrowing	40,000	(10,000)	(10,000)
Capital investment	50,000	0	0
Subtotal	**119,685**	**22,128**	**22,096**
Less:			
Change in accounts receivable	26,719	8,719	2,531
Change in other assets	8,000	0	0
Fixed assets	34,500	11,500	11,000
Change in other assets	1,000	0	0
Subtotal	**70,219**	**20,219**	**13,531**
Net Cash Flow	**72,951**	**34,234**	**73,605**
Cash Balance	**72,951**	**107,185**	**180,790**

S & J Advertising: Fixed Asset Detail

Note B

		Year 1	Year 2	Year 3
Furniture & Equipment Open Balance				
Computer hardware		7,500	0	0
Computer software		1,500	0	0
Audio production software		12,500	0	0
Video editing equipment		8,000	0	0
Office furniture		5,000	0	0
Leasehold improvement		0	0	0
Total		34,500	0	0
Purchasing				
Computer hardware		0	10,000	10,000
Computer software		0	500	1,000
Audio production software		0	0	0
Video editing equipment		0	0	0
Office furniture		0	0	0
Leasehold improvement		0	1,000	0
Total Purchasing		0	11,500	11,000
Furniture & Equipment Closing Balance				
Computer hardware		7,500	17,500	27,500
Computer software		1,500	2,000	3,000
Audio production software		12,500	12,500	12,500
Video editing equipment		8,000	8,000	8,000
Office furniture		5,000	5,000	5,000
Leasehold improvement		0	1,000	1,000
Total Fixed Assets		34,500	46,000	57,000
Depreciation	% Per Year			
Open balance		0	3,075	8,300
Yearly				
Computer hardware	20%	1,500	3,500	5,500
Computer software	20%	300	400	600
Audio production software	5%	625	625	625
Video editing equipment	5%	400	400	400
Office furniture	5%	250	250	250
Leasehold improvement	5%	0	50	50
Total Yearly Depreciation		3,075	5,225	7,425
Total Accumulated Depreciation		3,075	8,300	15,725

RATIO ANALYSIS FOR S&J AND COMPARISON WITH RMA DATA FOR ADVERTISING AGENCIES

Projected Balance Sheet	Year 1	Year 2	Year 3	Years 1–3 as Percentages of Assets			
				Year 1	Year 2	Year 3	RMA 2001
ASSETS							
Current assets:							
Cash & cash equivalents	72,951	107,185	180,790	52.1%	56.6%	67.2%	11.7%
Accounts receivable	26,719	35,438	37,969	19.1%	18.7%	14.1%	25.5%
Inventory	0	0	0	0.0%	0.0%	0.0%	5.4%
Other short-term assets	8,000	8,000	8,000	5.7%	4.2%	3.0%	5.1%
Total current assets	107,670	150,623	226,759	76.9%	79.6%	84.3%	47.7%
Fixed assets:							
Furniture & equipment, cost	34,500	46,000	57,000				
Less accumulative depreciation	3,075	8,300	15,725				
Total fixed assets	31,425	37,700	41,275	22.4%	19.9%	15.3%	32.5%
Other assets:							
Intangibles	0	0	0	0.0%	0.0%	0.0%	6.9%
Other assets and miscellaneous investments	1,000	1,000	1,000	0.7%	0.5%	0.4%	12.9%
Total other assets	1,000	1,000	1,000				
TOTAL ASSETS	**140,095**	**189,323**	**269,034**	**100.0%**	**100.0%**	**100.0%**	**100.0%**
LIABILITIES & STOCKHOLDERS' EQUITY							
Current liabilities:							
Accounts payable	26,610	53,513	78,184	19%	28%	29%	47.1%
Trade payable	0	0	0	0%	0%	0%	16.7%

Short-term bank borrowing	0	0	0	0%	0%	0%	2.3%
Other short-term liabilities	0	0	0	0%	0%	0%	24.3%
Total current liabilities	26,610	53,513	78,184	19%	28%	29%	90.4%
Noncurrent liabilities:							
Long-term debt	40,000	30,000	20,000	29%	16%	35%	28.7%
Other	0	0	0	0%	0%	0%	6.1%
Total non current liabilities	40,000	30,000	20,000	29%	16%	7%	34.8%
Stockholders' equity:							
Common stock	50,000	50,000	50,000				
Retained earning	0	23,485	55,810				
Earnings	23,485	32,325	65,040				
Total stockholders' equity	73,485	105,810	40,850	-52%	-56%	-15%	-25.2%
TOTAL LIABILITIES & STOCKHOLDERS'EQUITY	**140,095**	**189,323**	**269,034**				
KEY FINANCIAL RATIOS							
Net profit margin	15.66%	11.97%	16.06%				
Quick ratio	4.05	2.31	2.90	RMA Avg: 0.8%			
Cash flow/Interest expenses	570%	906%	2268%				
Net commissions /Revenue	150,000	270,000	405,000	100.0%	100.0%	100.0%	100.0%
Total operating expenses/Revenue	121,515	233,675	336,960	81%	87%	83%	92.8%
Income/Revenue	28,485	36,325	68,040	19%	13%	17%	7.2%
Income before taxes/Revenue	23,485	32,325	65,040	16%	12%	16%	1.2%
Cash Flow	**28,489**	**36,328**	**68,043**				
Interest Expense	5,000	4,000	3,000				

Five-Year Projections: S & J Agency

Startup Expenses

Computer hardware	$7,500
Computer software	1,500
Production studio construction	12,500
Video-editing equipment	8,000
Audio production equipment	6,000
Office furniture	5,000
Office rent deposit	3,000
Phone deposit	1,200
Stationery, etc.	600
Misc.	4,500
TOTAL	**$49,800**

Monthly Expenses

Fixed Expenses

Rent	$1,500
Phone	500
Travel and entertainment	1,500
Office manager	3,000
Jones salary	1,000 (Salaries go up when possible)
Smith salary	1,000
Employee fringe (35%)	1,750
Insurance	400

Variable Expenses

Studio producers 10 hours/ week @$30	1,300
TOTAL	**$11,950**

Professional Services—Advertising Agencies SIC # 7311 (NAICS 54181)

	Current Data Sorted By Assets						Comparative Historical Data	
		54 (4/1-9/30/01)	297 (10/1'01-3/31/02)					
Type of Statement								
Unqualified	31	3	5	4		1	48	39
Reviewed	26	6	41	2		1	97	80
Compiled	22	33	30	22			104	106
Tax Returns		11	3				30	48
Other	7	44	44	7	3	4	81	114
	0-500M	500M-2MM	2-10MM	10-50MM	50-100MM	100-250MM	4/1/97-3/31/98 ALL	4/1/98-3/31/99 ALL
NUMBER OF STATEMENTS	86	97	123	35	4	6	360	387
	%	%	%	%	%	%	%	%
ASSETS								
Cash & Equivalents	21.0	11.8	13.0	20.2			14.0	15.1
Trade Receivables (net)	34.5	50.3	51.3	45.9			51.6	48.5
Inventory	2.3	2.4	1.7	2.3			3.7	3.2
All Other Current	4.1	2.9	4.9	2.7			3.2	3.6
Total Current	61.8	67.4	70.8	71.0			72.4	70.4
Fixed Assets (net)	26.0	18.7	15.4	13.6			16.3	17.8
Intangibles (net)	5.4	6.4	5.4	6.4			3.9	4.2
All Other Non-Current	6.9	7.5	8.4	9.0			7.4	7.6
Total	100.0	100.0	100.0	100.0			100.0	100.0
LIABILITIES								
Notes Payable-Short Term	14.9	11.6	7.7	1.9			7.7	9.9
Cur. Mat.-L/T/D	4.4	2.3	3.1	3.0			2.7	3.5
Trade Payables	23.7	33.0	39.0	34.9			34.4	32.8
Income Taxes Payable	.3	.2	.5	.4			.5	.5
All Other Current	20.2	15.7	18.7	24.9			15.4	16.2
Total Current	63.6	62.9	69.0	65.2			60.8	62.8
Long Term Debt	15.7	10.2	8.8	9.2			7.5	12.4
Deferred Taxes	.2		.3	.2			.8	.7
All Other Non-Current	3.3	7.3	2.8	4.7			3.8	3.4
Net Worth	17.3	19.3	19.1	20.8			27.1	20.7
Total Liabilities & Net Worth	100.0	100.0	100.0	100.0			100.0	100.0
INCOME DATA								
Net Sales	100.0	100.0	100.0	100.0			100.0	100.0
Gross Profit								
Operating Expenses	97.5	97.3	98.2	97.8			96.5	95.7
Operating Profit	2.5	2.7	1.8	2.2			3.5	4.3
All Other Expenses (net)	1.0	.8	.8	1.1			.4	5.3
Profit Before Taxes	1.5	1.9	1.0	1.1			3.1	-1.1
RATIOS								
Current	2.1	1.8	1.2	1.7			1.6	1.5
	1.1	1.2	1.0	1.1			1.2	1.1
	.5	.8	.9	.9			1.0	.9
Quick	2.0	1.6	1.1	1.4			1.4	1.4
	1.0	1.0	1.0	.9			1.1	1.0
	.5	.7	.8	.8			.9	.8

(Continued)

Professional Services—Advertising Agencies SIC # 7311 (NAICS 54181) (*Continued*)

Current Data Sorted By Assets | | | | | | Comparative Historical Data

	C1 (UND)	C2	C3	C4	C5	C6		H1	H2
Statement counts	0 / 26 / 45	29 / 43 / 71	42 / 64 / 96	38 / 65 / 147				34 / 51 / 79	32 / 50 / 74
Sales/Receivables		12.4 / 8.5 / 5.2	8.7 / 5.7 / 3.8	9.5 / 5.6 / 2.5				10.7 / 7.1 / 4.6	11.4 / 7.3 / 4.9
Cost of Sales/Inventory									
Cost of Sales/Payables									
Sales/Working Capital	18.0 / 273.9 / -21.5	11.3 / 51.5 / -27.5	22.3 / 999.8 / -33.9	10.0 / 74.2 / -14.2				11.9 / 36.9 / -119.0	13.1 / 44.6 / -92.0
EBIT/Interest	(62) 11.1 / 1.9 / -2.7	(78) 11.0 / 2.9 / -1.6	(106) 7.8 / 1.7 / -2.4	(27) 8.3 / 2.6 / -1.8				(306) 19.3 / 6.0 / 2.1	(321) 15.7 / 5.0 / 1.5
Net Profit + Depr., Dep., Amort./Cur. Mat. L/T/D	(16) 4.8 / 1.6 / .1	(24) 12.7 / 3.3 / .4						(104) 6.9 / 3.2 / 1.5	(100) 8.7 / 2.8 / 1.4
Fixed/Worth	.2 / .9 / -1.8	.3 / 1.3 / -2.1	.3 / 1.0 / -6.6	.4 / 1.4 / -1.7				.2 / .6 / 2.1	.3 / .7 / 2.8
Debt/Worth	.8 / 2.5 / -8.3	1.4 / 4.7 / -10.0	2.7 / 5.4 / -66.3	1.9 / 11.8 / -35.2				1.4 / 3.3 / 13.5	1.6 / 4.2 / 16.9
% Profit Before Taxes/Tangible Net Worth	(57) 72.8 / 18.5 / -13.1	(64) 68.1 / 31.1 / 3.5	(90) 46.5 / 10.6 / -15.3	(26) 80.5 / 38.9 / 9.6				(297) 73.5 / 28.7 / 9.4	(318) 84.9 / 32.6 / 8.3
% Profit Before Taxes/Total Assets	21.1 / 3.9 / -10.5	14.0 / 2.7 / -3.0	7.4 / 1.4 / -4.1	9.4 / 4.9 / -1.2				16.3 / 6.9 / 1.9	19.4 / 5.9 / 1.1
Sales/Net Fixed Assets	114.0 / 36.8 / 16.7	52.1 / 28.1 / 14.8	68.8 / 30.2 / 12.8	53.0 / 25.0 / 8.6				69.1 / 31.8 / 15.7	70.5 / 31.3 / 14.7
Sales/Total Assets	8.3 / 5.4 / 3.5	5.2 / 4.1 / 2.7	4.0 / 2.7 / 1.5	3.4 / 2.5 / 1.0				5.4 / 3.7 / 2.3	5.2 / 3.7 / 2.5
% Depr., Dep., Amort./Sales	(55) .7 / 1.3 / 2.7	(84) .9 / 1.3 / 2.1	(104) .4 / 1.1 / 2.6	(32) .5 / 1.2 / 3.8				(307) .6 / 1.1 / 2.2	(324) .6 / 1.1 / 2.1
% Officers', Directors', Owners' Comp/Sales	(55) 6.8 / 11.2 / 18.6	(47) 4.0 / 6.5 / 10.9	(42) 2.4 / 4.6 / 8.6					(160) 4.0 / 6.7 / 11.2	(182) 3.5 / 6.4 / 11.5
Net Sales ($)	135549M	459823M	277379M	1547675M	2026068M	1975565M		5955708M	5898823M
Total Assets ($)	19059M	107708M	256440M	524693M	744267M	919058M		2480927M	1931390M

M = $thousand   MM = $million

Comparative Historical Data   **Current Data Sorted By Sales**

	4/1/99-3/31/00 ALL	4/1/00-3/31/01 ALL	4/1/01-3/31/02 ALL	0-1MM	54 (4/1-9/30/01) 1-3MM	3-5MM	297 (10/1/01-3/31/02) 5-10MM	10-25MM	25MM & O VER
Type of Statement									
Unqualified	37	23	17	1	10	1	3	8	10
Reviewed	72	82	65	11	30	13	16	17	9
Compiled	86	95	91			13	11	12	4
Tax Returns	49	52	36	13	11	4	10	2	
Other	102	131	142	16	39	8	27	26	26
NUMBER OF STATEMENTS	346	383	351	41	90	39	67	65	49
	%	%	%	%	%	%	%	%	%
ASSETS									
Cash & Equivalents	15.1	12.8	15.3	20.2	15.0	15.1	11.8	14.5	17.9
Trade Receivables (net)	48.3	47.6	45.9	24.0	47.0	49.2	47.1	53.1	48.1
Inventory	3.5	3.1	2.1	2.8	2.8	2.5	1.5	1.3	1.9
All Other Current	4.0	4.1	4.0	5.8	2.7	2.8	5.3	4.0	3.8
Total Current	70.9	67.6	67.2	52.8	67.5	69.6	65.7	72.8	71.6
Fixed Assets (net)	16.1	18.7	18.8	34.1	18.4	17.7	19.6	14.0	12.9
Intangibles (net)	5.5	5.4	6.3	6.2	6.9	4.8	5.6	5.4	8.7
All Other Non-Current	7.5	8.3	7.7	7.2	7.2	8.0	9.2	7.7	6.9
Total	100.0	100.0	100.0	100.0	100.0	100.0	100.0	100.0	100.0
LIABILITIES									
Notes Payable-Short Term	9.2	14.2	10.1	13.7	13.2	9.1	13.6	5.5	3.4
Cur. Mat.-L/T/D	3.3	2.5	3.2	2.9	3.9	3.6	2.0	3.9	2.3
Trade Payables	32.0	31.2	32.9	14.4	30.9	32.2	34.5	39.8	41.5
Income Taxes Payable	.4	.5	.4	.5	.3	.8	.3	.2	.3
All Other Current	18.0	17.4	18.8	19.9	18.3	17.3	19.8	18.2	19.3
Total Current	62.9	65.7	65.3	51.5	66.6	63.0	70.2	67.6	66.9
Long Term Debt	8.8	10.6	11.0	22.7	12.3	4.7	9.7	8.9	8.4
Deferred Taxes	.5	.6	.3	.2	.2	.8	.4	.1	.1
All Other Non-Current	4.9	4.4	4.3	5.8	4.1	2.3	7.0	2.5	3.5
Net Worth	22.9	18.7	19.2	20.1	16.9	29.2	12.7	21.0	21.1
Total Liabilities & Net Worth	100.0	100.0	100.0	100.0	100.0	100.0	100.0	100.0	100.0
INCOME DATA									
Net Sales	100.0	100.0	100.0	100.0	100.0	100.0	100.0	100.0	100.0
Gross Profit									
Operating Expenses	95.6	95.6	97.7	91.2	98.9	98.9	98.8	97.8	98.3
Operating Profit	4.4	4.4	2.3	8.8	1.1	1.1	1.2	2.2	1.7
All Other Expenses (net)	.8	1.2	1.2	5.5	.5	.2	1.2	.4	.8
Profit Before Taxes	3.5	3.2	1.1	3.3	.5	.9	.0	1.8	.9
RATIOS									
Current	1.6	1.6	1.5	3.1	2.0	1.5	1.2	1.3	1.3
	1.1	1.1	1.0	1.3	1.1	1.0	1.0	1.1	1.0
	.9	.9	.8	.5	.7	.9	.7	.9	.9
Quick	1.5	1.5	1.3	2.3	1.8	1.4	1.1	1.2	1.2
	1.0	1.0	1.0	1.1	1.0	1.0	.9	1.0	1.0
	.8	.8	.7	.4	.6	.8	.7	.9	.8

(Continued)

Professional Services—Advertising Agencies SIC # 7311 (NAICS 54181) (Continued)

Comparative Historical Data

	33 / 55 / 83	32 / 51 / 78	28 / 49 / 74
Sales/Receivables	11.1 / 6.7 / 4.4	11.4 / 7.2 / 4.7	12.8 / 7.4 / 4.9
Cost of Sales/Inventory			
Cost of Sales/Payables			
Sales/Working Capital	12.0 / 40.2 / -46.4	12.5 / 57.2 / -41.4	17.3 / 167.7 / -27.7
EBIT/Interest	(278) 20.6 / 4.8 / 1.4	(316) 13.3 / 4.2 / 1.2	(281) 8.5 / 2.1 / -2.2
Net Profit + Depr., Dep., Amort./Cur. Mat. L/T/D	(82) 8.2 / 3.3 / 1.2	(73) 11.0 / 3.2 / 1.7	(57) 6.8 / 2.2 / .3
Fixed/Worth	.2 / .6 / 5.8	.3 / .8 / 7.0	.3 / 1.1 / -3.9
Debt/Worth	1.3 / 4.2 / 53.7	1.3 / 4.0 / 83.5	1.7 / 5.0 / -18.3
% Profit Before Taxes/Tangible Net Worth	(266) 90.5 / 38.1 / 9.6	(291) 77.3 / 32.2 / 8.3	(243) 65.4 / 19.0 / -1.6
% Profit Before Taxes/Total Assets	18.9 / 6.4 / 1.0	17.9 / 6.0 / .7	12.3 / 2.3 / -3.8
Sales/Net Fixed Assets	77.0 / 30.8 / 14.4	66.3 / 29.3 / 13.2	68.0 / 29.5 / 12.8
Sales/Total Assets	5.0 / 3.4 / 2.2	5.3 / 3.5 / 2.3	5.2 / 3.5 / 2.2
% Depr., Dep., Amort./Sales	(288) .6 / 1.2 / 2.1	(308) .6 / 1.2 / 2.2	(281) .6 / 1.3 / 2.7
% Officers', Directors', Owners' Comp/Sales	(138) 3.4 / 5.9 / 11.4	(172) 3.6 / 6.3 / 11.6	(149) 3.9 / 7.5 / 13.6
Net Sales ($)	5142105M	6296183M	6422005M
Total Assets ($)	2167001M	2730871M	2571225M

Current Data Sorted By Sales

	0 UND 20 / 48	25 / 43 / 72	35 / 59 / 83	35 / 58 / 82	32 / 52 / 78	35 / 56 / 96
Sales/Receivables	UND / 17.9 / 7.7	14.4 / 8.5 / 5.1	10.4 / 6.2 / 4.4	10.5 / 6.3 / 4.5	11.4 / 7.0 / 4.7	10.3 / 6.6 / 3.8
Cost of Sales/Inventory						
Cost of Sales/Payables						
Sales/Working Capital	6.6 / 85.6 / -13.2	12.0 / 107.7 / -18.0	17.0 / 205.2 / -35.1	23.4 / -157.7 / -13.4	27.5 / 116.5 / -69.1	16.4 / 184.3 / -34.6
EBIT/Interest	(24) 19.8 / 2.0 / -2.1	(76) 9.7 / 1.5 / -3.3	(32) 7.2 / 2.4 / -2.8	(55) 8.5 / 1.3 / -2.8	(56) 13.4 / 2.5 / -.2	(38) 8.8 / 3.0 / -1.3
Net Profit + Depr., Dep., Amort./Cur. Mat. L/T/D		(10) 6.2 / 2.3 / -18.5	(10) 5.8 / 2.5 / .5		(15) 15.0 / 3.0 / -.3	(13) 9.1 / 2.7 / .9
Fixed/Worth	.1 / 1.2 / -5.5	.3 / .9 / -1.1	.3 / .9 / 3.5	.5 / 1.8 / -1.0	.3 / .8 / NM	.4 / 1.4 / -6.2
Debt/Worth	.5 / 3.1 / -6.7	1.4 / 3.4 / -9.3	1.1 / 3.3 / 43.4	2.8 / 7.9 / -8.0	2.1 / 3.8 / NM	2.9 / 12.9 / -39.6
% Profit Before Taxes/Tangible Net Worth	(26) 65.7 / 20.0 / -4.7	(60) 81.5 / 15.3 / -10.4	(30) 41.2 / 6.0 / .8	(44) 60.7 / 18.1 / -10.7	(49) 70.6 / 26.1 / 7.1	(34) 69.3 / 27.5 / 2.1
% Profit Before Taxes/Total Assets	18.6 / 3.8 / -8.4	15.4 / 1.6 / -7.7	8.3 / 2.1 / -1.7	6.9 / 1.0 / -9.8	14.5 / 4.9 / .2	7.5 / 2.4 / -2.5
Sales/Net Fixed Assets	97.5 / 17.5 / 5.2	71.4 / 33.6 / 15.6	41.1 / 21.1 / 12.6	51.5 / 32.1 / 13.6	107.7 / 37.5 / 16.6	61.5 / 33.3 / 11.9
Sales/Total Assets	5.3 / 3.4 / 2.3	6.3 / 4.2 / 2.3	4.9 / 3.1 / 1.8	4.7 / 3.3 / 2.2	5.1 / 3.7 / 2.6	5.4 / 3.1 / 1.3
% Depr., Dep., Amort./Sales	(26) 1.2 / 3.4 / 10.4	(66) .5 / 1.4 / 2.4	(36) .8 / 1.4 / 2.5	(55) .9 / 1.4 / 2.3	(56) .4 / .8 / 1.9	(42) .5 / 1.0 / 3.1
% Officers', Directors', Owners' Comp/Sales	(19) 12.5 / 15.5 / 21.1	(51) 8.5 / 15.5 / 15.7	(19) 3.6 / 6.5 / 10.6	(29) 2.6 / 5.7 / 11.3	(21) 2.9 / 5.1 / 8.0	(10) 1.4 / 3.4 / 17.0
Net Sales ($)	21859M	185355M	160263M	468208M	1036796M	4549578M
Total Assets ($)	11315M	78002M	70221M	184925M	349171M	187591M

M = $ thousand   MM = $million

Outline for a Complex Business Plan

This outline is a comprehensive list of subjects you *may* wish to include in your plan. No plan needs to be this detailed, but you should read the outline and select those topics that relate to your business. Some topics are repeated because they should be considered in multiple areas, such as pricing and descriptions of competitors, but duplicating these issues in your final business plan is not necessary.

I. Cover Sheet

II. Table of Contents
   1. A single page list of key sections and appendices and the page numbers on which they appear. You may also put the table of contents before the executive summary.

III. Executive Summary
   A. The Purpose of the Plan
      1. Obtain a bank loan
      2. Attract investors
      3. Document an operational plan for controlling the business
      4. Test the financial feasibility of a business concept
      5. Attract partners, vendors, or suppliers
   B. The Company
      1. Overview of the needs the company will meet
      2. The products or services you will offer to meet those needs
      3. Legal structure
   C. Market Analysis
      1. The characteristics of your target market (demographic, geographic, etc.)
      2. The size of your target market
   D. Market Research
      1. Market research that you have carried out to test and prove key elements of your plan including product or service characteristics, location viability, pricing, packaging, or target market acceptance
   E. Product or Service Research and Development
      1. Major milestones in product development and progress in meeting them

F. Marketing and Sales Activities
  1. Marketing strategy
  2. Sales strategy
  3. Keys to success in your competitive environment
  4. Sales and marketing efforts to date
G. Organization and Personnel
  1. Key managers, owners, directors, advisors, and employees
  2. Organizational structure
H. Financial Data
  1. Funds required and their use
  2. Historical financial summary
  3. Prospective financial summary (including a justification for prospective sales levels)
  4. Projected returns for equity investors
  5. Debt coverage levels

IV. Company Description
  A. Nature of Your Business
    1. Marketplace needs to be satisfied
    2. Method(s) of need satisfaction
    3. Key specific customers or market niches
  B. Your Distinctive Competencies and Competitive Advantages (primary factors that will lead to your success)
    1. Elements of superior customer-need satisfaction
    2. Cost advantages, such as production/service delivery efficiencies
    3. Personnel
    4. Distribution
    5. Marketing program
    6. Sales organization
    7. Patents, copyrights, brand names that you own
    8. Location strengths
    9. Experience, knowledge, or reputation of founders
  C. Operational Strategies
    1. Organizational structure
    2. Key financial incentives for your employees, partners, distributors, market reps, and sales force
    3. Control and feedback structures to ensure that goals are being met

    4. Accountants, lawyers, consultants, directors and the expertise they provide

V. Market Analysis
  A. Industry Description and Outlook
    1. Description of industry and primary competitors
    2. List of competitors, including their financial information, strategies, histories, competitive strengths and weaknesses, products, and pricing
    3. Size of the industry, currently, historically, and in projections
    4. Industry characteristics: history and trends
      a. technology changes
      b. life cycle (is industry growing, maturing, consolidating, shrinking?)
        1. historically
        2. currently
        3. in the future
    5. Major customer groups
      a. businesses
      b. governments
      c. consumers
  B. Target Markets
    1. Description and characteristics of target markets
      a. critical needs to be filled
      b. extent to which those needs are currently being met
      c. demographic characteristics such as age, gender, race, ethnicity
      d. geographic location
      e. purchase decision makers and influencers
      f. seasonal/cyclical trends
    2. Primary target market size
      a. number of prospective customers
      b. annual purchases of products or services meeting the same or similar needs as your products or services
      c. geographic area
      d. demographic characteristics
      e. anticipated market growth
    3. Market penetration goals
      a. market share
      b. number of customers

      c. geographic coverage

      d. rationale for market penetration estimates, including research, testing, and competitors' experiences

   4. Pricing/gross margin targets

      a. price levels

      b. gross-margin levels

      c. discount structure (volume, promptness, payment terms, etc.)

   5. Methods by which specific members of your target market can be identified

      a. directories

      b. trade association publications

      c. government documents

   6. Media plan

      a. publications

      b. radio/television/Internet ads and promotion

      c. sources of influence/advice

      d. specific media plan including budgets, sample ad copy, and plan to monitor ad results

   7. Purchasing cycle of potential customers

   8. Key trends and anticipated changes within your primary target markets

   9. Secondary target markets and key attributes

      a. needs

      b. demographics

      c. significant future trends

C. Market Test Results

   1. Potential customers contacted

   2. Information/demonstrations given to potential customers

   3. Reaction of potential customers

   4. Importance of satisfaction of targeted needs

   5. Test group's willingness to purchase products/services at various price levels

D. Lead Times (amount of time between customer order placement and product/service delivery)

   1. Initial orders

   2. Reorders

   3. Volume purchases

E. Competition
  1. Identification (by product line or service and market segment)
     a. existing
     b. market share
     c. potential (How long will your window of opportunity last before your initial success breeds new competition? Who are your new competitors likely to be?)
     d. direct
     e. indirect
  2. Strengths (competitive advantages)
     a. ability to satisfy customer needs
     b. market penetration
     c. track record and reputation
     d. staying power (financial resources)
     e. key personnel
  3. Weaknesses (competitive disadvantages)
     a. ability to satisfy customer needs
     b. market penetration
     c. track record and reputation
     d. staying power (financial resources)
     e. key personnel
  4. Importance of your target market to your competition
  5. Barriers to entry into the market
     a. cost (investment)
     b. time
     c. technology
     d. key personnel
     e. customer inertia (brand loyalty, existing relationships, etc.)
     f. existing patents and trademarks
F. Regulation
  1. Customer or governmental regulatory requirements
     a. methods of meeting the requirements
     b. timing involved in meeting the requirements
     c. cost of meeting the requirements
  2. Anticipated changes in regulatory requirements
  3. Positives of regulations
     a. barriers to entry for potential competitors
     b. patent, copyright, trademark protection

      c. government support of industry
      d. trade protections for industry

VI. Products and Services
   A. Detailed Product/Service Description (from the users' perspective)
     1. Specific benefits of product/service
     2. Ability to meet needs
     3. Competitive advantages
     4. Present stage (idea, prototype, small production runs, etc.)
   B. Product Life Cycle
     1. Describe the product/service's current position within its life cycle
     2. Factors that might change the anticipated life cycle
       a. lengthen it
       b. shorten it
   C. Copyrights, Patents and Trade Secrets
     1. Existing or pending copyrights or patents
     2. Anticipated copyright and patent filings
     3. Key aspects of your products or services which cannot be patented or copyrighted
     4. Key aspects of your products or services which qualify as trade secrets
     5. Existing legal agreements with owners and employees
       a. nondisclosure
       b. non-compete agreements
   D. Research and Development Activities
     1. Activities in process at this time
     2. Future activities (include milestones)
     3. Anticipated results of future research and development activities
       a. new products or services
       b. new generations of existing products or services
       c. complimentary products or services
       d. replacement products or services
     4. Research and development activities of others in your industry
       a. direct competitors
       b. indirect competitors
       c. suppliers
       d. customers

VII. Marketing and Sales Activities
  A. Overall Marketing Strategy
      1. Competitive advantages
          a. pricing
          b. delivery time
          c. service
          d. product features
          e. brand name
          f. reputation
          g. status
      2. Market penetration strategy
          a. high profitability
          b. significant market share
      3. Growth strategy
          a. internal
          b. acquisition
          c. franchise
          d. horizontal (providing similar products to different users)
          e. vertical (providing the products at different levels of the distribution chain)
      4. Distribution channels (include discount/profitability levels at each stage)
          a. original equipment manufacturers
          b. distributors
          c. retailers
      5. Communication
          a. promotion
          b. advertising, including detailed media plan
          c. public relations
          d. personal selling
          e. printed materials (catalogs, brochures, etc.)
  B. Sales Strategies
      1. Sales force
          a. internal vs. independent representatives (advantages and disadvantages of your strategy)
          b. size
          c. recruitment and training
          d. compensation
      2. Prospecting
          a. identifying prospects
          b. prioritizing prospects

    c. qualifying prospects (separating prospects from suspects)

   3. Sales activities

    a. number of sales calls made per period

    b. average number of sales calls per sale

    c. average dollar size per sale

    d. average dollar size per reorder

VIII. Operations

  A. Production and Service Delivery Procedures

   1. Internal

   2. External (subcontractors)

  B. Production/Service Delivery Capacity

   1. Internal

   2. External (subcontractors)

   3. Anticipated increases in capacity

    a. investment

    b new cost factors (direct and indirect)

    c. logistics (will expansion force you to slow or stop production for a time?)

    d. timing

  C. Operating Competitive Advantages

   1. Techniques

   2. Experience

   3. Economies of scale

   4. Lower direct costs

  D. Suppliers

   1. Identify suppliers of critical elements of production

    a. primary

    b. secondary

   2. Lead-time requirements

   3. Evaluate risks of critical element shortages

   4. Describe existing and anticipated contractual relationships with suppliers

 IX. Management and Ownership

  A. Management Staff Structure

   1. Management staff organization chart

   2. Narrative description of the chart

  B. Key Managers (complete resumes should be presented in an appendix to the business plan)

1. Name
2. Position
3. Primary responsibilities and authority in your company
4. Primary responsibilities and authority with previous employers
5. Unique skills and experiences that add to your company's distinctive competencies
6. Compensation basis and levels
C. Planned Additions to the Management Staff
   1. Position
   2. Primary responsibilities and authority
   3. Requisite skills and experience
   4. Recruitment process
   5. Timing of employment
   6. Anticipated contribution to the company's success
   7. Compensation basis and levels (be sure that they are in line with the market)
D. Legal Structure of the Business
   1. Corporation
      a. C corporation
      b. S corporation
      c. limited liability corporation
   2. Partnership
      a. general partnership
      b. limited partnership
      c. limited liability partnership
   3. Sole Proprietorship
E. Owners
   1. Names
   2. Percentage of ownership
   3. Extent of involvement with the company
   4. Form of ownership
      a. common stock
      b. preferred stock
      c. general partner
      d. limited partner
   5. Outstanding equity equivalents
      a. options
      b. warrants
      c. convertible debt

          6. Common stock
            a. authorized
            b. issued
   F. Board of Directors
          1. Names
          2. Position on the board
          3. Extent of involvement with the company
          4. Backgrounds
          5. Contribution to the company's success
            a. historically
            b. in the future

X. Organization and Personnel
   A. Complete Organization Chart
          1. Positions
          2. Reporting relationships
          3. Narrative description of the organization chart
   B. Brief Position Descriptions
          1. Primary duties
          2. Recruitment and training
          3. Staffing levels
          4. Compensation
            a. method
            b. level
   C. Anticipated Human Resource Requirements
          1. Organization chart
          2. Staffing levels by position
          3. Changes in compensation levels and/or methods

XI. Funds Required and Their Uses
   A. Current Funding Requirements
          1. Amount
          2. Timing
          3. Type
            a. equity
            b. debt
            c. mezzanine
          4. Terms
   B. Funding Requirements Over the Next Five Years
          1. Amount
          2. Timing

   3. Type
      a. equity
      b. debt
   4. Terms
  C. Use of Funds
   1. Capital expenditures
   2. Working capital
   3. Debt retirement
   4. Acquisitions
  D. Impact of the New Funds on the Company's Financial
     Position
   1. Dilution of ownership
   2. Change in leverage levels (debt to equity ratio)
  E. Long-Range Financial and Exit Strategies
   1. Going public
   2. Leveraged buyout
   3. Acquisition by another company
   4. Debt service levels and timing
   5. Liquidation of the venture

XII. Financial Data
  A. Historical Financial Data (past three to five years, if available)
   1. Annual summaries
      a. income statement
      b. balance sheet
      c. cash flow statement or statement of changes in finan-
         cial position
      d. comparison to industry standards such as RMA data
   2. Level of CPA involvement (and name of firm)
      a. audit
      b. review
      c. compilation
  B. Prospective Financial Data (next five years)
   1. Next year (by month or quarter)
      a. income statement
      b. balance sheet
      c. cash flow statement
      d. capital expenditure budget
      e. returns analysis
      f. debt service schedule

    2. Remaining four years (by quarter and/or year)
      a. income statement
      b. balance sheet
      c. cash flow statement
      d. capital-expenditure budget
      e. returns analysis
      f. debt-service schedule
    3. Summary of significant assumptions
    4. Type of prospective financial data
      a. forecast (management's best estimate)
      b. projection (what-if scenarios)

XIII. Appendices or Exhibits
    A. Resumes of Key Managers
    B. Pictures of Products
    C. Professional References
    D. Market Studies
    E. Pertinent Published Information
      1. Magazine articles
      2. Books
    F. Patents
    G. Significant Contracts
      1. Leases
      2. Sales contracts
      3. Purchases contracts
      4. Partnership/ownership agreements
      5. Stock option agreements
      6. Employment/compensation agreements
      7. Non-compete agreements
      8. Insurance
        a. product liability
        b. officers' and directors' liability
        c. general liability
    H. Financial Commitments
      1. Letters of intent from funding sources
      2. Bank commitment letter
      3. Letters of interest from potential customers

A Complex Business Plan:
Zif Medical Devices

Business Plan

Company Contact Information
Zif Medical Devices

David M. Bean
President
135 East Street
Middletown, MA 10949

Joseph C. Schroeder
Vice President
3860 Hickoryview Drive
Indian Springs, OH 45011

Table of Contents

- Financial Analysis
- Risks

Attachments
- Investment and Depreciation Schedule by Phase
- Capital Expenditure Summary
- Balance Sheets
- Income Statements
- Cash Flow Statement
- Product Costing
- Fixed Overhead Costs
- Total Fixed and Unit Costs
- Net Present Value Calculation

EXECUTIVE SUMMARY

Zif Medical Devices will produce medical syringes with the strategic product benefits of automatic safety, ease of use, and low cost. Zif (Zero Incident Frequency) will initially target the psychiatric hospital market followed by the pre-filled nuclear medicine syringe, family practice, and hospital markets.

Market Need

There are an estimated one million needle-sticks (accidentally getting stuck with an exposed needle during a medical procedure) per year. This costs the medical industry over $3 billion annually to test and treat injured health care workers. The worldwide needle-syringe market is $1.5 billion (12 billion units). Safety syringes have less than a 10% penetration into the syringe market. 80% of the market in the year 2000 will be comprised of safety syringes.[1] The market potential for the year 2000 is 9.6 billion safety syringes. This leaves 70 percent market-share potential from now until the year 2000. The demand in the U.S. for conventional syringes was 4.8 billion in 1994 representing $700 million in revenues.

Currently there are several syringes on the market that claim some form of safety. These syringes have had little impact on this market mainly because of their high cost compared to standard syringes, and their inconvenient design. Additionally, most of these safety syringes provide few safety benefits because they require manual intervention to ensure safe operation.

Product Development

Zif's unique product design is based upon extensive market research. Zif's competitive advantages include automatic safety, ease of use, and low cost.

---

[1] Theta Group Research report.

The Zif design is in the process of being submitted for patent protection. The firm of Woodard, Emhardt, Naughton, Moriarty & McNett of Indianapolis completed the initial patent search and found that Zif has several claims that can be patented. Additionally, Zif has developed two prototypes and has held focus groups with medical personnel at several locations including psychiatric and full-service hospitals. Zif is in the process of testing a second prototype.

Commercialization

Zif will pursue one of the following commercial options:

1. License the technology to an established medical device company.
2. Build specialized tooling and contract manufacturing and distribution functions.

Option #1

Zif currently needs $250,000 to complete the patent application, field trials, and Food & Drug Administration approvals. Upon FDA approval, $150,000 is required to commercially license this technology. Thus, $400,000 is required to commercialize this product under Option #1.

Option #2

Pursuit of commercial Option #2 will require $400,000 in year one for the development costs as stated in option #1. $1.47 million is required in year two to launch mass production of this new product. Zif plans to grow through the investment of retained earnings, thus no further capital outlays will be needed.

Zif plans to capture 15% market share of the U.S. psychiatric hospitals and pre-filled nuclear medicine syringe market within three years of operation and 9% market share of the overall U.S. safety syringe market by year five. Further growth will then be pursued through penetrating the overall hospital market.

Financials

	Option #1	Option #2
Approach	License	Manufacture
Capital Investment	$400,000/20% equity	$1.87 million/30% equity
Overall NPV[2]	$1.3 million	$4.4 million
Return on Initial Investment[3]	191%	176%

[2]Options are discounted at 50% and 30% respectively.
[3]Compounded annual return. Based on industry average P/E Multiple of 20.

Management Team

Zif will be incorporated in order to effectively raise capital and limit shareholder liability. The president of the company will be David Bean. Mr. Bean has a BS in Mechanical Engineering, extensive experience in engineering and manufacturing in the plastics industry, and is acquiring an MBA at Purdue University. Mr. Bean will be responsible for the company's general management, and contract printing, assembling and packaging needs. Hank Catalini, an expert mold designer and project engineer with 15 years experience, will be vice president in charge of mold design, procurement, start-up, processing and customer relations. Joe Schroeder, who holds a BA and an MBA in marketing, will be vice president in charge of sales, marketing, distribution, and human resources. Tom Evans, with an MBA in Finance and extensive experience as a corporate controller, will be vice president in charge of finance and accounting. As the company grows, additional professional help will be hired as the need becomes significant and justifiable.

PRODUCT DESIGN & USER BENEFITS

The Zif safety syringe is designed to provide maximum safety to the user while maintaining the ease of use that health providers expect. Zif syringes are provided to the user with the sheath locked over the needle tip. This assures initial safety during unpackaging and medical preparation. The sheath can easily be unlocked and positioned to allow the user to draw the injection fluid. Once the liquid is drawn, the needle can be covered by rotating the sheath back in place. When the injection is to be administered, the sheath is unlocked and the injection is performed in the usual manner. During the shot, the sheath is automatically set to the locking position, so when the needle is retracted from the patient, the sheath locks in place. This prevents any subsequent needle-sticks (accidentally getting stuck with an exposed needle during a medical procedure).[4]

The three major benefits of Zif syringes are:

1. Automatic safety.
2. Ease of use.
3. Excellent value for the price.

MARKET ANALYSIS

Industry Costs

The annual worldwide market for needle syringe devices is estimated at $1.5 billion. There are an estimated one million needle-sticks a year. This accident rate costs the medical industry $1.2 billion annually. Studies published to date indicate there is a real chance of acquiring HIV through occupational exposures. As of October 1993, 39 cases of HIV seroconversions of healthcare workers resulting from documented occupational transmission have been reported in the United States, and 81 additional cases of HIV seroconversions are considered to have possibly resulted from occupational transmission. Although the fear of contracting AIDS has overshadowed the concern about acquiring the hepatitis B virus (HBV) through an accidental needle-stick, the risk of acquiring and dying from HBV is much greater. Every time health care workers get a needle-stick, they must immediately document the incident and begin a regular testing program to determine if a virus was contracted via the needle-stick. This can range from a few months of testing for hepatitis, to several years of testing for the HIV virus. Another $1.8 billion is spent annually to treat workers who have actually contracted viruses from needle-sticks. Thus, the healthcare industry is

---

[4]Patent rules prohibit further disclosure of the actual product design without proper disclosure documentation.

spending a total of $3 billion on needle-stick accidents, twice the amount spent on needle syringes. Based on this, safety needles could be financially justifiable at twice the cost of standard needle syringes. In response to this, the medical industry is seeking ways to prevent needlesticks, despite the higher costs for safer medical supplies. This is demonstrated in the intravenous (I.V.) market, where health organizations are paying three times the traditional costs of needle injections by using a needleless I.V. interface.

Personnel at Risk

Medical workers currently use needle syringes for subquetanious, intramuscular, and Hickman Catheter injections. In a 1993 study of 1,245 healthcare workers with exposure to HIV-infected blood, the authors found that nurses were the most likely group to have received an exposure (64% of the study population) and that the vast majority of the exposures were the result of needle-stick injuries.[5] This study also found that 34% of the percutaneous injuries were caused by sticks from syringe devices. In another journal report by the Infection Control Department,[6] seventeen metropolitan Washington, DC, area hospitals were surveyed on all workers reporting needle-stick injuries during February 1990. The results were that 45.8% of the needle-sticks were to registered nurses. Recapping the needle accounted for a higher percentage than any other activity at 14.1%. Of the needle-sticks, 60.6% were after use and before disposal. The conclusion of the study was that safer needle devices would make a safer workplace. The Center for Disease Control and Prevention (CDC) recommmended that needles not be recapped and, if they must be recapped, that a method other than the traditional two-handed technique be used.

Numerous studies show that conventional, two-handed recapping is the cause of a significant portion of all needle-stick injuries. The alternatives to recapping include the use of safety syringes or the disposal of uncapped needles into permanent sealable containers (e.g., sharps containers). Also, while disposing of uncapped needles into sealable containers (sharps containers) sounds like an ideal solution to

---

[5]"Needle-stick Prevention Devises." *Health Devices*. August-September, 1994.
[6]"Reported hospital needle-stick injuries in relation to knowledge/skill, design, and management problems," *Infection Control Hospital Epidemiol*, May 1993, pp. 259-264.

the needle-stick problem, in actual practice, not all needles are properly disposed of, and needles stuffed into overfilled containers may still be dangerous. Again, this strengthens the need for safety syringes and the tremendous opportunity that Zif safety syringes will have in this environment.

About one out of every four needle-stick injuries involves IV therapy equipment. A sizable number of these injuries result during the disassembly, but needle-sticks also occur along every step of the assembly/use/discard process, including insertion into drip chambers, injection ports, and IV bags, for example. Needles attached to discontinued lines is another problem: sometimes the needles are concealed in bedding. At other times, nurses discontinue devices and hang tubing, with needles attached, over IV poles.

Another study done by the Pacific Presbyterian Medical Center for Infection Control[7] evaluated the impact of a shielded 3cc safety syringe on needle-stick injuries among healthcare workers. The study found that the overall rate of needle-sticks involving 3cc syringes decreased from 14 per 100,000 inventory units to 2 per 100,000 inventory units due to shielded 3cc safety syringes. This evidence demonstrates that there is a tremendous need for a protection of health care providers from exposure to bloodborne pathogens and helps us identify the target end-user.

Regulations and Recommendations

Currently, needle-stick prevention devices (safety syringes) are not required by OSHA. There is however, a large scale, voluntary effort—known as the Exposure Prevention Information Network (EPINet)—under way to compile a national database of device specific injury information. In addition, ECRI, a health services research agency, recently released a detailed evaluation of 30 needlestick-prevention products. On December 6, 1991, OSHA published "Occupational Exposure to Bloodborne Pathogens: Final Rule" (29 CFR Part 1910.1030). This standard requires that healthcare facilities use engineering controls (e.g., sharps containers) and safe work practices to protect their em-

---

[7]"Impact of a shielded safety syringe on needle-stick injuries among healthcare workers," *Infection Control Hospital Epidemiol*, June 1992, pp. 349-353.

ployees from all bloodborne pathogens. In addition, OSHA inspectors will be considering whether an institution has reviewed the feasibility of implementing more advanced engineering controls, such as needle-stick prevention devices (safety syringes). OSHA may also impose fines of up to $70,000 (for repeat violations) on facilities that fail to take adequate measures to protect workers. Between March 1,1992, and February 28, 1993, OSHA conducted more than 1,000 inspections in healthcare institutions and handed out more than 1,700 citations—fines totaling $1.3 million—for violations of the bloodborne pathogen standard. Of the 1,700 violations, 78 were given for failure to use engineering controls and safe working practices, including the unnecessary recapping of needles and failure to use mechanical devices for needle recapping or removal. This is a clear signal of regulatory change and the future demand for safety syringes.

On March 9, 1993 Congress reintroduced Anti-Needle-Stick legislation (H.R. 1304). The bill proposed an imposition of a tax on conventional syringes, thereby providing a price encouragement for acceptance of the safety syringe devices. The bill was referred to the House Committee on Ways and Means and no further committee action has been scheduled. Additionally, OSHA's requirement of needleless injection I.V. systems, may carry over to the syringe market. In other words, OSHA may require the adoption of safety syringes in the near future. Additional legislation and regulation is expected to continue the trend toward safety syringes.

MARKET OPPORTUNITY

The worldwide market for needle-syringes is 12 billion units annually. The demand per hospital bed per year is 1200 syringes. Unit demand for needle-syringes is rising at 7.1% per year[8]. Currently the market for safety syringes has less than a 10% market penetration. Industry experts are speculating that the worldwide market for safety syringes will be over 5 billion units by the year 1998. A Theta group research report suggests that 80% of the needle-syringe market in the year 2000 will be comprised

---

[8]"Safer syringes boost molder opportunities," *Plastics World*, August, 1993.

of safety syringes. This means the market potential for the year 2000 is 9.6 billion units. With a current market penetration of less than 10%, this leaves 70% market share potential from now until the year 2000.

The sales of traditional syringes are expected to contract by 12.8% a year through increased use of safety syringes and needleless IV systems. The replacement of the traditional syringes is constrained somewhat by cost since hospitals are not as concerned with the cost savings associated with safe needles due to insurance coverage; thus, the market has not moved as fast as it could. However, the potential for hospital liability after a needle-stick may increase with the availability of products, especially if the hospital fails to provide such devices. As the AIDS epidemic increases, health care providers and insurers alike are expected to move towards the safer syringes.

Problems associated with the safety syringe products have primarily focused on their higher cost versus standard syringes. Other problems with the safety syringes have been their user unfriendly design, additional disposal bulk, and their availability in limited sizes. We will address these issues more closely in Competitor Analysis, Customer Needs, and Marketing Strategy.

The 3cc syringe dominates the market because most doses require 2 cc injections. Next to the 3cc syringe, demand is greatest for the 1cc version followed by the 5cc and 10cc syringes.

The demand in the U.S. was 4.8 billion syringes in 1994 for a total of more than U.S. $700 million. Zif's initial target markets will be U.S. psychiatric facilities and pre-filled chemotherapy and nuclear medicine companies. The estimated sales potential for these markets are 145 million units and 20 million units, respectively. The rationale for choosing these markets and further analysis of our initial target markets is as follows:

Market Segments

The conventional U.S. syringe market is broken down as is shown on the following page[9]:

---

[9]Market segmentation estimates are based upon number of beds times usage rate per beds per segment. Discussions with distributors and nurse managers were also factored in.

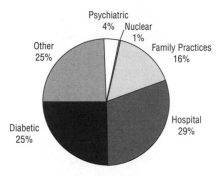

The safety syringe market segments are as follows:

1. *Psychiatric Hospitals (early adopters)*—Low volume users, however high usage rate—75% safety syringes. The reason for the high usage rate is due to concern with the hazard of needlesticks due to the potential for chaos in the hospital as well as rooms not being equipped with sharps containers. They are inclined to utilize distributors, although much less so than hospitals. In addition, they are less price sensitive than the hospitals.

2. *Nuclear Medicine (early adopters)*—Low volume users, however companies are pursuing the use of safety syringes to differentiate their products. Zif has had discussions with Syncor (60% market share) and Amersham (40%) regarding the design of safety syringes for their needs.

3. *Physicians (Family Practices) (early majority)*—Low volume users; utilize the 3cc syringe most, although, 1cc syringes are most common in pediatrics. This segment of the market is less tied to their distributors and may be more inclined to purchase safety syringes due to the high cost of insurance for small practices. They are also willing to pay a significant premium for safer syringes.

4. *Hospital and HMO's (late majority)*—High volume users, however late adopters. This overall hospital and HMO group primarily utilizes the 3cc syringes due to the fact that most doses given are 2cc doses. As prices continue to decline and realization of the cost benefits increases, hospital usage of safety syringes is expected to escalate dramatically. Hospitals and HMO's are highly tied to their group purchasing organizations and distributors for a multiple source of medical supplies.

5. *Diabetics (laggards/non-users)*—Low volume user. This segment of the market is only concerned with the retail price, and is not inclined to purchase safety syringes because they are using the needles on themselves.

Customer Needs

Current products offered in the market are weak relative to the market's key needs for ease of use and automatic safety. Based on focus groups and in-depth interviews the desired end-user product features/needs are:

- a transparent safety device requiring no additional steps to operate
- the ability to lock and unlock the protective sheath
- the ability to change the needle on the syringe
- the ability to cover the needle for sterility
- one handed operation
- a low cost product; it must have a good cost/benefit analysis
- a safety syringe in which the graduations can be easily read
- easy removal from the package
- needle mated with syringe—not separate
- to be able to hold the barrel directly

These features define the key attributes of:

- ease of use
- automatic safety
- syringe and needle included together
- size availability (1cc, 3cc, 5cc)

A complete primary data research report can be made available upon receipt of the non-disclosure form.

Competitor Analysis

Currently there are several syringes in the market that claim some form of safety. These syringes have had little impact on this market mainly because they are "clumsy" to use which make it more difficult for the health care worker to perform the injection. Additionally, most of these safe syringes provide few safety benefits because they require manual intervention to ensure safe operation. Manufacturer's of these safety syringes have yet to develop the perfect safety syringe that has both the benefits of ease of use and automatic needle-stick protection.

The competition can be separated into two distinct segments: (1) those pursuing an automatic safety syringe, and (2) those that are manufacturing a manually operated "safe" syringe. The following is a description of the competitors offerings separated by design:

(1) Automatic Safety Design Products

Med-Design.   Med-Design has a library of patents and is working on the development of various new products. Early in 1996 the company received its first FDA clearance to market a safety syringe, and the company has another 510(k) application filed and pending. The company also received approval for some patents in the European Community. Their syringe is a complicated retractable needle device that utilizes a spring to retract the needle. To enact the retraction mechanism, the medication contents of the syringe are dispensed by pushing the plunger into the syringe barrel. By pushing the plunger further into the barrel, like the click of a retractable ball-point pen, a spring loaded system is triggered which pulls the needle back into the syringe body, protecting the worker from accidentally sticking him or herself. It also serves to package the needle in a handy container for disposal which minimizes the contact of any bio-hazardous materials which might be present. Med-Design will pursue an 18 cent price and expects to obtain 10% of the syringe market. The company is concentrating on product development and design while leaving manufacturing and marketing to strategic partners. Med-Design's product costs will most likely be significantly higher based on the product's complexity and its incompatibility with existing assembly equipment.

Injectimeds—The Protector.   The Protector uses a spring-loaded, flexible, four-armed plastic sheath to cover the needle. The four arms bend and fold during injection and then automatically drive the end-cap to cover and lock over the needle after withdrawal. Currently they have discontinued production and are redesigning their product. The company is striving for a price of under 20 cents for their new product. Their product, however, is a needle-only system, and must be mated to a syringe for use. This is a convenience problem because the user will have to purchase syringes separate from the needle and then attach the needle to the syringe. This can also create an emergency issue situation were the user will not have the syringe ready for use when needed, which could be a significant problem in psychiatric hospitals. Injectimed intends to market its final product to small distributors and use a marketing pull strategy to draw demand from the end user. A significant problem with The Protector is that its needle guard flaps may interfere with its use at skin connection.

Sterimatic Medical Corp.—Sterimatic Safety Needle. Sterimatic's automatic system is much like that of The Protector above. The Sterimatic is removed from a sterile package and fitted to any size conventional syringe. A protective sheath is then removed to reveal the needlepoint. The needlepoint is injected into the patient and a spring-loaded inner sleeve retracts freely to allow the required penetration. As the needle is withdrawn, the sleeve automatically slides forward to cover the whole length of the needle and locks permanently. This device, however, is inconvenient because, like The Protector, it is sold as a needle-only system and must be fitted to a separate syringe. Again this can create a potential emergency readiness issue. It also requires a Leur-end vial adapter to draw the medication into the syringe. The Sterimatic's guard can be accidentally activated during use, creating a potential safety problem. Sterimatic prices this device at about 30 cents.

(2) Manually Locking Safety Design Products

North American Medical Products—Safepoint. Safepoint is a manually activated needle guard that extends and locks in place over the needle. Its Luer end must be attached to a syringe. The needle guard has a cutout that allows it to lock onto a Y-site once it has been activated. The advantages to Safepoint is that it is available in many different size needles and the manufacturer will provide customized packages of different syringe sizes. Some disadvantages cited are that the recessed needle function is not obvious without training, the length between user's hand and needle may make use more awkward. Safepoint's price with needle and syringe: 58 cents to $1.97 (depending on the size of the syringe).

Sims Smith Industries—Needle-Pro. The Needle-Pro is a manually activated needle guard; the needle protection device fits onto a Luer-lock syringe, and the needle is then twisted onto the male Luer-lock fitting on the Needle-Pro's base. After use, the user snaps the sheath against a hard surface. The biggest advantage Needle-Pro has is its price, only 12 cents (17 cents with syringe). Another advantage is that Needle-Pro can be activated with only one hand. The major disadvantages are that a needle-stick can occur if its guard is not closed on an appropriate surface. Also, a Luer-end vial adapter is needed if medication is to be drawn up into the syringe.

Becton Dickinson—Safety-Lok. Becton Dickinson's (BD) Safety-Lok syringe design is such that the user must manually move the plastic sheath over the needle when they are done with the injection. They also have to manually lock the sheath into place. This is a distinct disadvantage and a safety problem because of its inherent unsafe needle exposure after injection and before the user moves the sheath into place. This is also a convenience problem because the sheath does not automatically cover the needle.

BD holds 54% of the safety syringe market. BD's sliding sleeve syringe (Safety-Lok) accounts for approximately $70 million in sales. BD is currently undercutting all other safety syringes by pricing their product at 14 cents to hospitals. Overall, their safety syringe prices range from 14 cents to 26 cents.

BD has a powerful relationship with large distributors giving it a great distribution advantage and the potential ability to prevent the entry of smaller competitors into these channels. Additionally, BD takes advantage of its broad product lineup and size by bundling their syringes with other items when selling to large distributors. In this way, BD has some flexibility to undercut pricing of one product to increase revenues of its entire line. Syringes have often been used in this way to grow BD's overall product volume.

Sherwood Medical Co.—Monoject. Sherwood's Monoject product is similar to BD's and has the same convenience and safety problems. Sherwood has 43% market share, a strong relationship with distributors, and the advantage of product bundling. Sherwood sells its Monoject to hospitals for 14 cents.

U.S. Medical Instruments Inc.—Safesnap. U.S. Medical Instrument's (USMI) Safesnap is a retractable needle safety syringe. After injection, the user pushes the plunger fully into the barrel of the syringe until it locks onto the needle. The user then pulls the needle back into the syringe barrel. Once the needle is fully retracted, the plunger is snapped off and inserted into the open barrel, thus sealing the needle within the syringe. This also has the convenience and safety problems of the above syringes due to the manual operation and inherent needle exposure. Safesnap costs between 15 and 20 cents.

The Medtech Group—Entrap.   Entrap is similar to the Safesnap in that it is a retractable needle syringe. Its design allows for the contaminated needle to be withdrawn inside the syringe barrel following use. The needle automatically tilts sideways during retraction, thus preventing needle re-exit and possible needle-sticks. Again, this product has the convenience and safety problems we have seen with the other manual systems. Medtech had planned to sell Entrap for 30 cents, but was forced to withdraw from the market due to patent infringement lawsuits. They remain a potential future competitor.

Other Competitors.   Besides these well established companies, there are many start-up companies venturing into the anti-needle-stick market— since 1992 the U.S. Patent Office has approved more than 300 patents for safety features for syringes and needles. One of these start-up companies is *Unique Management Enterprises Inc.*, of Albany, NY. Anthony Vallelunga, the company owner, has sunk four years and $70,000 in borrowed money into development of a safety syringe. He has four patents on his product, with another waiting the go-ahead. The Food & Drug Administration has also given him a green light to go to market. *Medisys Technologies, Inc.*, Baton Rouge, Louisiana, as of July 15, 1996 has completed functional prototypes of the CoverTip™ safety syringe. CoverTip is a needle and syringe which automatically encloses the needle in a protective micro-thin sheath before the hypodermic is withdrawn from the patient's body thereby eliminating exposure to a potentially contaminated sharp needle point. *UnoLife Syringe Technologies, Inc.*, Hollywood, California, as of July 1, 1996, has patented a single-use self-destructing safety syringe which has received FDA 510(k) Pre-Market Notification clearance. The company's product is a retractable needle syringe, where the needle is retracted into the syringe barrel and incorporates a self-destructing feature. UnoLife is seeking funding to provide for commercial-test manufacturing run, marketing and sales development, and full production by contract manufacturing and distribution.

Competitor Analysis Summary

Below, we have summarized the strengths and weaknesses of competitors' products on key customer driven product attributes based on secondary and primary market research data. As shown a + indicates a strength on this attribute while a - indicates a weakness in this attribute. As shown, the Zif product will capture all of the key customer attributes.

	Market Share[10]	Price (cents)	Auto-matic	Ease of Use	Includes Syringe	Size Avail.
Injectimed—Protector	0%	25	+	-	-	-
Sterimatic—Sterimatic	1%	35	+	-	-	+
NAMP Safepoint	0%	58	-	-	+	+
Sims Needle-pro	0%	17	-	+	-	-
BD—Safety-Lok	54%	14 to 26	-	-	+	+
Sherwood—Monject	43%	14 to 26	-	-	+	+
USMI—Safesnap	2%	15 to 25	-	-	+	+
Medtech—Entrap	0%	30	-	-	+	-
MedDesign	0%	18	+	-	+	-
Zif—Zif	**N/A**	**14-18**	**+**	**+**	**+**	**-**

Primary Target Market

Zif's initial target will be U.S. psychiatric hospitals due to 1) their early adopters status 2) their high percent usage of safety syringes (70 to 100% of syringes used in these areas are safety syringes) 3) their dissatisfaction with the current safety syringes, and 4) Zif product features meeting their needs.

As of 1992 there were 5,498 mental health facilities in the U.S.[11] These hospitals/wards comprise 121,000 beds. Utilizing the usage figures per bed per hospital of 1200 units, we find the unit sales potential of this market to be 145 million units per year.

---

[10]"Safety syringe sales may reach 4 billion units a year by 1998," *Health Products News*, May 15, 1994, pg. 6.
[11]American Hospital Association, Chicago, IL, *Hospital Stat.* 1995-96.

Secondary Target Market

Our secondary initial target will be the chemotherapy and nuclear medicine pre-filled syringe market with an estimated market size of 20 million units. Medi-Physics (40% market share and subsidiary of Amersham) has indicated a strong desire for a safety syringe to differentiate their product and provide safety from accidental needle-sticks. In addition, Syncor also has indicated a strong desire to pursue safety syringes. Further research has found the overall pre-filled syringe market to be 6 billion units.

COMMERCIAL OPTIONS

Commercialization

Zif will pursue one of the following commercial options:

1. License the technology to an established medical device company.
2. Build specialized tooling and contract manufacturing and distribution functions.
3. Build specialized tooling, printing, and assembly equipment. Contract custom molding and distributor functions.

Option #1

Zif currently needs $250,000 to complete the patent application, field trials, and Food and Drug Administration approvals. Upon FDA approval, $150,000 is required to commercially license this technology. Thus, $400,000 is required to commercialize this product under Option #1.

Option #2

Pursuit of commercial Option #2 will require $400,000 in year one for the development costs as stated in Option #1. $1.47 million is required in year two to launch mass production of this new product. Zif plans to grow through the investment of retained earnings, thus no further capital outlays will be needed.

Commercial Flow Chart

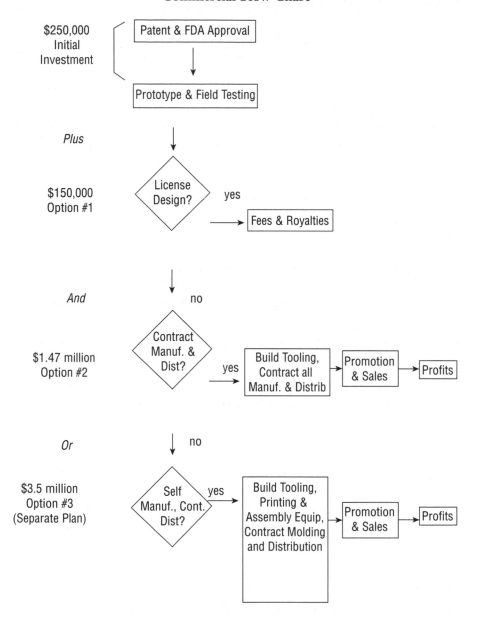

Option #3

This option involves purchasing all the product specific tooling and auxiliary equipment. This option is more capital intensive, but eliminates the need for contracting high value printing, assembly and packaging operations with a potential competitor. This option is developed fully in a separate business plan. This higher risk plan will be utilized only in the case of strong investor preference, or lack of success with options #1 and #2.

MARKETING STRATEGY

Zif will initially pursue a niche marketing strategy targeting psychiatric and pre-filled nuclear medicine syringe markets. After penetrating these niche markets Zif will then expand to the overall syringe market.

Product Positioning

Zif will be positioned as an automatically safe, easy-to-use product, with a competitive price. Competitors' products lack one or both of these features (refer to Competitor Analysis section). The Zif syringe provides maximum safety with ease of use through these two features:

1. The Zif syringe is one unit and can easily be unlocked, re-locked, and positioned to allow the user to load the injection fluid.

2. During the shot, the sheath is automatically set to the locking position. Then, when the needle is retracted, the sheath automatically covers the needle and locks into place over the needle, thus, ensuring that the needle is never exposed after the shot is administered.

Zif's automatic design[12] will differentiate it substantially from the major players, BD and Sherwood (97% combined market share). In addition to its automatic feature, Zif beats BD and Sherwood on ease of use, and can match them on price and availability.

---

[12]Zif syringe drawings and prototypes can be made available upon receipt of the non-disclosure form (last page).

Price

Zif will price its safety syringe at a competitive 16 cents. In the safety syringe market, Zif will be priced at a slight premium compared to the lowest price of Becton Dickinson's Safety-Lok and Sherwood's Monoject, while beating or matching the prices of other competitors in the market. Zif's superior customer-driven product design will enable a premium pricing as compared to the Safety-Lok and Monoject. However, market research has indicated a clear need for low cost, and a substantial benefit versus cost requirement. Therefore, Zif has chosen a pricing position that establishes a premium compared to Safety-Lok and Monoject, yet lower than other products whose design is also superior to Safety-Lok and Monoject. In addition, the low price will allow Zif to build market share quickly against small competitors, while ramping up production. These prices will likely be adjusted as factors such as market demand, name recognition, plant capacity and marketing channels change. In addition, the pricing will depend upon the options that are pursued and the partnership agreements.

In terms of future prices, according to a recent pricing survey, increases in the price that hospitals and group purchasing organizations pay for needles and syringes have slowed to a virtual standstill, with average prices for syringes rising only 0.9% and average prices for needles rising only 0.7%. This reverses the trend of rapid price increases seen in 1994's survey of this high-volume, low price commodity item, when prices increased an average of 6.6% over 1993. Not one of the executives responding expects prices to rise any time soon. While competition is the most significant factor keeping the lid on prices, two respondents—both group purchasing organizations—cited the rising cost of materials as exerting an upward pressure on costs.

Below is an analysis of the unit economics for option #1 (license) and option #2 (manufacture).

Option #1 (License)—Unit Economics

Based upon royalty arrangements similar to industry practices, Zif's royalty share will be 3.0 cents per unit (see below). The basic assumptions in this analysis are that:

1. The value premium for safety products is determined by subtracting the average price of non-safety products from the average price of existing safety products on the market.

2. The incremental manufacturing cost of safety products is subtracted from the net sales premium determined in step one.

3. Zif will negotiate a royalty fee equal to 40% of the net premium derived in step 2.

Option #2 (Manufacturing)—Unit Economics

Based on product costing analysis (below), a 3cc Zif safety syringe will have a variable cost of 7.2 cents. The distribution partnership mark-up is estimated at 20%. This leaves Zif with a wholesale price of 13.3 cents. This will provide a gross margin of 46% or 6.1 cents.

	Opt. #1 License	Opt. #2 Manuf.
Avg. Sale Price	0.160	0.160
Distributor Margin	0.015	0.027
Contracted Cost	0.070	—
Contract Expense	—	0.070
Avg. Depreciation	—	0.002
Gross Margin	0.075	0.061
Royalty (40% GM)	0.030	—
Zif Gross Margin	**0.030**	**0.061**

Promotion and Distribution

Promotion of Zif will be targeted towards psychiatric hospitals, and nuclear medicine suppliers as well as to potential strategic partners with expertise in marketing and/or manufacturing.

Selling in the industry entails three separate alternatives which are:

1. *Selling directly to the end-user.* This alternative will require a large sales force. Sales would increase at a slow pace and significant promotional expense is required.

2. *Selling to small distributors who service the medical industry.* Again, this alternative involves obtaining a large amount of testing, product research, and end-user data to get them to carry Zif. The average costs in this alternative is a 10% distributor markup.

3. *Selling to Group Purchasing Organizations(GPO's).* The role of a GPO is to negotiate favorable contracts with manufacturers through

exclusive contracts for the hospitals they represent. GPO's are prevalent in the industry and most full-line hospitals are members of GPO's. In addition, psychiatric hospitals are moving more towards membership with GPO's. The selling to a GPO entails obtaining a large amount of testing, product research, and end-user data. In addition, a low price is key to an acceptance of a bid proposal. "Invitations to Bid" on a particular product are sent to vendors on their bid list then the bids and product samples are sent to a committee who decides on what products and companies with whom to develop agreements. Most agreements have two-year firm prices. The average costs involved in this alternative is a "3% of sales" fee to the GPO and a 10% or less markup to the distributor. This alternative would require the least amount of sales force; however, large amounts of end-user acceptance data will be required. Zif has made initial contact with Tenet and Amerinet, two of the largest GPO's with over 1500 hospital memberships each. In addition, Zif has discussed "Invitation to Bid" procedures with Hospital Purchasing Service located in Michigan with a membership of over 150 hospitals.

In addition, the selling of product to state owned psychiatric hospitals requires either: 1) selling to the state through the process of waiting for the state to put out a bid, submitting a bid, then waiting for the state to decide on the items they would like to place on their list of items the hospitals are allowed to purchase and/or 2) pulling the product through the channel by selling directly to hospitals, then, if the hospital wants the product, waiting for them to request the state to put the item on the state's list or the hospital will buy direct.

The most effective form of selling to psychiatric hospitals is through direct contact with hospital nursing managers, hospital infection control managers, and purchasing managers, thus pulling our product through the channel via end-user demand for our product. In addition, the use of samples and testing is key to decision making. Based on these findings, Zif will pursue strong marketing partnerships for the promotion of the Zif safety syringe.

Sales Strategy

Option #1—License

In year one, with an initial investment of $400,000, Zif plans to spend $150,000 on the direct selling efforts to end-users and strategic partners.

The remaining will go to prototype development, pilot production, and field tests. Zif plans to utilize four sales representatives with previous sales experience in the medical field. The pursuit of licensing will involve targeting key manufacturers interested in extending their product line or looking for product improvement. After a licensing agreement is reached, no sales representative will be required. (See marketing budget.)

Option #2—Manufacture

In year one, with an initial investment of $400,000, Zif plans to spend $150,000 on the direct selling efforts to end-users and marketing partners, while the remaining will go to prototype development, pilot production, and field tests. As in option #1, Zif plans to utilize four sales representatives with previous sales experience in the medical field. Two will pursue end-user acceptance and order generation through trade promotions, while two will pursue marketing partnerships. The pursuit of a marketing partnership will involve the targeting of key distributors. An overall 20% mark-up allowance has been made for the costs of the distribution partnerships. This is an overall doubling of the current industry distribution mark-up allowance between manufacturer and distributor. In subsequent years, we have allocated a 10% annual growth in marketing expenditures. (See marketing budget.)

Sales Forecasts

Zif expects to capture a 5%, 10%, and 15% of the psychiatric hospital and nuclear pre-filled syringe markets in years one through three. We will follow this initial market penetration by expanding into the family practice and hospital markets. Zif estimates that in years four and five it will capture 5%, and 9% of the overall U.S. syringe market. (See below for calculations.)

MANUFACTURING IMPLEMENTATION

Technology

The Zif syringe is designed to be manufactured on existing syringe equipment. Thus, Zif will use the following existing technologies to manufacture syringes:

- Clean room manufacturing environment
- Plastic injection molding
- Vertical continuous-motion rotary syringe barrel printing
- High-speed spring winding
- Continuous motion rotary syringe assembly
- Horizontal continuous packaging equipment

Zif will work with contractors and/or licensees to integrate these technologies into a streamlined manufacturing process that will make use of Just-In-Time principles. This arrangement is proven to provide the greatest quality at the lowest cost. Additionally, this process will allow Zif and its partners to operate with very low inventory levels, low overhead costs, and with excellent space utilization.

Syringe manufacturing is a complicated, but well-established in its field. Six individual pieces, as shown below, must be manufactured or sourced, then printed, assembled and packaged in an efficient manner.

Syringe Manufacturing Flow

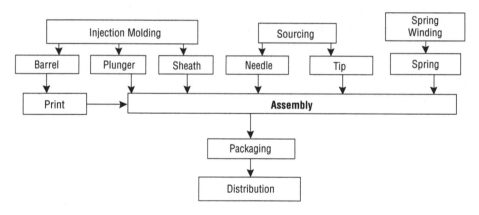

Buy/Source Decisions

The specific part buy/source decisions are as follows:

- *Plunger tip, needle:* purchased parts
- *Barrel, sheath, plunger:* purchase molds and use custom molder
- *Spring:* purchase spring winding machine to integrate w/ assembly

- *Printing*: Leverage w/existing player
- *Assembly*: Leverage existing player's equipment
- *Distribution*: Partnership

Project Implementation

The manufacturing plan will be implemented in three phases (also refer to Timeline):

Phase I: Prototype, Patent, and Apply for FDA Approval (Options #1 and #2)

This includes filing for patent protection, applying for FDA approval, and developing small scale production for field testing and promotions. Upon completion of Phase I, managers and investors will determine whether to pursue the licensing option (Option #1) or continue on to Phase II.

Phase II: 3cc Production Line (Option #2 Only)

This phase is designed to begin full-line production with a minimal capital investment. This includes the purchase of specialty spring winding equipment, and plastic injection molds for the syringe barrel, sheath, and plunger. The plastic molding of the syringe parts will be contracted out to a custom molding company. The printing and assembly of the syringe will also be contracted out. Zif will work as the management tie between the contract manufacturing, and the distribution partner(s).

Phase III: 1cc Production Line (Option #2 Only)

Positive cash flow from the first line will be reinvested into line #2. This phase duplicates previous efforts to develop and commercialize a 1cc version of the Zif safety syringe. See timeline for details.

ORGANIZATION AND ADMINISTRATION

Zif will be incorporated in order to effectively raise capital and limit shareholder liability. The president of the company will be David Bean. Mr. Bean has a BS in Mechanical Engineering, extensive experience in engineering and manufacturing in the plastics industry, and is acquiring an MBA at Purdue University. He has the practical experience and educational background required to make this venture successful.

Initially, Mr. Bean will be responsible for the company's general management, financing, and contract printing, assembling, and packaging needs. Hank Catalini, an expert mold designer and project engineer with 15 years experience, will be vice president in charge of mold design, procurement, start-up, and processing. Additionally, Mr. Catalini will be responsible for the coordination of contract molding. Joe Schroeder, BA and MBA in marketing, will be vice president in charge of sales, marketing, distribution, and human resources. Mr. Schroeder has broad experience in each of these areas and is well positioned to meet the company's early and ongoing service requirements. Tom Evans, MBA in Finance, will be vice president in charge of finance and accounting. Mr. Evans has extensive experience as a corporate controller.

Initially, a temporary hourly workforce will be hired for administrative tasks. Employees will be offered permanent salaried positions once they have demonstrated technical proficiency and are determined to be a good fit for Zif's team-based environment. Professional services such as accounting and engineering will be leveraged as needed. As the company grows, professional help will be hired as the need becomes significant and justifiable.

Organization Chart

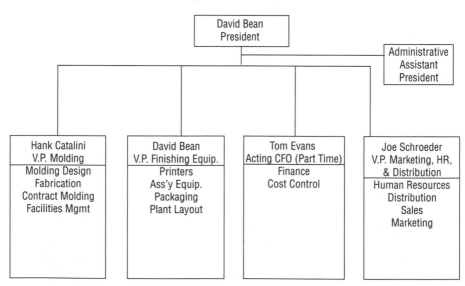

CORPORATE VALUES, VISION, AND MISSION

Zif will operate with the following corporate values, vision, and mission statement:

Values:

Integrity	Nothing but the highest level of integrity will be acceptable.
Teamwork	Effective teamwork is key to our company's success.
Individuality	Individuals are valued, trusted and respected assets of the corporation.
Performance	We expect a high level of achievement and contribution from all employees. Employees will be compensated based on individual and team performance.
Community	We will contribute a percentage of our time and resources to improving the community in which we live and work.
Vision:	To make obsolete the standard syringe through superior design, performance, and value.
Mission:	To provide a high return on investment through the marketing of safe, reliable, and effective medical syringes.

FINANCIAL PLAN

Capital Investment Strategy

Commercial option #1 (License) will require an initial capital investment of $400,000 for patent protection, FDA approval, field testing, prototype development, and promotion. See itemized budget listing.

Commercial option #2 (Manufacture) will require an initial capital investment of $400,000 for promotion, prototype development, and field testing, and an additional $1.47 million for the implementation of

	Cost	Life-Yrs[14]	Year 1	2	3	4	5
No. of Production Lines			0	1	1	2	2
Proprietary Groundwork:							
Prototype Molds (2)	120	0	120	0	0	120	0
Patent Costs	10	10	10	0	0	0	0
FDA Application	10	0	10	0	0	10	0
Field Tests	10	0	10	0	0	10	0
Molds:							
48 Cavity Barrel Mold	200	10	0	200	0	200	0
48 Cavity Plunger Mold	180	10	0	180	0	180	0
48 Cavity Sheath Mold	200	10	0	200	0	200	0
Assembly:							
Spring Windings	250	10	0	250	0	250	0
Special Assembly Equip.	n/a	10	0	255	0	255	0
Office Equipment	n/a	4	0	15	0	5	0
Total Capital		150	150	1,100	0	1,230	0

the first production line. The Option #2 capital summary[13] (in thousands of dollars) is as follows:

All capital expenditures beyond the first two years will be financed through retained earnings. Zif plans to grow through the investment of retained earnings, thus no dividends are expected to be paid out in the first six years of operations. A friendly acquisition or an initial public offering will be made by year six to allow initial investors to divest from Zif.

In general, Zif will invest very conservatively to minimize risk and to not outgrow its resources or capacity to expand. Based on investor opinions, company resources, and realized profits, Zif may grow faster than outlined below through the acquisition of debt beyond the 10% debt to equity established in this plan.

---

[13]Does not include marketing expenses and salaries.
[14]See page 226 for Depreciation Schedule.

Equity Offering

	Equity Investment	Equity Share
Option #1 (License)	$ 400,000	20%
Option #2 (Manufacture)	$1,870,000	30%

Financial Analysis

Option #1—License

Cash flow statements (following) show that Zif will have positive cash beginning in year 2. Income statements show profit growth from $27,000 in year 2, to $4.8 million in year 6. Balance sheets following show a strong return on equity, and no debt will be incurred with this option.

	Optimistic	Most Likely	Pessimistic
Product Price ($)	0.18	0.16	0.14
NPV (mil $)[15]	1.7	1.3	0.94
IRR	152%	135%	115%
ROE (5 yr avg.)	72%	71%	60%
Return on Initial Investment[16]	198%	191%	182%
5 Year Multiple of 20% Equity	61	49	37

Option #2—Manufacture

Cash flow statements below show that Zif will create positive cash flows within two years of operation. Income statements show geometric profit growth from $(7,000) in year 2, to $9.3 million in y ear 6. Balance sheets show strong return on equity, and no debt will be incurred.

Based on the scenarios above, all cases provide excellent financial results with minimal leverage.

---

[15]Calculated with a discount rate of 50%.
[16]Compounded annual return of 20% equity stake. Based on industry average P/E Multiple of 20.

	Optimistic	Most Likely	Pessimistic
Product Price ($)	0.18	0.16	0.14
Contracted Cost per unit ($)[17]	.067	.072	.08
Dist. Mark-up (% Sales)	15%	20%	25%
NPV (mil $)[18]	6.1	4.4	2.3
IRR	92%	84%	71%
ROE (5 yr avg.)	38%	33%	23%
Debt/Equity (year 6)	0%	0%	0%
Return on Initial Investment[19]	186%	176%	160%
5 Year Multiple of 30% Equity	41	30	17

Risks

The risks associated with this plan are as follows:

Design problems (5%)   This will be minimized through extensive proto-typing and field testing.

Patent infringement/litigation (15%)   Several firms have patented safety syringe ideas, but none are identical or very close to the Zif design. Litigation based on prior art may cost the firm in terms of a licensing fee settlement which would hurt profitability, but most likely allow the firm to remain profitable. Additionally, frivolous litigation may be initiated by a competitor as a means of predatory action. The cost of this litigation is unknown.

Manufacturing failure (5%)   Proven technology will be used to manufacture this product. The major risk involved here is in the combination of these technologies feeding one directly into the other without buffer zones. This may pose initial start-up difficulties as machine outputs may suffer.

---

[17]Variation based upon negotiated contract.
[18]Calculated with a discount rate of 30%.
[19]Compounded annual return of 30% equity stake. Based on industry average P/E Multiple of 20.

Poor market reaction (5%)   Zif must market itself effectively and provide a sense of product quality, security and reliability. If the market is negatively effected by competitive "propaganda" or initial quality problems, Zif could quickly lose hold in the marketplace. This is a small risk because the large pent-up demand for safe syringes will encourage users to try new brands. Additionally, Zif will focus on initial and ongoing product quality as a way of doing business to ensure its products meet the strictest user requirements.

FDA rejection (5%)   Due to the safe nature of this product, tremendous market demand, existing manufacturing technology, and soon to be established field results, this risk is small.

Overall, the combined risk assessment is 35%. This risk can have an impact on the initial profitability; however, these setbacks, if realized, are expected to be minimized and eventually eliminated within the first five years of operation.

Investment and Depreciation Schedules by Phases

Phase I (Year #1 Investment)—Prototype, Patent, Incorporate, and FDA Appl.

Description	Cost	Depr. Life	1	2	3	4	5	6	7	8	9	10
							Depreciation Schedule in Years					
Prototype Molds (2)	80	0										
Patent Costs	10	10	1	1	1	1	1	1	1	1	1	1
FDA Application	10	0										
Field Tests	10	0										
Total Capital Phase I	**110**		1	1	1	1	1	1	1	1	1	1

Phase II (Year #2 Investment)—Start-up Production Line #1 w/Minimal Capital

Description	Cost	Depr. Life	1	2	3	4	5	6	7	8	9	10
Molds:												
48 Cavity Barrel Mold	160	10	16	16	16	16	16	16	16	16	16	16
48 Cavity Plunger Mold	180	10	18	18	18	18	18	18	18	18	18	18
48 Cavity Sheath Mold	150	10	15	15	15	15	15	15	15	15	15	15
60 Cavity Rubber Mold	200	10	20	20	20	20	20	20	20	20	20	20
Assembly:												
High Speed Barrel Printer	500	5	100	100	100	100	100	0	0	0	0	0
High Speed Assembly Equipment	950	5	190	190	190	190	190	0	0	0	0	0
Sorting Equipment	100	5	20	20	20	20	20	0	0	0	0	0
Conveying Equipment	50	5	10	10	10	10	10	0	0	0	0	0

Packaging:

Horizontal Wrapper Equip.	140	5	28	28	28	28	28	0	0	0	0
Fork Truck	20	10	2	2	2	2	2	2	2	2	2
Misc.											
Manual Bridgeport Mill	10	10	1	1	1	1	1	1	1	1	1
Manual Lathe	10	10	1	1	1	1	1	1	1	1	1
Maintenance Equipment	15	10	1.5	1.5	1.5	1.5	1.5	1.5	1.5	1.5	1.5
Office Equipment	15	4	3.75	3.75	3.75	3.75	3.75				
Total Capital Phase II	**2500**	**426.25**	**426.25**	**426**	**426**	**423**	**75**	**75**	**75**	**75**	**75**

Phase III (Year #3 Investment)—Buy Facility & Equip Line #2

Building/Facility:											
30.000 Sqft Bld w/ Clean Rm 4,000	30	133	133	133	133	133	133	133	133	133	133
Silo & Mat'l Handling	87	10	8.7	8.7	8.7	8.7	8.7	8.7	8.7	8.7	8.7
Molding Machines:											
225 Ton Inj. Mold Machine (2)	500	10	50	50	50	50	50	50	50	50	50

(Continued)

223

Investment and Depreciation Schedules by Phases (*Continued*)

Phase III (*Continued*)

Description	Cost	Depr. Life	Depreciation Schedule									
			1	2	3	4	5	6	7	8	9	10
Molds:												
48 Cavity Barrel Mold	160	10	16	16	16	16	16	16	16	16	16	16
48 Cavity Plunger Mold	180	10	18	18	18	18	18	18	18	18	18	18
48 Cavity Sheath Mold	150	10	15	15	15	15	15	15	15	15	15	15
60 Cavity Rubber Mold	200	10	20	20	20	20	20	20	20	20	20	20
Assembly:												
High Speed Barrel Printer	500	5	100	100	100	100	100	0	0	0	0	0
High Speed Assembly Equip	950	5	190	190	190	190	190	0	0	0	0	0
Sorting Equipment	100	5	20	20	20	20	20	0	0	0	0	0
Conveying Equipment	50	5	10	10	10	10	10	0	0	0	0	0
Packaging:												
Horizontal Wrapper Equip.	120	5	24	24	24	24	24	0	0	0	0	0
Misc:												
Mold Prep Equipment	20	10	2	2	2	2	2	2	2	2	2	2
Grinding Machine	25	10	2.5	2.5	2.5	2.5	2.5	2.5	2.5	2.5	2.5	2.5
CNC Milling Machine	80	10	8	8	8	8	8	8	8	8	8	8
Total Capital Phase III	**7122**	**621**	**623**	**624**	**625**	**626**	**283**	**284**	**285**	**286**	**287**	**147**

Phase IV (Year #4 Investment)—Equip Line #3 & Bring all Molding In-House

Molding Machines:

225 Ton Inj. Molding Mach. (4)	1500	10	150	150	150	150	150	150	150	150	150
Molds:											
48 Cavity Barrel Mold	320	10	32	32	32	32	32	32	32	32	32
48 Cavity Plunger Mold	360	10	36	36	36	36	36	36	36	36	36
48 Cavity Sheath Mold	300	10	30	30	30	30	30	30	30	30	30
60 Cavity Rubber Mold	400	10	40	40	40	40	40	40	40	40	40
Assembly:	0										
High Speed Barrel Printer	1000	5	200	200	200	200	200	0	0	0	0
High Speed Assembly Equip	1900	5	380	380	380	380	380	0	0	0	0
Sorting Equipment	200	5	40	40	40	40	40	0	0	0	0
Conveying Equipment	100	5	20	20	20	20	20	0	0	0	0
Packaging:											
Horizontal Wrapper Equip.	240	5	48	48	48	48	48	0	0	0	0
Total Capital Phase VI	**6320**	**981**	**982**	**983**	**984**	**985**	**298**	**299**	**300**	**301**	**302**

(Continued)

Investment and Depreciation Schedules by Phases (Continued)

Phase V (Year #5 Investment)—Equip Line #4

Description	Cost	Depr. Life	Depreciation Schedule									
			1	2	3	4	5	6	7	8	9	10
Molding Machines:												
225 Ton Inj. Molding Mach. (4)	2000	10	200	200	200	200	200	200	200	200	200	200
Molds:												
48 Cavity Barrel Mold	640	10	64	64	64	64	64	64	64	64	64	64
48 Cavity Plunger Mold	720	10	72	72	72	72	72	72	72	72	72	72
48 Cavity Sheath Mold	600	10	60	60	60	60	60	60	60	60	60	60
60 Cavity Rubber Mold	800	10	80	80	80	80	80	80	80	80	80	80
Assembly:	0											
High Speed Barrel Printer	2000	5	400	400	400	400	400					
High Speed Assembly Equip	3800	5	760	760	760	760	760					
Sorting Equipment	400	5	80	80	80	80	80					
Conveying Equipment	200	5	40	40	40	40	40					
Packaging:												
Horizontal Wrapper Equip.	480	5	96	96	96	96	96					
Total Depr. Schedule	1		1852	1852	1852	1852	1852	276	276	276	276	276

Capital Expenditure Summary
in thousands of dollars

	Unit Cost	Deprec. Life (yrs)	YEAR				
			1	2	3	4	5
No. of Incremental Prod. Lines			0	1	1	2	4
Proprietary Groundwork:							
Prototype Molds (2)	80	0	80	-	-	-	-
Patent Costs	10	10	10	-	-	-	-
FDA Application	10	0	10	-	-	-	-
Field Tests	10	0	10	-	-	-	-
Molds:							
48 Cavity Barrel Mold	160	10	-	160	160	320	640
48 Cavity Plunger Mold	180	10	-	180	180	360	720
48 Cavity Sheath Mold	150	10	-	150	150	300	600
60 Cavity Rubber Mold	200	10	-	200	200	400	800
Assembly:							
High Speed Barrel Printer	500	5	-	500	500	1000	2000
High Speed Assembly Equip	950	5	-	950	950	1900	3800
Sorting Equipment	100	5	-	100	100	200	400
Conveying Equipment	50	5	-	50	50	100	200
Packaging Equipment	120	5	-	140	120	240	480
Building/Facility:							
30,000 Sqft Bld w/ Clean Rm	4000	30	-	-	4000	-	-
Silo & Material Handling	43.5	10	-	-	87	-	-
Molding Machines:							
225 Ton Inj. Mold Machine	250	10	-	-	500	1500	2000
Misc.							
Maintenance Equipment	n/a	10	-	55	125	-	-
Office Equipment	n/a	4	-	15	5	5	5
Total Capital			**110**	**2,500**	**7,127**	**6,325**	**11,645**

Balance Sheets
(thousands of dollars)

	YEAR					
	1	2	3	4	5	6
Cash	10	907	1,814	3,629	7,258	14,515
Short Term Securities	-	789	573	894	2,836	30,204
Accounts Receivable	-	1,512	1,512	3,024	6,048	12,096
Inventories	-	87	174	348	696	1,393
Current Assets	10	3,295	4,073	7,895	16,838	58,208
Equipment, Land, & Facil.	10	2,510	9,637	15,962	27,607	27,607
Less Accum. Depreciation	0	(1)	(428)	(1,477)	(3,508)	(7,399)
Total Assets	20	5,804	13,282	22,379	40,938	78,417
Accounts Payable	-	725	725	1,451	2,902	5,803
Bank Loan: short term	-	500	-	-	-	-
Current Liabilities	-	1,225	725	1,451	2,902	5,803
Long Term Debt	-	-	4,000	4,000	4,000	4,000
Total Liabilities	-	1,225	4,725	5,451	6,902	9,803
Capital Investments	120	2,620	2,620	2,620	2,620	2,620
Retained Earnings	(100)	1,958	5,937	14,309	31,416	65,993
Total Owner's Equity	20	4,578	8,557	16,929	34,036	68,613
Total Liabilities + OE	20	5,804	13,282	22,379	40,938	78,417
Return on Equity		45%	46%	49%	50%	50%
Debt to Equity	0%	11%	47%	24%	12%	6%

Assumptions:

Price/units	$0.140
Cost/unit	$0.067
Distribution costs/unit	15% Sales Price
A/R period	30 days
A/P period	30 days
Bank Loan Interest	10%
Cash	10% Sales

Income Statements
(thousands of dollars)

			YEAR			
	1	2	3	4	5	6
Units Sold (millions)	-	65	130	259	518	1,037
Net Sales	-	9,072	18,144	36,288	72,576	145,152
Cost of Goods Sold	-	4,352	8,705	17,410	34,820	69,639
Gross Profit	-	4,720	9,439	18,878	37,756	75,513
Distribution Expense	0	1,360	2,721	5,443	10,886	21,772
S&A Expenses	20	160	160	120	120	120
Product Liab. Insurance	-	50	100	200	400	800
R&D	80	30	30	30	30	30
Operating Earnings	(100)	3,119	6,428	13,085	26,320	52,790
Interest Expense	-	-	400	400	400	400
Earnings Before Tax	(100)	3,119	6,028	12,685	25,920	52,390
Income Tax	-	1,060	2,049	4,313	8,813	17,813
Net Earnings	**(100)**	**2,058**	**3,978**	**8,372**	**17,107**	**34,578**

Statements of Cash Flows
(thousands of dollars)

Operating Activity

Net Income	(100)	2,058	3,978	8,372	17,107	34,578
Adj: A/R	-	(1,512)	-	(1,512)	(3,024)	(6,048)
A/P	-	725	-	725	1,451	2,902
Depreciation	-	1	427	1,049	2,031	3,891
Inventory Change	-	(87)	(87)	(174)	(348)	(696)
Net Cash fm Operations	(100)	1,186	4,318	8,460	17,217	34,626

Investing Activity

Purchase of Equipment & Land/Facil.	(10)	(2,500)	(7,127)	(6,325)	(11,645)	-
Short Term Securities	-	(789)	216	(321)	(1,943)	(27,368)

Financing Activity

Equity Investments	120	2,500	-	-	-	-
Acquired Short Term Debt	-	500	(500)	-	-	-
Acquired Long Term Debt	-	-	4,000	-	-	-
Total Change in Cash	10	897	907	1,814	3,629	7,258
Cash fm Begin. of Year	0	10	907	1,814	3,629	7,258
Cash at End of Year	10	907	1,814	3,629	7,258	14,515

Product Costing

Material:				Direct Labor:		
	Material Wght gm	Material $/gm	Cost		$/hr	Unit Cost
Barrel	2.05	0.0015	0.0031	Operator	15.00	0.00083
Plunger	0.95	0.0015	0.0014	Assembler	15.00	0.00083
Sheath	1.50	0.0015	0.0023	Packaging	15.00	0.00083
Rubber	0.20	0.0009	0.0002	Quality Control	15.00	0.00083
Contract Molding	n/a	n/a	0.0083	Maintenance	15.00	0.00083
Spring	n/a	n/a	0.01	Shipping/Recieving	15.00	0.00083
Needle	n/a	n/a	0.020	**Total Labor Cost/Unit**	**0.0050**	
Packaging Film	n/a	n/a	0.001			
Shipper 1/100	n/a	n/a	0.01			
Total Material Cost/Unit			**0.0562**	**Total Variable Costs**		**$0.061**

Total Fixed and Unit Costs

Fixed Overhead Costs:

	1	2	3	4	5	6	7	8
No. of Prod. Lines	0	0.5	1	2	4	8	8	8
Salaries & Wages	-	150,000	150,000	200,000	250,000	300,000	300,000	300,000
Salaried Benefits	-	75,000	75,000	100,000	125,000	150,000	150,000	150,000
Supply & Quality	-	30,000	60,000	60,000	100,000	100,000	100,000	100,000
Office Supplies	400	800	800	800	800	800	800	800
Engin. Impvmnts	-	80,000	80,000	80,000	150,000	150,000	150,000	150,000
Rent	-	6,000	6,000	6,000	-	-	-	-
Utilities	-	5,000	10,000	20,000	40,000	80,000	80,000	80,000
Equip. Maintenance	-	110,000	220,000	440,000	880,000	880,000	880,000	-
Depreciation	-	1,000	427,250	1,048,783	2,030,783	3,890,783	3,890,033	3,545,033
Total Fixed Costs	**400**	**402,800**	**919,050**	**1,735,583**	**3,136,583**	**5,551,583**	**5,550,833**	**5,205,833**

Total Unit Costs:

Year	1	2	3	4	5	6	7	8
Pcs Produced (MM)	0	64.8	129.6	259.2	518.4	1036.8	1036.8	1036.8
Total Var. Cst (mil)	0.00	3.97	7.93	15.86	31.73	63.45	63.45	63.45
Total Fixed Cst (mil)	0.00	0.40	0.92	1.74	3.14	5.55	5.55	5.21
Total Costs (mil)	0.00	4.37	8.85	17.60	34.86	69.00	69.00	68.66
Total Unit Cost	**n/a**	**$0.067**	**$0.068**	**$0.068**	**$0.067**	**$0.067**	**$0.067**	**$0.066**

(Continued)

231

Total Fixed and Unit Costs (Continued)

Assumptions:

Manufacturing Ass'y Rate (yield)	300	parts/minute
Product Line Capacity	129.6	million/yr
Propolyene Material Costs	0.68	$/pound
Rubber Material Costs	0.40	$/pound
Needle Material Cost	0.010	$/Unit
Spring Wire costs	0.01	$/Unit
Operator Hourly Wage	10.00	
Benefit Multiplier	50%	
Income Tax Rate	34%	
Maintenance Per Line (annual)	110000	$per line
Prod. Liability Insurance (annual)	100000	$per line
Packaging Film	0.001	per unit
Shipper costs	1.00	
Inventory	20	Days COGS

453		grams/lb
0.00150110	=	$/gram
0.00088300	=	$/gram

Year	1	2	3	4	5	6	7	8
Inventory	-	87,049	174,098	348,195	696,390	1,392,781	1,392,781	1,392,781
Inventory Build	-	87,049	87,049	174,098	348,195	696,390	-	-
R & D	80,000	30,000	30,000	30,000	30,000	30,000	30,000	30,000
Product Liab. Insur.	-	50,000	100,000	200,000	400,000	800,000	800,000	800,000
Marketing/Advert.	-	50,000	50,000	10,000	10,000	10,000	10,000	10,000
Sales Expense	20,000	100,000	100,000	100,000	100,000	100,000	100,000	100,000
Travel	-	5,000	5,000	5,000	5,000	5,000	5,000	5,000
Legal & Prof.	-	5,000	5,000	5,000	5,000	5,000	5,000	5,000
Total S&A Expenses	**20,000**	**160,000**	**160,000**	**120,000**	**120,000**	**120,000**	**120,000**	**120,000**
Total/Final Unit Cost		**0.072**	**0.071**	**0.070**	**0.069**	**0.068**	**0.067**	**0.067**

Time Lines

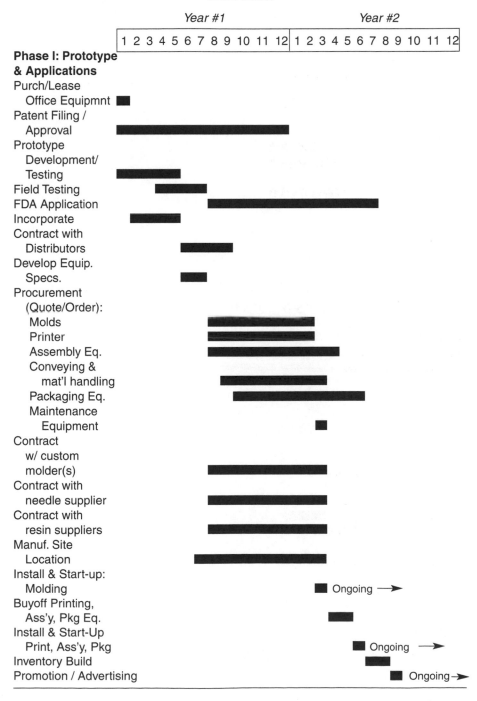

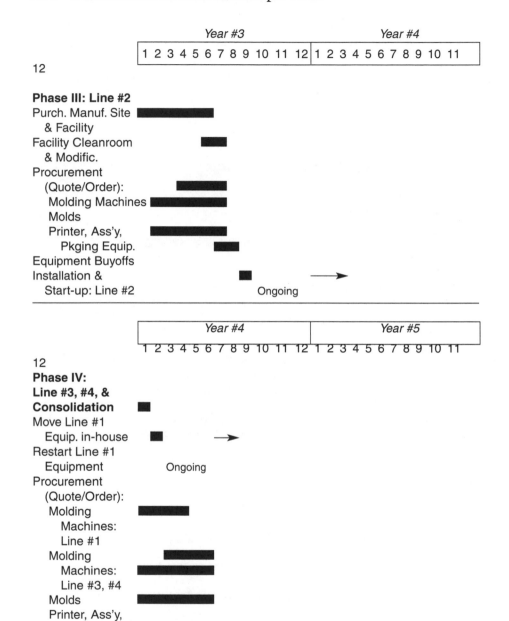

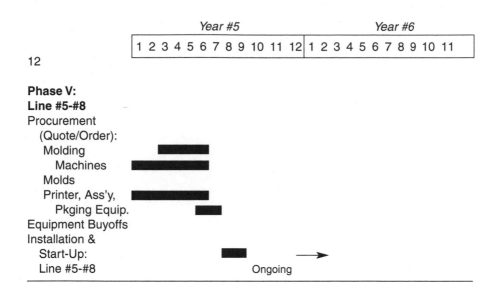

Phase V:
Line #5-#8
Procurement
   (Quote/Order):
    Molding
      Machines
    Molds
    Printer, Ass'y,
      Pkging Equip.
Equipment Buyoffs
Installation &
    Start-Up:
    Line #5-#8

Net Present Value (NPV) Calculation

Cash Flows:	1	2	3	4	5	Perpetuity 6		Aquisition 6
Cash Flow	0	0	0	0	0	34,578	Ongoing	145,152
PV of perpetuity T6						115,258		
Capital Investments	-120	-2,500	0	0	0			
PV Factor	0.7692308	0.592	0.455	0.35	0.269	0.20718		0.2072
Present Values	-92.307692	-1,479	0	0	0	23,878.8		30,072

NPV—Perpetuity	**22,307**
NPV—Acquisition	**28,500**

Discount Rate 30%

	Optimistic	Most Likely	Pess.
NPV (mil)	50.9	22.4	4.7
IRR w/ perpituity	119%	92%	57%
IRR w/ aquisition	195%	168%	131%

References

CHAPTER/ACTION STEP 4: Analyze Your Market: *Who will want your product or service?*

The Encyclopedia of Associations, published by Gale-Thomson, is available in book form or on the web through libraries that subscribe to it. It is a good place to find out if your industry has an association that might publish industry background information.

Thomson Register of American Manufacturers, also published by Gale-Thomson, is similarly available in book form or free on the web at www.thomasregister.com. If you need to locate possible suppliers for your business, it is an efficient place to begin.

Hoovers.com at www.hoovers.com, provides company and industry data and various useful links. Some information is provided at no charge; other data is on a fee basis.

Financial and Operating Results of Department and Speciality Stores, published by the National Retail Merchants Association, is an annual presentation of detailed financial information that can serve as useful guidance and comparison.

The U.S. Census Bureau at www.census.gov is a source for literally billions of dollars of high-quality research on population, industries, employment, and ethnic groups, most of which is available for all localities throughout the United States. Industry reports compiled by the Census Bureau can be searched by NAICS code (see chapter 10 for an explanation of the coding systems) at www.census.gov/ftp/pub/cir/www. There is so much information, that it may take a while to sort through it all, but it's worth the time, and the price is right . . . it's free.

Other ways to search the vast array of government offerings include the *Catalog of Federal Domestic Assistance* at www.cfda.gov; the **Government Printing Of-**

fice at www.gpo.gov; **FedStats** at www.fedstats.gov; **First Gov**, at www.first-gov.com, also offers state and local information; the **National Associations of Counties** at www.naco.org/counties/.

The Small Business Administration, www.sba.gov, is loaded with useful information, reports, financing worksheets, background on government programs, and many links. It is somewhat cumbersome to navigate, but worth the time. Some of the same information is available more directly through another SBA site, the **U.S. Small Business Advisor**, www.business.gov.

Information on public companies in your industry can provide good background or comparisons with your own plans. **The Securities and Exchange Commission** site, www.sec.gov/edgar.html, provides fast access to all public company filings. **Quicken** and **CNNfn** with their sites, quicken.com and cnnfn.com, provide current and historical financial information for public companies.

General business background information is available through www.factiva.com, which is the site for searching the **Reuters** and **Dow Jones** business publications at http://www.factiva.com/. **Lexisnexis.com** at www.lexis.com offers data from public records, newspapers, and magazines. **Standard and Poor's** has various industry reports at its site, www.standardandpoors.com. You can use all three of these sites free at a library that subscribes to these services, or on a basis fee on the web.

Kompass at www.kompass.com provides product and contact information for 1.7 million companies throughout the world. It is searchable using their product-classification system.

Economy.com at www.economy.com/freelunch/ offers links to nearly a million sources of economic and financial data on industries, consumers, and government statistics.

Many libraries offer information directly over the web, or provide links to business references. Among the better ones are:

> **The Library of Congress** at http://lcweb.loc.gov
>
> **U.S. Public Libraries on the Web** at http://sunsite.berkeley.edu/Libweb/Public_main.html
>
> **The American Library Association** guide to best business websites at www.ala.org/rusa/brass/besthome.html
>
> **The Libarian's Index to the Internet** at www.lii.org/

CHAPTER/ACTION STEP 5:   Develop a Strong Marketing Campaign: *How will you reach your customers and what will you say to them?*

The Successful Marketing Plan, 2nd Edition. Roman F. Hiebing, Jr. and Scott W. Cooper. NTC Business Books, Chicago, 1996. This is a very clear and detailed explanation of the marketing aspect of a business plan.

The 33 Ruthless Rules of Local Advertising. Michael Corbett with Dave Stili. Pinnacle Books, New York, 2001. I have worked with Michael Corbett and Dave

Stili for more than 20 years, including writing a book with Michael Corbett. No one understands the issues of marketing a small business better than Corbett and Stili. This book is indispensable for businesses that need to rely on local advertising to be successful.

The American Marketing Association at www.marketingpower.com has a site with many reports, most of which are free, and useful links, all of which are related to marketing strategies.

CHAPTER/ACTION STEP 7:   Design Your Company: *How will you hire and organize your work force?*

American Association of Franchisees and Dealers, www.aafd.org, has a very useful website that includes both free information and an online bookstore with publications about franchises.

Franchising 101, edited by Ann Dugan. Upstart Publishing Company, Chicago, 1998. This is an excellent collection of articles by experts on various aspects of franchising.

CHAPTER/ACTION STEP 9:   Explain Your Financial Data: *How will you convince others to invest in your endeavor?*

Venture Economics annually publishes *Pratt's Guide to Venture Capital Sources*, which provides a comprehensive list of venture capital companies, along with their investment criteria and areas of focus.

The National Venture Capital Association publishes a similar directory, *National Venture Capital Association Directory*, also available on the web at www.nvca.org.

A useful site for information on bank lending, current rates and credit cards is **Bank Rate.com** at www.bankrate.com.

The Commerce Clearing House (CCH) website at www.toolkit.cch.com, has a great deal of useful and easy to find information including model spreadsheets, sample business plans, reports on topics of importance to small business, and legal and tax information.

One of the best financial tools for business plans that I have come across is called **Active Money** and it's available at the website of the Columbus Enterprise Development Corporation, www.cedcorp.com/activemoney/start_cd.htm. Key Bank also makes this available as a CD. Active Money takes you through the process of building financial projections in a clear, simple, straightforward, and sensible way.

Nolo.com, www.nolo.com, is a site that specializes in legal issues. Sample documents, such as contracts, are available for a fee, but most of their background material on legal issues is available at no charge.

The Entrepreneurial Edge, http://edge.lowe.org, is a service of the Edward Lowe Foundation, which promotes entrepreneurship. There is an extensive library of reports and numerous links to other business sites.

The Kauffman Center for Entrepreneurial Leadership, www.entreworld. org, has a great number of resources for entrepreneurs, including access to its business financial benchmarking system at, www.businessekg.com.

Winning business plans from the **University of Texas MOOTCORP Competition**, like the Zif Medical Devices plan presented here, are available at their Web site, www.businessplan.org.

Accounting help, including break-even analysis, returns analysis, and creating statements, can be found in *Introduction to Management Accounting*, 12th Edition, Charles T. Horngren, Gary L. Sundem and William O. Stratton. Prentice-Hall, 2002.

Salary.com and **Hr-guide.com** are useful in getting a handle on some of the many costs for businesses related to salary. They are easy-to-use, free sites that provide average salary information. Their addresses are and www.salary.com and www.hr-guide.com; the latter is also a useful site for issues related to human resources, such as benefits and incentive plans, **Work Index.com** at http://workindex.com/.

CHAPTER 12:   How to Create a Time Line

Project Management: A Systems Approach to Planning, Scheduling and Controlling, 7th Edition, Harold Kerzner. John Wiley & Sons, Inc., 2001. This is a textbook that clearly and comprehensively covers project-management tools. For your own application, you will probably only need to refer to a few pages, so you may want to review it at a library.

The Fast Forward MBA in Project Management, Eric Verzuh. John Wiley & Sons Inc., 2001. This is an overview of project-management tools, and will be helpful in determining which of these tools will be appropriate to your needs.

Teach Yourself Microsoft Project 2000, Vickey L. Quinn. Hungry Minds, Inc., 2001. This is a good guide that will get you up and running quickly.

CHAPTER 15:   Present Yourself in the Best Light

How to Say It In a Job Search: Choice Words, Phrases, Sentences, for Resumes, Cover Letters, and Interviews, Robbie Miller Kaplan. Prentice Hall, 2002. A helpful guide to presenting your skills and background.

CHAPTER 16:   Make a Great In-Person Presentation

The Entrepreneurial Conversation: How Entrepreneurs Think, Talk, and Listen to Build Successful Businesses, Edward G. Rogoff, Michael Corbett, and Perry-Lynn Moffitt. Pinnacle Press, New York, to be published in 2003.

Index